Faculty Bargaining

Faculty Bargaining
CHANGE AND CONFLICT

by Joseph W. Garbarino

Director, Institute of Business and Economic Research
and Professor of Business Administration
University of California, Berkeley

in association with Bill Aussieker

Assistant Professor in Administration
California State College, San Bernardino

A Report Prepared for
The Carnegie Commission on Higher Education
and
The Ford Foundation

McGRAW-HILL BOOK COMPANY
New York   St. Louis   San Francisco
Düsseldorf   Johannesburg   Kuala Lumpur   London   Mexico
Montreal   New Delhi   Panama   Paris   São Paulo
Singapore   Sydney   Tokyo   Toronto

The Carnegie Commission on Higher Education,
2150 Shattuck Avenue, Berkeley, California 94704,
has sponsored preparation of this volume as
part of a continuing effort to obtain and present
significant information for public discussion.
The views expressed are those of the authors.

FACULTY BARGAINING
Change and Conflict

This book was set in Palatino by University Graphics Inc.
It was printed and bound by The Maple Press Company.
The designer was Elliot Epstein. The editors were
Nancy Tressel and Michael Hennelly for McGraw-Hill
Book Company and Verne A. Stadtman for the Carnegie
Commission on Higher Education. Audre Hanneman edited
the index. Milton J. Heiberg supervised the production.

Library of Congress Cataloging in Publication Data
Garbarino, Joseph William, date
Faculty bargaining.

Bibliography: p.
Includes index.
1. Collective bargaining—College teachers.
I. Aussieker, Bill, joint author. II. Carnegie
Commission on Higher Education. III. Ford Foun-
dation. IV. Title.

LB2334.G37   331.89′041′37812   75-8661
ISBN 0-07-010111-6

123456789 MAMM798765

Contents

Foreword, vii

Acknowledgments, ix

1 *The Challenge of Institutional Change,* 1

Changes in size ▪ Changes in structure ▪ Changes in function ▪ The accountability complex ▪ The new legal environment ▪ Overview

2 *Patterns of Faculty Representation in Governance,* 23

Management and governance ▪ Enter collective bargaining ▪ The governance-bargaining continuum ▪ Alternative models of representation ▪ Recapitulation

3 *Faculty Unions: Patterns of Organization,* 51

Dimensions of support for unionism ▪ Growth trends of faculty unionism ▪ The anatomy of unionism ▪ Institutional correlates of faculty unionism ▪ Institutional structure and the unions ▪ The public-private dichotomy ▪ The quality conundrum ▪ Summary

4 *Collective Bargaining: The Parties and Their Relationships,* 83

The American Association of University Professors ▪ The American Federation of Teachers ▪ The National Education Association ▪ Other organizations ▪ Mergers and coalitions ▪ Rejections of unionism ▪ The reluctant dues payers ▪ Structuring the relationship ▪ Faculty bargaining as multilateral bargaining ▪ The elusive employer ▪ Managerial bargaining models

5 *Collective Bargaining: Evaluating the Issues,* 135

Guild unions and comprehensive unions ▪ Unions and governance ▪ Unions and university management ▪ Unions and status equalization

6 *Community Colleges Without Community,* by Bill Aussieker 179

Institutional similarities ▪ The effects of bargaining laws ▪ Financial difficulty and educational reform ▪ Organizational change and rapid growth ▪ Insidious comparisons ▪ Something for nothing?

7 *Academic Unionism in Great Britain,* 213

The structure of the system ▪ Developing the mechanics of representation ▪ Collective bargaining in practice ▪ An evaluation

033922

8 *A Recapitulation,* 251

Why do the faculty of colleges and universities organize? ■ Is faculty unionism inevitable? ■ Is faculty unionism irreversible? ■ What are the principal effects of faculty unionism?

References, 261

Index, 269

Foreword

Among the truly new—but probably permanent—factors in American academic life are organizations patterned on the models of industrial unions to represent teachers and scholars in negotiations with colleges and universities on matters of compensation and working conditions. It is not yet clear that the new patterns will be all pervasive. The best guess is that they will not, but that there will always be fertile soil for them, at least on campuses where faculty participation in institutional governance is minimal.

Regardless of how extensive the new forms of organization may be, they will be accompanied by important changes. There will be changes in the ways in which faculty members regard themselves—as professionals, and in relation to administrators, students, trustees, fellow workers who are not academics, and to faculty members at other institutions where academics are not organized. There will also be changes in the ways colleges and universities operate, with shifts in the character of campus policies regarded as matters of shared faculty and administrative responsibility.

The Carnegie Commission on Higher Education neither condemned nor advocated the movement toward faculty bargaining. What we said on this subject in our report on *Governance of Higher Education: Six Priority Problems* bears repeating here. Our basic recommendations on the subject (in a slightly different order than originally presented) were:

Faculties should be granted, where they do not already have it, the general level of authority as recommended by the American Association of University Professors.

State laws, where they do not now permit it, should provide faculty members in public institutions the opportunity of obtaining collective bargaining rights. One alternative under such laws should be choice of no bargaining unit.

Representation and bargaining units should be composed of faculty members, including department chairmen.

The approach to contract coverage should be one of restraint, with the contract covering economic benefits and with academic affairs left (or put) in the hands of the faculty senate or equivalent council.

A separate federal law and separate state laws should be enacted governing collective bargaining by faculty members in both private and public institutions and should be responsive to the special circumstances that surround their employment. If this is not possible, then separate provisions should be made in more general laws, or leeway should be provided for special administrative interpretations.

Faculties in each institution should undertake the most careful analysis of the implications of collective bargaining and, more broadly, of which of the alternative forms of governance they prefer.

This book should make a significant contribution to any analysis made by faculty members or administrators in response to this last recommendation. Its principal author is an exceptionally able economist with considerable experience as an academic and as a labor arbitrator and consultant to various companies, non-profit corporations, and government agencies. His view of academic bargaining benefits enormously from these perspectives. We are pleased that we could join with the Ford Foundation in supporting his work.

Clark Kerr

Chairman
Carnegie Commission
on Higher Education

April 1975

Acknowledgments

The research reported in this book involved a lengthy period of monitoring the development of faculty unionism and collective bargaining through campus visits, interviews with participants, participation as an observer in meetings and conferences, the collection and analysis of contracts and other written materials, and the compilation of statistical material. Many persons were of great assistance during the period without, of course, bearing any responsibility for errors of fact or interpretation in the final product.

In addition to preparing Chapter 6, Bill Aussieker was in charge of data collection throughout the project. The number of persons who made a material contribution to my understanding of the problem is too large to permit individual acknowledgment, but special mention is due Robert Fisk, Caesar Naples, Robert Granger, and Lawrence De Lucia for material on the State University of New York; Arnold Cantor, Maurice Benewitz, Israel Kugler and David Newton for material on the City University of New York; Neil Bucklew of Central Michigan University; Anthony John and Joseph Orze of Southeastern Massachusetts University; Donald Walters of the Massachusetts State Colleges; William Weinberg of Rutgers University; and Richard Peairs of the American Association of University Professors. The chapter on British experience owes a great deal to the cooperation of Adrienne Aziz of the Association of University Teachers; Derek Ware of the Universities Authorities Panel; and Gareth Williams of the Higher Education Research Unit at the London School of Economics and Political Science.

Editorial assistance was provided by Nancy Blumenstock.

Joseph W. Garbarino

1. The Challenge of Institutional Change

"The 1970s may belong to faculty activism as the 1960s did to student activism," concluded the Carnegie Commission on Higher Education in its final report after six years of prodigious activity under Clark Kerr. The Commission identified four sources of potential new initiatives in higher education in the United States and predicted that "those originating with faculties, and particularly collective bargaining, may be the dominant ones in the near future" (1973b, p. 56).

The Commission's conclusions could be supported by citation of the more than 330 institutions of higher education whose faculties had chosen exclusive bargaining agents by late 1974. Possibly of more long-run significance is the finding that two-thirds of all faculty members responding to a massive survey of faculty opinion agreed that collective bargaining by faculty had a place in colleges and universities.

The faculty union movement will be analyzed in this book primarily as a response to the dramatic institutional changes that occurred with great rapidity beginning at the end of the 1950s. These changes included an expansion in size and a change in the structure and the functions of the systems of higher education, changes in student and public attitudes, and, on a different level, changes in public policy toward collective bargaining by public employees. Most of the changes took place during the single decade of the 1960s, and at its close the faculty union movement was well established and steadily growing.

The opening years of the decade were marked by burgeoning population growth in the college-age groups and an increase in the proportion of those groups choosing to attend college. Demonstrations by economists seemed to prove that investment in "human capital" in the form of more years of schooling yielded attractive monetary returns both to individuals and to society. The launching of the Soviet Sputnik created an atmosphere of international competition in science and technology that led to massive increases in federal support for education and for programs of research and production that directly increased the demand for the services of highly trained manpower. This international competition had its domestic counterpart as major states began to view their university establishments as counters in the contest of attracting research and development contracts and follow-up manufacturing activities. The administrations of Presidents Kennedy and Johnson drew heavily on the universities and the periphery of other intellectual institutions, such as foundations and research organizations, for personnel and for policy proposals. The proposition that the real power of the large corporation had passed into the hands of an expert and highly educated technostructure came to be taken seriously, and, on the theory that the apparent dynamism of American business was in some manner attributable to what went on in American universities, versions of such mundane institutions as business schools were transplanted to the exotic environments of several foreign countries. The scramble of business and government employers for the graduates of science departments and of professional schools such as engineering and business administration was of unprecedented intensity, perhaps exceeded only by the frenetic efforts of the universities themselves to recruit faculty to cope with the flood of students and to become recognized as "centers of excellence."

The quantitative impact of the decade of growth was impressive. The number of institutions of higher education rose by one-quarter; their current expenditures almost quadrupled; the number of students enrolled increased $1\frac{1}{4}$ times; the number of faculty doubled; and the average faculty salary at the end of the decade was at least 75 percent higher than it had been in 1959.[1] A stereotype developed of the academic entrepreneur, someone more or less continuously airborne with a briefcase filled with

[1]The corresponding increases in the 1950s were: number of institutions, 8 percent; expenditures, 125 percent; students, 25 percent; faculty, 60 percent; and salaries, 63 percent (U.S. Office of Education, *Digest*, 1972; American Association of University Professors, 1973).

research and consulting contracts, invitations to international conferences, proposals for foundation grants, and competitive offers from a variety of institutions. Although only a microscopic fraction of the entire profession ever came close to fitting this description, the presence of the more successful practitioners of academic gamesmanship in the major graduate schools provided a new vision of the potentialities of an academic career for thousands of graduate students destined to staff the expanded system of higher education. The drift of institutional power in the direction of the faculty was so pronounced that two prominent analysts proclaimed the existence of an academic revolution and identified the revolution as one "in which the academic profession had freed itself from effective lay control" (Jencks and Riesman, 1968, p. viii). Overall, the prestige of university faculty and of university education had never been higher.

It was a brief golden age.

The backward swing of the pendulum began before the middle of the decade with the eruption of student unrest. Although an important part of the discontent undoubtedly was based on educational issues, the sources of the disturbances were primarily social and political and were located off campus. The effect on the personal relations and the institutional structures on campus and on the attitudes of the public and political constituencies of the colleges and universities was serious and long-lasting. At about the same time, a growing concern for the social problems of race, health, and poverty challenged the position of education in the minds of the public and in the budgets of government. There were also other more direct changes in the environment. The sustained economic boom that characterized most of the sixties lost its buoyancy in 1969; the wave of new students crested and a trough was clearly visible; the massive stimulus of defense and space expenditures subsided; and the inevitable retardation in the unprecedented and unsustainable rates of growth set in. In part, these were the consequences of higher education's success: between 1960 and 1970 the number of bachelor's degrees granted doubled, while the number of master's and doctoral degrees each tripled.[2] Of

---

[2]By contrast, between 1950 and 1960 the number of bachelor's degrees granted actually declined, master's degrees increased 20 percent, and doctoral degrees 50 percent (USOE, *Digest of Educational Statistics,* 1972).

particular significance to the position of faculty were the large, absolute numbers of doctoral degrees awarded: 30,000 in 1970, for example.

It was in this context that faculty unionism surfaced as a major new development, owing its prominence primarily to the formal recognition of two unions as bargaining representatives for the academic staff at the City University of New York in 1968. By 1974 more than one-fifth of the full-time teaching faculty in higher education were represented by recognized bargaining agents.

It would be a mistake to assume that faculty unionism in higher education resulted primarily from a worsening of conditions of service or even from a general failure of conditions to improve. If the unionization of faculty is fundamentally a response to change in higher education, the stresses produced are probably easier to bear when the modifications accompany the golden worries of budgetary affluence and expansion than when they are forced by stringency and "no growth" situations, but the strains are real in both instances.

Significant change will continue in higher education for the foreseeable future, and the dreary probability is that it will occur in an atmosphere of financial depression. This suggests that unionism will continue to grow, although the growth may be sporadic in time and uneven in extent. Some of the dimensions of change that seem to be particularly important to the creation of an external environment for higher education favorable to faculty unionism will be described in the following sections.

CHANGES IN SIZE We have already noted that the number of institutions of higher education increased much more slowly than student enrollment during the 1960s; therefore most of the expansion must have taken place in the existing institutions.[3] Between 1960 and 1970

---

[3]A note on definitions: In the statistics of the U.S. Office of Education, *institutions* of higher education are units that offer at least a two-year residence program of college-level studies that are in some fashion accredited. A *campus* is a location of an institution or a part of an institution. A *multicampus institution* is either an institution with two or more administratively equal campuses responsible to a central administration (which may or may not be located on one of the campuses) or an institution having a main campus and one or more branch campuses. An *institutional system* is a complex of two or more institutions, each separately organized or independently complete, under the supervision of a single administrative body (U.S. Office of Education, National Center for Educational Statistics, *Education Directory, 1972–73*, pp. xii–xiii).

the mean enrollment in the average institution almost doubled, but the growth in the importance of the large institutions in the upper size ranges was more impressive. The number with more than 10,000 students in 1960 had almost tripled by 1970 (74 to 209), and they accounted for almost exactly half of all students. The 30 largest institutions, each with more than 30,000 students, enrolled 1 of every 6 students.[4]

The total number of faculty grew somewhat more slowly than the total number of students, probably reflecting a combination of shifts in the distributions of the students among the various types of institutions with differing faculty-student ratios and an increase in the ratios over the decade. Faculty engaged in resident instruction at the beginning of the decade were estimated to number just under 300,000; at the end, the total was estimated to have about doubled. The distribution of faculties by size appears to be just as skewed toward large units as is the distribution of students. Our best estimate is that more than half of all faculty were members of faculties with more than 500 colleagues in 1970, while more than a quarter of all faculty were members of groups of more than 1,500.[5]

One result of the growth in numbers of faculty in higher education during the 1960s was the presence of a large proportion of relatively young persons. According to the Carnegie Commission *National Survey of Faculty and Student Opinion*,[6] in 1969 one-third of all respondents were 35 years old or younger, indicating that probably they had been hired during the preceding 10 years of institutional expansion.

As is well known, the public sector of higher education grew more rapidly than the private sector over this period. The number of public institutions grew four times as fast as the number of private institutions. As a result, at the beginning of the 1970s three-fourths of all the students and about two-thirds of all the faculty were in public institutions.

[4]Unless otherwise noted, the data in this section are assembled from the U.S. Office of Education publications, *Opening Fall Enrollment . . . , Education Directory . . . ,* and the *Digest of Educational Statistics, 1971.* There are a great many problems of consistency and classification in the statistical definitions that might be challenged, e.g., the University of California appears as a single nine-campus institution.

[5]Calculated from data in the *World Almanac, 1971.*

[6]This survey of undergraduates in 189 institutions, graduate students in 158, and faculty in 303 institutions was conducted with the cooperation of the American Council on Education and the U.S. Office of Education.

In summary, at the beginning of the 1970s the typical faculty member was teaching in a large public institution, one that was about twice as large as it had been a decade earlier. He was a member of a very large professional group that had doubled in total size under very favorable conditions in 10 years and was working in a faculty unit of more than 500 members.

CHANGES IN STRUCTURE

One of the most important structural changes in the 1960s was the development of various types of institutional systems that brought together numbers of campuses into larger administrative units.[7] Table 1 illustrates the importance of the different types of multicampus systems and the changes in growth that occurred over the period 1962–63 to 1970–71. The broad classes of multicampus institutions that have been identified are comprehensive systems that include institutions offering both two- and four-year degrees, segmented systems that may be composed either of all two-year or of all four-year institutions, and multicampus institutions made up of a recognized main branch with direct administrative control over subordinate campuses.

The data in Table 1 show that the number of multicampus institutions increased more than $1\frac{1}{2}$ times, while the number of campuses included doubled in the eight-year period under review. By the end of the period, more than one of every five campuses were part of a larger administrative structure. The most rapid growth occurred among the segmented systems of institutions of higher education, which went from 6 in 1962–63 to 40 in 1970–71. In one important sense Table 1 understates the movement that took place within the overall structure of the system. The relative stability in the numbers of main-branch institutions, for example, does not mean that little change took place among the institutions that made up this classification in 1962–63. Many of the institutions and campuses that were in this category at the beginning of the period became part of comprehensive or segmented systems while other former single-campus institutions took their places.

Since our interest is in the status of faculty members, we have tried in Table 2 to estimate the distribution of faculty among the various categories of institutions at the end of the period. The most striking finding is that the approximately 20 percent of all

[7]See Lee and Bowen (1971) for a study of one set of multicampus institutions.

TABLE 1 *Structural changes in higher education*

	1962–63	1970–71
Comprehensive systems	6	12
Institutions	44	139
Campuses	56	167
Segmented systems	6	40
Institutions	7	135
Campuses	23	196
Main-branch institutions	78	74
Campuses	225	235

	Number	*Percent of total*	*Number*	*Percent of total*
Total multicampus institutions	129	6.2	348	13.6
Total campuses	304	13.4	598	21.3

KEY: A comprehensive institutional system is a complex of two or more institutions offering different levels of degree programs (e.g., two-year, four-year) each separately organized or independently complete, under the control or supervision of a single administrative body. Example, the City University of New York.

A segmented institutional system is a complex of two or more institutions offering a single level of degree programs (e.g., two-year or four-year and graduate programs), each separately organized or independently complete, under the control or supervision of a single administrative body. Example, the Los Angeles City College system. It also includes the U.S. Office of Education category of multicampus institution defined as an organization, resembling an institutional system but unequivocally designated as a single institution having two or more campuses responsible to a central administration. Example, the University of California.

A main-branch institution is an institution having a main campus with one or more branch campuses attached to it and administered from the main campus. Example, Rutgers University.

SOURCE: U.S. Office of Education, *Education Directory,* appropriate years.

TABLE 2 *Distribution of faculty by structural type of institution 1970 to 1971 (percent)*

	Comprehensive	*Segmented*	*Main branch*	*Single campus*
Public four-year	9	11	15	9
Public two-year	2	3	4	9
Private four-year	—	—	8	23
Private two-year	—	—	—	2
Other*	—	—	—	5

*Other refers to special-purpose institutions.

SOURCE: U.S. Office of Education, *Digest of Educational Statistics.* Data refer to full-time faculty. For definitions see Table 1.

campuses that are part of multicampus institutions have more than half of all the full-time faculty. The other significant fact revealed by these data is that at least 70 percent of all faculty in public institutions are in multicampus units.[8] These are the institutions in which faculty bargaining has grown most rapidly.

Coordinating agencies   One more form of structural change can be noted. The increase in structural complexity just described in terms of the growth of institutional systems and of multicampus institutions is related to, but is different from, changes in the overall coordinating bodies that states have established to coordinate their systems of higher education. These coordinating agencies sometimes function as "superboards" in that, on occasion, they have the responsibility of supervising sets of institutions, each of which may have its own board of trustees. The boards may thus represent an administrative layer situated above even the boards of the comprehensive institutional systems listed in Table 1 (as in New York State). In smaller states the coordinating agency may take the form of a single governing board with responsibility for all public higher education in the state with intervening layers of supervision. Robert Berdahl conducted a comprehensive review of the types of coordinating bodies for higher education that existed in each state as of 1969 and traced their evolution over the years (Berdahl, 1971, p. 35). Berdahl identified six different levels of coordination progressing from the first level, in which no state coordinating agency existed, to a sixth, representing a full-fledged, consolidated governing board with regulatory power. Each separate level of coordination represented a step toward more central direction

[8]Following the definitions of the U.S. Office of Education produces an underestimate of the trend toward multi-institutional systems and multicampus institutions. Several segmented systems are not included because, although they are governed by a single statewide board, the several institutions are administered separately in the absence of an operating chief executive. Examples are the Minnesota community colleges and the state colleges of New Jersey, Nebraska, Pennsylvania, and Vermont. Similarly, although the California community colleges have a separate board and a chancellor, there is a low degree of central control so they have not been included. The more than 100 institutions that are included in this group of segmented systems are counted in our statistics as single-campus institutions. About 75 percent of all faculty in public institutions would be in multicampus units if these institutions were considered part of multicampus systems.

TABLE 3
***Number of states
by type of
coordinating
agency***

		1959	1964	1969
I.	No state agency	17	11	2
II.	Voluntary association	7	4	2
IIIa.	Coordinating board	2	3	2
IIIb.	Coordinating board	3	8	11
IIIc.	Coordinating board	5	7	14
IV.	Consolidated governing board	16	17	19

NOTE: IIIa: the board has an institutional majority and advisory powers; IIIb: the board has a public majority and advisory powers; IIIc: the board has a public majority and regulatory powers.
SOURCE: Adapted from Berdahl (1971, p. 35).

and control of higher education. A summary of some of Berdahl's data for the decade of the 1960s is reported in Table 3.

The record summarized in Table 3 is one of remarkably rapid centralization of direction in the state systems of higher education. As late as 1959, 17 states had no state agency performing a coordinating function for higher education. By 1969 this number had shrunk to 2. In 1959, 26 of the states had coordinating agencies classified in the lower half of the six-stage hierarchy of control classification; by 1969 all but 6 states had shifted to a form of coordination in the top half of the spectrum. The rate at which shifts occurred was particularly rapid during the last half of the decade; during this five-year period 9 states established a coordinating agency for the first time.

The upward drift has continued beyond the terminal date of 1969; for example, both California and Wisconsin currently rank higher than they did in 1969.

The consequences of change   The significance of the changes in size and structure detailed in the preceding analysis lies in their importance in affecting the ability of faculties to influence decisions on policy and programs in the system as a whole and on their own campuses in particular. This range of problems is typically discussed in terms of faculty participation in governance of the institution. Faculty members, like members of other traditional professional groups, feel that their expertise justifies a high degree of autonomy and self-government in the practice of their profession. The major universities, at which a large proportion of the career faculty receive their graduate training, usually provide their faculties with considerable power in academic matters, and the expectations of recruits to the profession have been formed by exposure to this model. Only a minority of leading institutions provide anything close to the ideal model of faculty participation in governance, but the mystique of professionalism is attractive and appears to permeate the educational profession even in the lower schools.

The growth in size of the typical institution probably has some effect in depersonalizing and formalizing relations in the basic academic units, the departments. The major change, however, is likely to be felt in the larger administrative units of colleges, schools and, most importantly, at the campus level. Increases in the size of the campus mean a proliferation of committees and a need for coordination and consultation that results in delay, compromise, and referrals before an action can be taken. Faculty organizations that formerly included all members in one unit are converted into representative bodies. From the standpoint of both the administrator and the individual faculty member the process of making a decision has become more cumbersome and more difficult to influence quickly and directly, and the administrative and social distance between the persons who make decisions and those whom these decisions affect has increased.

The increase in bureaucratization of the institution is multiplied in the multicampus institutions and the multi-institutional systems, which have grown so dramatically during the past two decades. In these systems the problems of participation and coordination on a single campus are compounded. The major elements of the faculty governance structure on the individual campuses have to be reproduced at the central administrative level. Here the problems of representation are increased because at least some of the representatives are not well known to one another and because difficulties are caused by infrequent meetings and geographical dispersion. The relations between the separate campus committees and senates and their central office counterparts are awkward to arrange in a way that preserves any feeling of individual or small group influence among the faculty. Even if the problems of control and coordination can be solved on the faculty side of the administrative structure, the multiple levels of the administrative structure mean that the levers of decision are taken from the campus administrators and shifted upward to the managers at the central office of the system.

The growth of consolidated governing bodies sketched in Berdahl's study adds still another layer of administrative control to the managerial pyramid. Faculty representation at the level of the "superboard" is likely to be minimal or nonexistent. Often local administrations have little more direct influence than local faculty groups. On many of the academic bread and butter issues that are of day-to-day concern to the faculty—matters of curriculum, for example—decisions are routinely delegated down to the local level, but major issues are almost certain to be considered on a systemwide basis and are often beyond the reach of local influence.

The growth in the size of institutions, the shift to public institutions, the creation of multicampus institutions and multi-institutional systems, and the trend toward consolidated coordinating agencies—all push decision making on major problems farther from the individual faculty member, his department, and other colleagues with common interests. In the process of adapting to these changes, strains are placed on existing faculty governance mechanisms, and one of the modifications of the traditional pattern that has appeared is the faculty union.

CHANGES IN FUNCTION An institution of higher education can be regarded as changing its function when it either changes the level of the highest degree awarded or changes the character of the programs it offers. Examples of the first change would be a community college that had previously limited itself to nondegree work or to granting a two-year degree converting into a four-year institution, or a four-year college adding a Ph.D. program. Examples of the second would be a trade-technical school that added liberal arts programs to what previously had been exclusively vocational courses, or a teachers' preparatory institution expanding to offer a general liberal arts program and adding professional schools. Many institutions, of course, have made both changes simultaneously. Between 1952 and 1966 Harold Hodgkinson found that a total of 1,178 institutions made at least one change in functions (Hodgkinson, 1971, pp. 64–65). (Institutions that made more than one change were counted only once.) The most common type of change involved moving to a liberal arts and general program, with more than half of all the moves falling into this category. Even though the period studied excluded the later years of the 1960s, which were probably years of greater than average movement, these data suggest that almost half of all the institutions of higher education existing in the period studied made one or more changes in function.

Changes in the function of an institution are important partly because they are usually associated with changes in size or structure, but even more because they typically result in a change in the character of the student body and the faculty. The changes that appear to have occurred most frequently are the addition of liberal arts programs to vocationally oriented junior colleges and the conversion of institutions that were primarily teachers colleges to general liberal arts campuses. In both instances, adding large numbers of faculty with background and training in the humanities, the physical sciences, and the social sciences is likely to produce significant internal conflicts. Potential sources of conflict are to be found in both academic and nonacademic matters, including such areas as courses and curricula, the mix of required and elective courses, and the criteria for admission of students and standards of performance, as well as the standards for recruitment of faculty, the administration of salaries, and the criteria for promotion. One common cause for faculty dissatisfaction in such evolving institutions seems to have been a lag in many instances in the adaptation of administration style and procedures to the new, more "academic" atmosphere.[9]

There were probably few institutions of higher education in the United States that did not make substantial changes in their system of internal governance procedures under the pressures of the structural and functional changes described in this section as well as the other myriad forces pressing for innovation in the 1960s. Almost 700 institutions instituted the single, major innovation of a broadly based senate alone (Hodgkinson, 1973*a*, p. 5). Many of the new systems represented adjustments in the internal balance of forces that met the needs of the moment without modifying the earlier arrangements in a fun-

---

[9]See American Association for Higher Education (1967), a report based on some 35 case studies.

damental way. Others were more radical departures from the mechanisms of an earlier era, and among these were the new systems of faculty collective bargaining.

THE ACCOUNTABIL-ITY COMPLEX The term *accountability* is used here to refer to demands that the institutions and the individuals that provide educational services must be "accountable" to one or more groups in some aspect of their behavior. Such aspects may include the validity of their objectives, the effectiveness of their expenditures, the day-to-day performance of their functions, or the educational results of their activities. The demand for accountability can be used as a catchall to cover quite different phenomena, all of which have in common a feeling that colleges and their faculties should have to "account" for their performance.

The pressures for accountability directed to faculty are based on a belief that faculty have not been responsive and responsible in their professional role. Legislatures and alumni fund sources complain that faculties are shirking their main task of teaching undergraduates, diverting their energies to the conduct of often dubious research projects, the cultivation of exotic special topics, and the cultivation of graduate student disciples. Periodically questions about the level of top faculty salaries and the amount of outside faculty income attract the interest of often relatively low-paid legislators and state officials.

Administrators are prone to assert that faculties are the principal obstacles to desirable academic reforms, ranging from the adoption of new teaching technologies to the use of new admission standards for students and hiring standards for faculty, the creation of new programs, and, on occasion, simply doing more work.

Students protest against pedagogical neglect, a lack of influence on curricula and course content, a routine approach to teaching, and competitive grading systems. They see no irony in calling for the abolition of formal grading for students while simultaneously proposing elaborate arrangements for student evaluation of faculty.

Over the years faculties have developed a set of defenses in depth to protect their positions. The principal bastions are the tradition of academic freedom, the prerogatives of professionalism, and the institution of academic tenure. In its most familiar manifestation academic freedom is seen as a protection of faculty from reprisal for political beliefs or expression. It also, however, is called on to protect the right of the faculty member to control course content, to allocate his time, and to choose his own research topics. The concepts of professionalism are used to buttress the exercise of professorial authority on issues such as grading methods and standards, the design of curricula and programs, peer influence in recruiting and promoting colleagues, a voice in the selection of administrators, and participation in policy making in the institution. The holder of a tenured position is protected against the termination of his appointment except for gross malfeasance or financial exigency of a degree not yet, but soon to be, tested in the courts.

One of the issues brought to the surface by the campus turmoil of the 1960s was the possibility that disciplinary action short of dismissal might be imposed on faculty. Termination is the equivalent of capital punishment in a system of employee discipline, and in the case of tenured faculty it has been used very rarely. The lack of anything like a comprehensive code of conduct or statement of responsibilities for faculty has meant that behavior or lack of cooperation not serious enough to warrant the ultimate sanction of discharge was very difficult to manage. Techniques for eliciting cooperation have tended to be limited to persuasion, administrative harassment, or the award of a positive inducement.

If faculty are to be held accountable by legislators, governing boards, administrators, or students, some part of these defenses must be neutralized. In varying degrees all three have suffered some erosion in recent years.

The ability of faculty members to control the content and the organization of their work in the name of academic freedom has been challenged to a minor extent. In some instances graduate student groups, notably the teaching assistants' union at the University of Wisconsin, have demanded a voice in determining course content and reading assignments in courses in which they carry on part of the instruction. Occasionally a claim has been advanced that an implied contract existed between a college and its students as to the advertised content of courses or the timely performance of duties. In an unknown but probably sizable number of universities student pressures have had substantial influence on course structure, teaching methods, and grading practices. The notion that a course description in a catalog or a printed schedule of classes could be regarded as a form of implied contract between the student, the faculty member, and the institution has had some impact.

In the area of professional prerogatives faculty control over curricula and course content has been reduced by limits on the number of required courses and by breaches in departmental boundaries that permit students to influence faculty behavior through enrollment choices. Grading is a potent method of controlling student behavior, and innovations such as pass/fail grading reduce its effectiveness. Student evaluation of teaching as a factor in promotion reduces the importance of peer review; student membership on appointment and promotion committees changes the character of the review process.

Tenure has been the subject of much attention and concern as the reduced growth rate in faculty positions threatens to reduce the capacity of the system to adapt to changing conditions. The pressures on tenure are high and rising and are taking the primary forms of induced or involuntary early retirement schemes and of term contracts for young faculty members. In addition, the boundaries of the areas protected by tenure are being probed by administrative action (for example, what is the administrative or program unit within which tenure is effective?). As the absolute protection formerly provided by the tenure system is challenged, and as the specification of faculty duties and responsibilities becomes more common, the consequences of noncooperation with administrative requests become uncertain.

The development of accountability, as noted previously, involves accountability to students, administrators, and governing boards. Legislators are moving toward accountability largely through the power of the purse. Even in the states where universities have constitutional autonomy, legislatures seldom find it difficult to get the university's undivided attention through budget action. At least some of the consolidation of governing bodies noted in Berdahl's study stems from the desire of legislatures to see a greater degree of rationalization and control over university operation exerted throughout the higher education sector. Legislatures seem particularly sensitive to questions of work load and utilization of facilities, but they have demonstrated a clear interest in many other aspects of university operation as well.

It is tempting to stress the effects of the financial depression on higher education in the discussion of the new environment. The leaner, less benign condition of university budgets in the late 1960s cast a pall over the exuberance of the earlier years of the decade. Although there has been a reduction in the rate of growth of support for higher education from all sources, overall appropriations have continued to expand even when calculated on a per-student basis. The dollar gains have been eroded by inflation, however, and the state totals conceal shifts in allocations among the various segments of higher education so that individual institutions have been worse off even in current dollars.

Similarly, average salaries for faculty have continued to rise, and, although the increases have fallen behind the rate of price inflation in recent years, this is hardly a phenomenon unique to faculty as an occupational group. In general there is evidence in the studies of individual instances of faculty unrest and faculty organization that the direct effects of financial stringency on the economic position of faculty have been subordinate to the other types of change discussed in this chapter. (It might be thought that the reports of cutbacks in faculty positions followed by an upsurge in interest in organization, such as have occurred in Oregon and Washington, provide evidence to the contrary, but most of these instances seem to have as their initiating cause a drop in student enrollment.) Further support for the proposition that noneconomic factors have been preeminent is the fact that the highest degree of unionization is to be found in the sector of higher education that has continued to enjoy the most bountiful economic environment, the public community colleges.

In summary, the introduction of the notion of accountability for institutions and their faculties is another form of institutional change that generated pressures that have been countervailed by faculty organizations. In a sense faculty unions are a way of demanding that administrations be "accountable" to the faculty for at least some of their actions.

THE NEW LEGAL ENVIRONMENT   The changes outlined to this point have been those that are internal to the system of higher education. Other developments external to the system had a major impact on the position of institutions of higher education and their faculties. Possibly the most important single external development was the rapid growth of the public employees' collective bargaining movement.

The United States adopted a policy of protecting the right of employees in the private sector of the economy to "organize and bargain collectively through representatives of their own choosing" with the passage of the Wagner Act in 1935. In most industrialized countries the unionization of public employees has been accepted for years as part of the movement toward collective bargaining as a system of industrial government.

When employees were granted the right to form associations, one of the conditions imposed was the prohibition of affiliation with an "outside" organization that might impose an obligation to strike or assist in the conduct of a strike. It became commonplace for governments not only to ban affiliation with outside organizations that might create a strike problem but also to require that the associations of government employees themselves refrain from asserting the right to strike as a condition for acceptance as legitimate employee representatives.

In spite of continuing concern with the strike issue throughout the 1950s, the campaign to secure adoption of a federal government policy more favorable to formal employee representation in the union pattern gained momentum. A major breakthrough occurred with the issuance of Executive Order 10988 by President Kennedy in 1962. Rather euphemistically titled "Employee-Management Cooperation in the Federal Service," Section 1 opened with a statement providing that employees were to be protected in the right to belong to organizations to improve working conditions while retaining the requirement that their organizations had to refrain from asserting the right to strike. This executive order was superseded by Order No. 11491 in 1969, and federal policy continues to evolve with increasing support for the enactment of a public employee counterpart of the National Labor Relations Act on a national level. By 1970 more than half of the 2.7 million federal employees were enrolled in unions or associations.[10]

At the state and local levels growth was larger in absolute terms, but distribution of membership in unions or associations was uneven, depending on the character of state law. The

---

[10]Statistical data are from Goldberg (1972, pp. 56–66).

upsurge of collective bargaining in state and local government began in large metropolitan centers. Over many years, Cincinnati and Philadelphia had gradually evolved systems of bargaining, and New York established a formal system of bargaining by executive order in 1958. The first state bargaining law was passed in 1959 in Wisconsin, and the legislation continued to spread during the 1960s and thus far in the 1970s. By the end of 1970, 25 states had laws which mandated collective negotiations for some sector of public employees, 15 more had laws which permitted negotiations or the presentation of proposals, 8 had no legislation, and 2 had laws prohibiting public-employee negotiations.

As this mix of legislation developed over the sixties, it produced an upsurge of union representation at the state and local level, with a membership rising to 2.67 million or 28 percent of all employees in 1970. These figures refer to the number of employees who were members of organizations, not the number of employees represented by unions or associations in actual negotiations. Many members work in agencies without collective bargaining, and many employees are represented by bargaining agents without being members.

Teachers were in the forefront of the organizing (and strike) activity of the last two decades. The American Federation of Teachers, the AFL-CIO affiliate among teacher organizations, boosted its membership from about 56,000 in 1960 to 205,000 in 1970 and claimed a membership of nearly 400,000 in 1974. At the beginning of the decade the National Education Association was regarded as a professional association. By 1970 it had become recognized as a bargaining organization along with several other professional and state employee associations. The inclusion of the NEA and other employee associations along with traditional unions in membership statistics provided by the Bureau of Labor Statistics helps to explain a large part of the growth in union membership in recent years, although large numbers of the NEA's million-plus membership undoubtedly view their new classification with mixed feelings.

By 1970 it was estimated that more than one-third of all public employees were union or association members.[11] This means that, in spite of the limited protection offered by the law

[11]The estimate of one-third for public employment is from Goldberg (1972, p. 56).

in public employment, union and association membership is already a higher proportion of all employment in the public sector than it is in the private nonagricultural sector of the American economy. [In 1970 union and association membership was equal to 30.1 percent of all private nonagricultural employment combined (U.S. Bureau of Labor Statistics, 1972, p. 72).] The prospects for future growth are undoubtedly substantially better in the public sector as well.

As suggested earlier, this new situation is a result of a combination of a growth in membership of public employees in traditional unions, such as the American Federation of Teachers, and the transformation of associations not previously regarded as unions to at least quasi-union status. The reasons for these developments are numerous, with one of the more important being the long-standing campaign by the traditional unions to extend to public employees the private sector policy of encouraging organization or at least protecting the right to organize. Faced by a low level of growth in the private sector since the 1950s, the union movement has seen the public sector as the most promising area of potential growth, not only because of its large absolute size but because public employment has been growing relatively faster than has private employment.

Another factor, and one that may be of greater importance in the future, is the effect of present growth on future growth. As organization in the public sector expands among some occupations and some agencies, and as collective bargaining and even strikes become accepted in law or in fact, it may appear that organization is necessary for defensive purposes in the battle of the budget, both within the government departments and between them.

As part of the same growth in the acceptance of collective bargaining, jurisdiction of the National Labor Relations Board in the private sector has been extended. In 1970 the board decided to take jurisdiction over private institutions of higher education with an annual gross revenue of more than $1 million, but through 1974 the effect of this decision has not been great. The rising wave of public-employee unionization created a favorable climate for faculty unionism. The teachers' union, the AFT, has been visible, aggressive, and successful in winning bargaining rights in the lower schools, and the NEA affiliates in many states have been converted to unionism. The community colleges, with their administrative and personnel links to the lower schools, have led the way to organization in higher education, and a slow but steady increase in union organization among four-year institutions has occurred. The associations' civil service approach to personnel administration, supplemented by lobbying and low-profile electoral politics, is being modified by collective bargaining and by more aggressive lobbying and election activity in the union style. In public higher education something of the same transformation is occurring both within the governance systems of individual institutions and in the legislative and budgetary process at the state level. Even when the result is not formal union representation, the old institutions of governance are being modified to function in a representative role in an explicit and more adversary manner.

OVERVIEW   The analysis in these sections has been intended to support the thesis that the American system of higher education experienced a greatly accelerated rate of change in institutional characteristics and in external environment beginning in the late 1950s and continuing to the present time. We have focused on changes in the size of institutions, on the growth of multicampus institutions and the consolidation of systems, on the shifts in the character of colleges and universities as indicated by type of program, on the increase in the demands for accountability, and finally on the revolution in public-employee relations that has occurred in most of the major industrial states.

With the possible exception of the growth in size, the changes have had their greatest impact on the public sector of higher education. This differential effect appears to be part of the explanation for the relative lack of union activity in the private sector.

It is hazardous to try to create a composite of the typical faculty member of the 1970s, but, if we concentrate primarily on his institutional role, he might be described as a male in his mid-thirties who is employed in a large public institution that is part of a multicampus system of similar institutions more or less loosely integrated into a framework of statewide higher education. Like the faculty member himself the college or university has been "upwardly mobile" in that it has expanded the range of the programs it offers and has increased the variety and the level of the degrees it grants. The composition of the student body and, to a lesser extent, the composition of the faculty have changed. Internally the institution has changed its governance system in the past decade, broadening the groups which participate and adding one or more administrative strata.

The faculty member and his colleagues have been the subject of a flood of task force and committee reports, the great bulk of which have questioned what the faculty were doing or the efficiency with which it was being done, or both. There is a 50 percent chance that the typical faculty member does not have tenure, in which case he foresees difficulty in acquiring it, although he can find solace in the routine description of his group as vital assets for whom a place must be found in the profession. If he has successfully crossed the border to the sanctuary of tenure, he knows there is a widespread suspicion that he is actual or incipient deadwood, and possibly expensive deadwood at that. In recent years he has seen the budget for his institution increase at a rate below that to which he had become accustomed as well as below the rate of inflation. At the same time he has been asked to work more and to consider giving up some of his prerogatives.

Given this recital of trials and tribulations, one may wonder why the colleges and universities have not seen a greater surge of interest in militant unionism than has occurred. The answer is that most faculty, as part of an individualistic professional group with a highly developed critical sense, seem reluctant to opt for one of the traditional forms of unionism. They enjoy an attractive style of life with relatively good salaries and an unusual amount of autonomy and self-direction of their work schedules. In addition, while the level of the academic quality of life has deteriorated in almost all institutions, the incidence of the deterioration has been uneven among institutions and among different groups in the same institution. Finally, colleges and universities have a variety of methods already existing for resolving individual and group grievances, and these may be strong and flexible enough to absorb the increasing pressures without the necessity for a sharp break with the institutional past.

2. Patterns of Faculty Representation in Governance

Much of the discussion of university governance in recent years has a solemn, deferential, and, occasionally, even a mystical character. Our approach is to see the conduct of the internal affairs of colleges and universities as a mixture of management in the traditional sense of control and direction by an administrative hierarchy, of governance in the sense of participation by colleagues in academic policy decisions and professional self-direction, and of bargaining as decision making by negotiation between interest groups with more-or-less formal representative roles. The term *governance* will be used in the customary way to refer to the total system of institutional administration, including relations among governing boards, administrators, and faculty organizations, as well as to the special form of governance involving internal faculty decisions mainly in academic and related matters. We will stress the mix of the three types of decision making found in higher education at any one time and the changes in the mix that are occurring over time.

MANAGEMENT AND GOVERNANCE Since there are more than 2,800 institutions of higher education in the United States, virtually every conceivable variety of administrative control and direction probably has existed somewhere. In a significant portion of these institutions, including most of the larger and better known of them, a fairly standard combination of management and governance evolved over many years. A generation ago the affairs of the institutions seemed to fall naturally into two fairly well-defined categories, the business and the academic. A relatively small body of administrators, often ex-academics, handled the external affairs of the college and performed the business functions and the housekeeping chores of the academic side of the organization.

While the administration exercised substantial influence over the general nature of academic affairs through their control over finances, most of the content of the academic program and many personnel matters were determined by the faculty. The teaching faculty accounted for the great majority of the professional staff, and teaching was the major activity both of the individual faculty member and of the institution as a whole. The faculty were a homogeneous group in terms of their training and their values, and they were in general agreement as to the nature of higher education and their professional role in it. In these circumstances the division of responsibility and function seemed to work fairly well, although instances of faculty-administration conflict were not unknown. *Management,* defined as administrative direction and control of business and external affairs in which actions are taken primarily at the initiative of the administrators, and *governance,* defined as the structure and processes of decision making primarily but not exclusively concerned with academic matters of program and curricula, were able to coexist.

In the postprosperity phase of higher education, pressures for more aggressive and more comprehensive management appeared. In the public sector these pressures took two forms: the already noted tendency to consolidate and coordinate what had previously been separate institutions or separate systems of institutions into larger, more comprehensive organizational patterns; and, in both the public and the private sectors, a move to more explicit and effective management control within individual institutions. As accountability became the watchword, the classic management principle required that the scope of responsibility be matched by the scope of authority.

There are several indications of an increase in the emphasis on management in colleges and universities. Although figures are difficult to come by, there has been a greater increase in the number and variety of administrative officers than in the number of institutions. Management internship programs have been funded and are in operation, and a professional association of administrators modeled after the American Association of University Professors, the American Association of University Administrators, has been organized. Perhaps the best quantitative evidence of the growth of management aggressiveness is the establishment of offices of institutional research.

Rare a few years ago, there are now several hundred, and a national organization, the Association for Institutional Research, has been established.[1] Talk of management information systems, operations analysis, program budgeting, cost-effectiveness studies, management gaming, and mathematical and computer simulation models of university operations fills the air. Educational consulting firms, management workshops, and professional publications proliferate and references to "undermanaged universities" are commonplace. Where there is so much organizational smoke, there must be some managerial fire.

At the same time that management activities were expanding in scope and diversifying in method, the traditional governance systems at many institutions showed signs of disintegration. In many colleges and universities, of course, decision making was always dominated by management, and governance in the form of shared authority had little scope in which to operate. In these institutions it would be misleading to speak of the disintegration of a governance system; here the process of change took the form of a general challenge to almost complete administrative authority. However, in the large number of colleges and universities with substantial faculty participation in decision making, the governance system was the embodiment of faculty power and a distinct entity that could be challenged in its own right.

The traditional mechanics of governance involve some form of faculty senate or council with financing through the institutional budget; with automatic, universal membership; with part-time, largely amateur leadership; and with powers delegated to it by the institution's governing board. The formal recommendations of the senate are advisory, but in practice their ratification is routine except in unusual circumstances.

On the surface it would appear that this system would not wield effective power, but in a great many institutions, including nearly all the prestigious ones, faculty power is an impressive reality in academic and personnel matters. The original

---

[1]A survey found that 337 institutions had "an office or unit" of institutional research in 1969–70, 27 others volunteered that they were starting one in 1970–71, and 97 other institutions used a similar office in a central agency. Of all institutions with enrollments of more than 5,000, more than 60 percent already had established their own offices (Pieper, 1971).

bases of this power were the buoyant labor market for faculty, the sensitivity of governing bodies to considerations of institutional prestige and reputation, the consensus among faculty as to educational goals and values, the tradition of filling administrative posts with faculty members (many of whom expect to return to faculty status), and the generally high regard for the academic profession held by the public at large.

The most publicized challenge to the traditional governance system has come from the students. They have criticized the content and the methods of the educational process, the system of selecting and evaluating the faculty, and often administrators and governing boards. Students have objected to faculty research and consulting, their professors' political involvement (or lack of involvement) in external affairs, and the relationship of the university to society at large. Activist students have tried to institutionalize their power by securing membership on educational policy and faculty personnel committees and by winning voting membership in faculty senates and governing bodies. They have had some success; for example, most of the almost 700 institutions Hodgkinson found with a "broadly based senate" in 1972 (defined as a legislative unit representing several constitutencies) included students (1973a, p. 5).

Other threats to the faculty position in the governance system may be more important, although less prominent. The basic threat is a decline in consensus among the faculty and a rise of differences in opinions and attitudes among the faculty as a whole. Many of the issues on which these differences are apparent parallel those that have agitated the students. They include research policy, policy toward minorities and women, open admissions, and the role of the university in society. In other instances conflicts arise because of the larger size and the greater diversity of activities that characterize the "multiversity." Universities are larger, and the typical institution has more specialized interests, more departments, more research institutes, more libraries and museums, and often whole new categories of professional employees, such as full-time researchers, computer specialists, counselors, and financial aid officers.

Along with the increase in the number of constituencies clamoring for a role in the governance process have come demands to increase the range of activities that are subject to codetermination and to minimize the influence of the administration. In short, the mixture of conflict and consensus that previously characterized the relationships among the faculty, the students, and the professional staff and between the administration and each of its several constituencies has changed in the direction of more conflict and less consensus.

With management expanding its area of activity and becoming more aggressive and with the traditional governance mechanism struggling with only partial success to adapt to new pressures and to a more varied constituency, a different and more diverse set of relationships is evolving. The key element in the new system is the introduction of collective bargaining by independent faculty organizations.

ENTER COLLECTIVE BARGAINING There is nothing new about bargaining as a method of reaching decisions in colleges and universities. It is hard to imagine a system of decision making by consensus that does not include some elements of implicit bargaining, and bargaining between interest groups in even the most traditional of universities is often quite explicit. Even if bargaining is interpreted in an employer-employee context and limited to negotiations over economic issues, a great deal of it has always gone on in institutions of higher education. Many faculty senates have had salary and "welfare" committees that have discussed pay and other benefits with administrative officers, and other faculty organizations, such as faculty associations, have often engaged in negotiations with governing bodies.

What is new in American higher education is the creation of organizations of faculty, outside and independent of the institutional structure, that are recognized as the official representatives of the faculty in formal negotiations over terms and conditions of employment. Collective bargaining also usually brings with it an array of practices that have evolved over the decades of experience with bargaining in the private sector of the economy and, more recently, in the public sector as well. These include exclusive bargaining rights; written, comprehensive contracts; formal grievance procedures; third-party intervention in grievance settlements and negotiation of impasses; compulsory financial contributions; and strikes and other direct pressure tactics.

It is important to remember, however, that although unions

in the United States have many organizational features in common, in practice they have been able to adapt their goals and methods of operation to very diverse circumstances. All organizations classed as unions and winning bargaining rights for faculty need not function in the same manner. The tendency to compare an idealized or stereotyped version of one alternative to the actual, functioning version of the other must be resisted. Although there is enough uniformity of behavior to make the concept of a union model of faculty bargaining a useful one, actual union behavior reflects the goals and the interests of the politically effective union members and not some inherent organizational logic. Faculty members voting for collective bargaining are choosing to use the union as a vehicle to achieve a potential solution to problems they already perceive to exist. Once established, by institutionalizing the management of discontent, the union may generate an independent organizational momentum that identifies or activates problems that might otherwise have remained dormant. Unless these problems are of real concern to substantial segments of the membership, however, they are unlikely to survive long in the harsh environment of tough bargaining.

A corollary of this reasoning is that unionism in higher education seldom represents a dramatic new development or a sharp discontinuity in existing administration-faculty relations. Almost all of the demands that the new unions at the City University of New York presented to the administration after winning bargaining rights had been proposed earlier by the predecessor faculty organizations. In this instance the passage of a new state bargaining law dramatically changed the context of the relationship between faculty and administration, but the substantive issues were largely familiar ones.

The conclusion to be drawn is that collective bargaining by faculty unions is a form of university governance, possibly *the* form of governance of the future over large areas of higher education. It is a new form that is a response to changes in the external environment of higher education, to changes in the structure and functions of the system itself, to changes in managerial style and tactics, and to a failure of the traditional forms of governance to adapt successfully to new problems. Because American colleges and universities are diverse with respect to location, control, size, structure, program, and the characteristics of their student and faculty populations, the resort to collective bargaining will not be universal, and the pattern will reflect a combination of many influences. The rate of expansion is likely to be slow, and periods of stagnation will occur, but persistent, long-term growth is the most likely prospect.

THE GOVERNANCE-BARGAINING CONTINUUM It is helpful to view the various structural arrangements through which faculty may represent their occupational interests and may participate in the governance of their institution as a whole (as distinct from their academic departments) as arrayed along a continuum ranging from the simple to the complex. The principal patterns of faculty-administration relations that have appeared are:

1 *Individual bargaining* This term is used to describe the situation in which the faculty deal with the administration as individuals, exercising only personal influence on institutional affairs and on their own conditions of employment. Some of the faculty may hold membership in national professional associations, such as the American Association of University Professors in its pre-collective-bargaining form, but these organizations do not engage in continuous, direct representation of the interests of the faculty as a whole. Their intervention in campus affairs is on an ad hoc basis, usually in response to a crisis of some sort when they seek to generate support from the larger body of faculty. Some form of individual bargaining always exists, even when an organization has formal bargaining rights.

2 *Organic internal organizations* These are the familiar senates or councils into which faculty are organized. They are organic in the sense that they are an integral part of the institutional structure and all faculty automatically are included; they are internal in that their membership is limited to the staff of a single institution or a single system of higher education.

3 *Independent internal organizations* These organizations are internal in the same sense that organic internal organizations are. They are, however, formally separate from the institutional structure and are membership organizations supported by their own funds. Their independence may or may not extend to advocating policies different from or opposing those of the administration. They may be, and often have been, close allies of the administration in dealing with outside interests, particularly state legislatures. Occasionally more than one such organization may exist on a single campus. Historically, particularly in

public institutions, this type of organization frequently came into existence before senates were established. Formation of senates has often been among their goals for internal governance.

4 *External organizations* These organizations are external to any individual institution because they include in their membership faculty from more than one unit or system of higher education. They are, therefore, also "independent." Unions are obvious examples of external organizations and, as before, more than one organization often exists on the same campus, even when one organization holds legal, exclusive bargaining rights. Once again, they may support the establishment of a senate style of internal system.

The concept of a governance continuum is a useful taxonomic device, but in an increasing number of institutions it is an oversimplification of a complex pattern of organization that is likely to persist in spite of proposals for mergers and affiliations among the various faculty groups.

In fact, none of the four categories is likely ever to be found as a pure type, with the possible exception of individual bargaining. Some version of a senate organization has been established on the great majority of campuses, and on many campuses the whole range of categories is represented, often in more than one version. Even where a faculty organization has won administrative recognition as an exclusive bargaining agent, senates usually continue to function, and often other competitors remain in existence and on occasion, as happened in the New Jersey State Colleges in 1973, succeed in supplanting the original choice of the staff.

Considered in general terms, some form of bargaining can exist in any of the four patterns, although unions such as the American Federation of Teachers are clearly the prototype of the "external organization" and lie at one end of the continuum, while individual bargaining is at the other. At what point on the spectrum is an institution to be considered as "unionized" for the purposes of this study?

The key factor that identifies a unionized institution is its administration's formal recognition of an independent organization as the exclusive bargaining representative of a group including the faculty. Neither the presence of one or more faculty unions on campus nor the administration's practice of meeting and negotiating with the various faculty organizations constitutes "unionization" by our definition. (Nor does the recognition of groups not including faculty.) Treating formal recognition and exclusive representation status as the essence of unionization may seem arbitrary at first glance, but it accords with the general consensus among educators. The CUNY unions existed and met regularly with the New York Board of Higher Education to present demands for years prior to the representation elections that led to the achievement of exclusive recognition, but these elections are rightly regarded as marking a sharp break with the past and the beginning of a dramatic new phase of the relationship. There have been at least five faculty organizations with substantial membership of faculty in the California State University and Colleges that have been meeting with the administration and engaging in a form of negotiations at least since 1965, yet no one, least of all the officers of the organizations, regards the system as unionized.[2]

ALTERNATIVE MODELS OF REPRESENTA- TION

Leaving individual bargaining aside, the other patterns of faculty-administrative relations include four principal types of faculty organizations. Two of these types, faculty senates and faculty associations, are internal, while the other two, professional associations and unions, are external to the institution. An evaluation of their characteristic features follows:

The Faculty Senate Model

The great majority of institutions of higher education use some version of an academic senate or faculty council to organize faculty participation in institutional affairs. Basic membership of these organizations is defined in terms of broad classes of occupational titles, and all persons in these titles are automatically included (although the legislative body itself may be a representative one). There are no dues because finances and facilities are provided by the institution. Some administrative officers are usually included in the membership; officers are unpaid and serve part time; and most business is conducted through standing committees. In recent years the pressures

[2]The signing of a bargaining agreement would be at least as defensible a criterion for unionization as recognition and in the long run would amount to the same thing. Recognition has been used to keep the data current, since, on occasion, more than a year has elapsed before a contract has been negotiated.

from nonfaculty employees have led to the establishment of mixed senates with members chosen from nonteaching professionals and sometimes students as well as faculty.

The powers of the senate are delegated to it by the administration and the governing boards and usually are exercised primarily in academic affairs, such as programs of instruction and curricula. Although they are not usually included in the formal senate organization, the committees through which faculty participate in the affairs of their departments and schools should be considered part of the senate system of representation. Personnel decisions on selection and promotion are considered in the departments, often with some senate participation in reviews or appeal procedures. Faculty welfare and salary committees of senates function in roles ranging from discussion to something close to negotiations.

The de jure powers of faculty senates vary greatly from institution to institution, and the de facto powers are even more difficult to ascertain and assess. One of the most comprehensive and careful studies of the character of faculty participation in governance was undertaken by the AAUP during the 1969–70 academic year—a time when unionization began its rapid growth in the four-year colleges and when expansion in the community colleges was fairly new. The AAUP surveyed all institutions in which chapters of the association were operating and received returns from 970 separate institutions, of which about 800 were four-year units ("Report of the Survey Subcommittee of Committee T," 1971). A list of 31 types of decisions was formulated, and the respondents were asked to indicate the proportion of specific instances of decisions of each type that fell into each of five levels of participation: faculty determination, joint action, consultation, discussion, and no participation.[3] A summary of the results is presented in Table 4, with the 31 items divided into three main classes, depending on whether they involved *personnel, academic,* or *administrative* matters. (The classification of the items is the author's, not the AAUP's.)

Although judgments as to which class a particular item might

[3]Questionnaires were sent to the chief administrative officer and the chapter president, who were encouraged to prepare a joint reply. Of those tabulated, there were 615 joint replies, 176 administration only, 93 chapter only, and 86 institutions from which two separate replies were received.

TABLE 4 *Average of institutional responses to governance questions, 970 survey institutions, 1969–70 (in percentages)*

Decisions relative to:	Forms of faculty participations*				
	Determination	Joint action	Consultation	Discussion	None
Personnel matters					
1 Appointments	4.3	25.1	28.1†	29.5	13.1
2 Reappointments or nonrenewal	4.3	20.9	29.8†	25.5	19.6
3 Promotions	4.9	26.4	30.8†	18.9	19.1
4 Tenure	5.4	29.0	29.1†	16.4	20.1
5 Dismissal for cause	4.9	29.5	32.3†	12.4	20.8
17 Faculty salary scales	0.4	10.4	24.0	18.8†	46.4
18 Individual faculty salaries	1.0	8.4	14.9	25.7	50.0†
Average	3.6	21.4	27.0†	21.0	27.0
Academic matters					
6 Curriculum	41.1	38.7	12.9	6.0	1.3
7 Degree requirements	43.4	35.1†	11.9	6.2	3.5
8 Academic performance of students	85.9†	8.7	2.9	1.8	0.7
9 Types of degrees offered	18.6	49.5†	15.7	8.0	8.2
10 Establish new educational programs	14.2	51.4†	18.2	10.9	5.4
11 Admission requirements	14.7	27.5	18.0†	16.0	23.8
22 Teaching assignments	13.9	49.6†	14.2	17.0	5.2
23 Specification department committees	41.0	24.8†	12.2	10.9	11.0
24 Membership departmental committees	47.1	21.2†	9.8	10.9	11.1
26 Specification senate committees	21.0	35.5†	17.8	10.1	15.6
27 Membership senate committees	32.2	28.2†	14.1	9.3	16.2
28 Academic discipline	26.0	35.9†	17.4	10.5	10.3
Average	33.3	33.8†	13.8	9.8	9.4
Administrative matters					
12 Relative staff sizes of disciplines	1.3	9.5	19.7	30.2†	39.3
13 Programs for buildings, facilities	0.4	7.3	28.4	38.3†	25.6
14 President	0.4	9.2	36.7	20.4†	33.3
15 Academic deans	0.5	12.2	32.4	24.0†	31.0
16 Department chairmen	6.8	15.7	26.6	24.9†	25.9
19 Short-range budgetary planning (1–3 yr.)	0.6	4.7	22.8	29.2†	42.8

TABLE 4 *(continued)*

| Decisions relative to: | Forms of faculty participations* | | | | |
	Determination	Joint action	Consultation	Discussion	None
20 Long-range budgetary planning	0.3	2.6	16.4	25.8	54.9†
21 Average teaching loads	4.1	21.2	22.3	29.6†	22.8
25 Authority of faculty in government	9.8	36.9	27.5†	7.2	18.6
29 Specification student extracurricular rules	5.0	25.0	22.3†	20.4	27.3
30 Extracurricular behavior	3.9	25.6	21.4†	18.1	31.0
31 Student role in institutional government	15.2	32.8	21.6†	15.5	14.8
Average	4.0	16.9	24.8	22.3†	30.6
Overall average	15.2	24.5	21.0†	17.2	21.6

*KEY: Determination—faculty has final authority. Joint action—formal agreement by both faculty and other components is required. Consultation—a formal procedure for recommendations, a vote or other expression of opinion. Discussion—informal expressions of opinion are solicited or formal opinions only from administration-selected committees. None—no faculty participation.

† Median response.

NOTE: Respondents from each of 970 institutions were asked to indicate for each item the proportion of the specific decisions of that type which fell into each level of participation: e.g., for item 1, appointments, 4.3 were decided by the faculty, 25.1 percent were the result of joint action, etc. The numbers are unweighted averages of institutional responses. The division of the 31 items into personnel, academic, and administrative matters was made by the author; the AAUP numbers for the items were retained by identification. The calculations of the average values for each class and the overall averages were made by the author.

SOURCE: Adapted from Table 1 and Appendix II, "Report of the Survey Subcommittee of Committee T," Spring 1971, pp. 68–124.

be assigned may differ, the calculation of the median level of participation for the items in each of the three classes reveals clear-cut differences in patterns of participation.

Personnel matters The process of "consultation," defined as the use of a formal procedure for eliciting faculty recommendations, a faculty vote, or other expression of opinion, clearly dominates in personnel affairs. The first five of the seven personnel items are handled in this way. The sixth item, faculty salary scales, is handled instead by "discussion," meaning that informal expressions of opinion are solicited from individuals or groups of faculty or that formal opinions are secured from committees whose members are appointed by the administration. The median response on the last question, that of individual faculty salaries, was "no participation" (actually exactly 50 percent fell into this category with the other half distributed over the four other responses). The reporting of the median responses exaggerates the difference between the extent to which faculty participate in the consideration of salary scales compared with individual salaries, since "no participation" accounted for more than 46 percent of the responses on salary scales as well.

Academic matters   The pattern for involvement in academic affairs is even more clear-cut. For 10 of the 12 items in this class the median participation was in the form of "joint action," defined as a procedure requiring formal agreement of both faculty and other components of the institution. For the other two items, the faculty "determines" one, that is, has final authority for evaluating the academic performance of the students and has consultation status with regard to the other admission requirements. As would be expected, faculty participation in decisions on academic matters is the highest of the three categories.

Administration   As would be expected, the pattern of participation in administrative matters is more varied, but on the whole, the faculty has least power in this area. Of the 12 items in this class, the faculty participates at the consultation level in 4, 3 of which involve nonacademic relations with students. The faculty participates at the discussion level for 7 other items and has no participation in one—long-range budgetary planning.

On paper then, faculty power was greatest in academic affairs, next strongest in faculty personnel matters, and lowest in administrative affairs.

One major qualification of the results reported by the AAUP ought to be noted. It is reasonable to suspect that the survey overstates significantly the average level of faculty participation in the entire population of institutions of higher education, since only those with chapters of the AAUP were included. This would produce, for example, an underrepresentation of the community colleges, in which faculty participation levels are likely to have been relatively low. It is also likely that four-year institutions in which AAUP chapters have not been established have a below-average level of participation as well, although there is no way of testing this assumption.

Even recognizing possible shortcomings in the data, the AAUP survey portrays a situation that has several important implications for the faculty unionization movement.

First, outright faculty "determination" is low on virtually all issues except the evaluation of the academic performance of students. On only four items (all of them academic matters) did the incidence of "faculty determination" reach 40 percent of the total. This is not surprising because the essence of the senate system is usually described as "shared authority," meaning in the American system of lay control of higher education that the governing boards share some of *their* authority.

Second, our classification is relatively conservative in the number of items considered to be academic; other analysts, including the AAUP, would probably classify some of the administrative items in Table 4 as academic. Nevertheless, the survey reveals that on the average faculty have not achieved as high a status as "joint action" on a single one of the 19 other nonacademic items. In other words, even though several items classed as nonacademic might be considered "academic" and therefore appropriate for joint action, in no instance was joint action the norm outside the academic sphere.

Third, in the light of the pressure for unionization, the relatively low level of faculty participation on personnel matters, particularly on salary questions, is important. Two-thirds of the responses reported no participation or participation at the level of discussion only on faculty salary scales, while three-fourths of the responses for individual salaries were found in these two categories. Much of the published discussion of "faculty power" assumes that the faculty dominates decisions in the areas represented by the first four of the personnel items: appointments, nonrenewals, promotions, and tenure decisions. For these four vital personnel issues the survey reveals that about one-third of all responses fell into the two lowest categories of participation, "discussion only" or "no participation." The suspicion arises that most of the usual analysis reflects the institutional location and experience of the relatively high-status authors of the published material. Undoubtedly many of the personnel recommendations produced under the rubric of formal consultation or joint action are routinely ratified by the administrative bodies, but, as the number of responses in the two lowest categories shows, the usual assumption of faculty dominance in personnel decisions does not apply to large absolute numbers of institutions.

Fourth, in the current climate of budgetary constraints combined with increasing demands for effective participation in a wider range of institutional decisions, the number of responses found in the low levels of participation categories in what we have called administrative decisions is highly significant. Over half of the institutional responses concerning decisions on the relative size of academic staffs by disciplines, on the selection of presidents, deans, and, particularly, chairmen of departments, on budgets, and on teaching loads fell into the "no participation" or "discussion only" categories.

Fifth, the survey emphasizes the diversity in the actual practice of governance in American institutions of higher education. There are many institutions whose replies on all or most of the governance items found in the table fall into the categories of joint action or a strong version of consultation, but there are large numbers that lie in the lower reaches of the spectrum of participation for most of the items. The authors of the AAUP report calculated a single index figure for individual institutions and found that the median level of participation was somewhat below "consultation." If the thesis is accepted that the 60 percent of all institutions not represented in the survey are on the average likely to have somewhat lower levels of participation, then the total number of institutions whose faculties have limited capacities to influence decisions is high indeed.[4] This thesis draws strong support from the fact that only about one-sixth of the community college population is included.

In 1969 the Carnegie Commission on Higher Education joined with the American Council on Education to sponsor a

[4]An examination of the institutions responding to the survey shows that they included seven of the eight Ivy League schools, nine of the Big Ten universities, all four university centers of the State University of New York, and a return covering all nine campuses of the University of California, as well as large numbers of prestigious smaller schools, such as Amherst, Williams, Wesleyan, Carnegie-Mellon, Rochester, Wellesley, Bryn Mawr, Reed, Haverford, Oberlin, and Swarthmore.

survey of the attitudes of a large sample of faculty on a wide variety of topics. Carr and Van Eyck (1973, Chap. 3) analyzed a few indications of faculty attitudes on issues suggested by the AAUP survey of the governance system that can be found in the Carnegie survey replies. The members of the sample were asked to evaluate "the effectiveness of your campus senate or faculty council" as either excellent, good, fair, or poor. Fewer than two-fifths (38.3 percent) rated their senates as excellent or good. Faculty opinions on effectiveness were negatively related to the degree of support for collective bargaining among the respondents. About 35 percent of those favoring collective bargaining thought well of their senates, while 45 percent of those opposing bargaining described them as effective. On other questions somewhat less than half of the respondents thought that faculty salary levels in general in their institutions were good or better than good, while something over half thought their own salaries were satisfactory.

The AAUP survey demonstrated wide disparities in the level of faculty participation in institutional decision making in 1969. This variety suggests that in many institutions faculty are likely to be content to rely on the traditional shared authority approach to governance, while in many others there is reason to suspect that there is a good deal of dissatisfaction with the existing degree of participation, a suspicion supported by the more than 60 percent of the faculty in the Carnegie survey that rated their senates' effectiveness as fair or poor.

Whether or not the senate system in a particular institution can perform the representation function to the satisfaction of the faculty depends on many factors, of which the most fundamental is the level and character of conflict between the faculty on the one hand and the administration and the governing boards on the other. Where differences are infrequent and vital issues are not involved, even a low level of faculty power may be regarded as adequate, but, where conflict is serious or disputes are continuous, even a senate with a high level of participation may be unsatisfactory to its constituents. There is no guarantee that a high level of participation will produce results satisfactory to the faculty.

The basic sources of senate weakness in situations of serious conflict are its delegated powers and its dependence on the institutional structure for financial and personnel resources. In a low-conflict situation the fact that powers are delegated may be a positive advantage. Where conflicts are few, a governing board may be willing to delegate a broad range of powers that in a rare emergency can be revoked unilaterally, but even where conflict levels are low, a board might be reluctant to grant such powers constitutionally or contractually except under great pressure.

In a handful of community colleges faculty senates have actually been recognized as bargaining agents, and in some of the California community colleges the senates engage in something close to bargaining without the outward trappings of the process. A faculty senate committee at the University of Michigan recommended that the senate there adopt a policy of "collective negotiations," changing the character rather than the form (or the financing) of their relationships with the administration. No real change has occurred at Michigan, and no senate at a four-year college has formal bargaining rights.

Unfortunately, the level of conflict between faculties and administrations has been increasing. The rate of salary increase has been slowing, promotions have been more difficult to come by, staff has been reduced, programs have been curtailed or eliminated, the principle of tenure has been challenged, and attempts have been made to increase teaching assignments. Faculty recommendations that had been routinely ratified are now questioned; the centers of decision making have been moved beyond the reach of the campus; and the weight attached to the consultation or discussion process has been reduced in favor of more administrative initiative.

In addition, attempts to modify the senate system to make it a more versatile and useful tool of governance by extending membership to other components of the university reduce its ability to represent the interests of the faculty as a specific occupational group.[5] Broadly based or mixed senates have a great attraction to administrations anxious to avoid an interminable series of consecutive consultations, but the faculty finds its power diluted and its interests muted in the struggle for organizational influence. Once again, almost any kind of senate can work satisfactorily if no serious issues are at stake.

---

[5]For a brief description of mixed senates at Cornell and Columbia, see Garbarino (1971).

When a serious threat to their occupational interests arises, however, faculties have enough difficulty dealing with divergent views within their own ranks without having to generate a unified front from a membership that may include students, nonteaching professionals, and the other diverse groups that have been admitted to academic citizenship in the town meeting versions of the senate. The faculty, of course, is not the only group that may find the version of the senate that administrations prefer for governance purposes inadequate for the job of representing their narrower group interests. Students or nonacademic employees also may find it necessary to maintain independent organizations to advance their interests.

If it is true that academic governance in the future will be concerned more with managing conflict than presiding over consensus, then traditional senates may find it hard to meet the desires of the faculty for a body representing their occupational interests. Faculties are frequently advised to rely on the internal senate approach to shared authority; one early example of such counsel may be found in the report of the Task Force on Faculty Representation (American Association for Higher Education, 1967). Much of this advice is directed to the wrong audience. Unfortunately, in a very large number of institutions the faculty really does not have a choice; the governing board and not the faculty must act to make the choice of an influential senate effective.

Even in a well-functioning system of shared authority, strains of serious conflicts over policy may be hard to handle. Without funds of their own, without guaranteed powers, and without professional staff, in a crisis senates may not be able to challenge administration unilateralism seriously. Under these circumstances experiments with other types of faculty organizations will be tried.

The Faculty Association Model   Although in the current era of organizational proliferation faculty associations have appeared in conjunction with or as adjuncts to faculty senates, many of them antedate senates in their institutions. So they are a familiar organizational form. A faculty association is a membership organization of faculty at a single institution or complex of institutions making up a single system and is not affiliated with a larger association. Prior to the spread of teacher unionism the associations were concentrated in public institutions and were primarily lobbying organizations, although they might on occasion negotiate some issues with their governing boards. Examples of this type of organization are the Association of California State College Professors (ACSCP) set up in the early 1950s in the California system of state colleges, then made up of individual units operating under the state board of education, and the Legislative Conference in CUNY, which dates back to the 1930s. As the examples cited suggest, associations were most likely to be found in large public institutions which do not have a well-developed internal senate organization—at least for the system as a whole—and which often are subject to fairly direct or detailed control by an administrative body.

The associations are the result of faculty recognition of the importance of legislative support and a belief that teacher interests could be served best by direct lobbying rather than by a complete reliance on the efforts and goodwill of an institution's administration lobbyists. Although conflicts between faculty and administration views of desirable policy occur, mutual agreement and support on many issues are common. Before unionism became a factor on campus, associations often supported the establishment and strengthening of faculty senates in their institutions. Where associations and senates both existed, a division of function seemed natural, with the association handling external affairs and the senates concerning themselves with internal academic matters. Very often the officers of the two groups were drawn from the same pool of faculty leaders.

The California association, the ACSCP, claimed partial credit for the establishment of senates in the state university and college system in the 1960s. When collective bargaining became an issue in the colleges in the mid-1960s, the ACSCP first offered itself as one of the candidates for representative status in competition with several external organizations. Later, as the situation changed, the association negotiated a partially successful merger with the American Federation of Teachers local. At CUNY the Legislative Conference converted itself into a collective bargaining arm when the opportunity arose and won the bargaining election for the faculty unit. It later affiliated with the New York State Teachers Association, the state NEA unit, and then went on to merge with the United Federation of

College Teachers, the New York version of the American Federation of Teachers.

A somewhat different pattern has emerged in recent years. When collective bargaining has surfaced as an issue on campuses, existing senates, faced with the problem of maintaining their status as the chosen instrument of shared authority while simultaneously covering all collective bargaining bets, have sometimes encouraged the formation of separate faculty associations. The associations can generate unencumbered dues income and take advantage of any rights and protections that may be provided by the relevant labor legislation in the various jurisdictions. As potential bargaining agents the associations have considerable attraction for many faculty. They give the appearance of being more subject to local control, they usually have lower dues than the national organizations, and they allow the faculty to get accustomed to the idea of adversary relationships without requiring them at the same time to choose among the competing national groups.

The local flavor and independence of ties to external groups that are among the main attractions of the associations can be a source of weakness as well. Once again, the key variable is the level and the character of conflict in the institution. As the mix of conflict and consensus in the administration-faculty relationship changes in the direction of more conflict, the associations' representation burden increases. Even an association representing a large public system of higher education may be hard put to provide the combination of lobbying activity and representation in proceedings before courts and administrative boards and in election campaigns; bargaining expertise; grievance handling; contract administration; and general organizational management that is needed in a full-fledged bargaining situation. There are economies of scale in the performance of such union functions (particularly in the public sector) as political, legal, and negotiation activities, and these economies encourage mergers and affiliations with larger groups. As the examples suggest, these functions are particularly important in the public sector of higher education.

Once again, there are undoubtedly institutions in which the combination of a senate handling internal academic matters and an association dealing with economic and external affairs will work out satisfactorily. The tendency for the officers of the two to be drawn from the same leadership pool may make a division of function workable. Having moved along the governance continuum to this point, many institutions may find it to be a stable equilibrium for long periods of time. To date, however, particularly in the large bargaining units, there has been a clear-cut tendency for independent faculty associations to merge or affiliate with one of the external organizations to secure political, financial, or organizational advantages.

The most prominent example of the second variant of the faculty association model, in which a senate sponsors the formation of an association, is found in the State University of New York. For tactical reasons the senate negotiated an alliance with an organization of nonteaching professionals to create the Senate Professional Association (SPA). After many vicissitudes (detailed in Chap. 4), the SPA ended up as part of a merged NEA-AFT organization.[6] In this instance the role of the SPA as a vehicle for easing the transition to external organization was brief.

The internal organizations, the senates, and the faculty associations may be able to function in a quasi-bargaining role without either needing or wanting formal recognition as a bargaining agent. Undoubtedly, many situations of this sort exist in the nation's colleges. Where the question of recognition as the official bargaining agent arose, internal associations represented the faculty in about 10 percent of all the bargaining units in early 1974. (See Chap. 3.) Almost all of these cases are in community colleges where the scope of activity of the bargaining agent permits a locally based, relatively small organization to handle the representation function.

The Professional Association Model As a device for representing faculty interests at the local campus level, the professional association may be in danger of becoming obsolete, or perhaps it might be more accurate to say that it never really operated that way. The American Federation of Teachers has always been forthright about its concept of itself as a trade union of professionals rather than a professional association. The local and state affiliates of the National Education Association began the by-now-complete retreat from the status of professional association as far as economic representa-

[6]Currently known as the United University Professors.

tion was concerned very early in the 1960s under the pressure from the American Federation of Teachers' locals in the large cities. The NEA and the AFT have engaged in merger negotiations that sooner or later are likely to lead to the creation of a single large and militant union organization. The AAUP retains a strong element of professional association coloration at the national level, although it has increasingly taken on a union tint at the local level as it competes in local elections and functions as a bargaining agent.

It is not unusual for proponents of orthodox unionism to express considerable scorn for the pretensions of "professionalism," particularly as they are articulated by members of occupations newly claiming professional status. *Professionalism* in this sense refers to certain attitudes and patterns of behavior; for example, it may be claimed that it is unprofessional to belong to a union affiliated with local labor councils or the AFL-CIO, to require union membership in a bargaining agent as a condition of employment, to oppose merit pay, or to go on strike. There may be some merit in at least some of these positions, but in any event the union spokesmen who minimize their importance are ignoring the fact that professionalism is not only a set of attitudes but also a system of "job control" that substantially overlaps the techniques of traditional craft unionism. Like craft unionism, under the proper circumstances professionalism has won substantial rewards for the members of occupational groups.

The techniques of professionalism were developed by the associations representing the traditionally self-employed professionals. Law and medicine are the leading examples, but there are other, more recent additions, such as accountancy. The essence of professionalism is autonomy and self-regulation of the conditions under which the profession is carried on, in return for which the professional accepts a form of fiduciary responsibility toward his or her clients. The arrangements are based on the assumption that the members of the profession are the only competent judges of the qualifications and the performance of the practitioners. In particular, the client is assumed to be incapable of making informed judgments on these matters.

Professional associations regulate the conditions under which services are performed in three major ways: control of supply of practitioners, control of work behavior, and control over work jurisdiction. Supply is controlled through some form of certification of competence. This may involve formal licensing by the state, as in the practice of medicine, but it need not. The Ph.D. degree, for example, has no legal standing, but it is close to being a requirement for holding a teaching position in a university of any standing. The essential element is that the profession's clients must be convinced that the certificate is a valid proof of quality, that there is an important difference between an M.D. and a herb doctor. Professional associations often certify the competence not only of the individual but also of the institutions which train them or in which they practice, for example, as the medical associations certify medical schools and hospitals. This obviously is an important part of the control of the supply of practitioners.

Work behavior is controlled usually through codes of ethics. These codes are portrayed with some justification as protections for the client, but at the same time they typically protect the practitioners from the competition of their fellows. Examples are the prohibition of advertising, the promulgation of recommended fee schedules, and the prohibition of corporate practice of the profession.

Control of work jurisdiction is necessary to keep controls of supply and work behavior from losing their effectiveness. If potential clients are permitted to secure services from other providers, the effectiveness of professional controls is reduced. Medical doctors must limit the activities of chiropractors, and lawyers must prevent accountants from encroaching on the practice of law.

The parallels with union apprenticeship regulations, union work rules, and union rules on work jurisdiction are obvious, but there is a vital difference. The traditional techniques of professionalism are not well designed for use by employed professionals. Professional associations are organized to deal with conditions affecting an occupation as a whole and have not been concerned with many conditions important to a specific individual who works on a specific job for a specific employer. Within the professional association there are no equivalents to the plant union; the detailed contract covering a wide range of local conditions; the shop steward at the work place; or the procedures for handling complaints about treatment by supervisors or for interpreting rights and obligations in the performance of day-to-day operations.

In its role as a professional association the AAUP has effectively used two devices to advance its members' interests.[7] One is the "self-grading" salary survey, under which the AAUP collects detailed salary data from institutions, calculates averages for different types of respondents, assigns grades according to the salary level within types, and publishes the results. It is a tribute to the tight faculty labor market of the 1950s and 1960s and to the shared values of faculty and administration that the survey shows continuing competition among institutions to improve their AAUP grades. (The governance survey of the AAUP, discussed in this chapter, was conceived in part as an attempt to develop a similar self-grading approach to governance standards.)

The other major contribution of the AAUP to the profession has been its success in formulating and gaining acceptance for the principles of faculty tenure and its related system of mediating and investigating threats to tenure and academic freedom on individual campuses by association officers and visiting committees of faculty. The AAUP stands ready to intervene on campus "where it appears likely that corporate or individual functions of the faculty have been seriously impaired or threatened" (AAUP, 1969, p. 31).

In effect the AAUP has added new weapons to the arsenal of professionalism by developing these tactics. In the relatively benign environment of the past two decades the AAUP has undoubtedly influenced the salary level at colleges and universities to some extent by facilitating and encouraging the process of invidious comparisons. Its "statements on principles" on tenure and other aspects of governance have set standards and have been the subject of a genteel form of bargaining between the AAUP and associations of colleges and universities; as a result, a number of these associations have recommended the adoption of various statements by their members.

The AAUP has been remarkably successful in attracting a high level of top leadership and of participating staff and faculty, and their efforts have produced statements and reports of impressive quality. The new techniques are designed to meet

[7]For a more complete account of the AAUP in this role, see Strauss (1965).

the needs of employed professionals in ways the traditional tactics of professionalism could not, but these techniques have serious shortcomings as a system of representation.

The salary surveys are useful to a negotiating team, but their effectiveness depends on local initiative and pressure, to which the national AAUP makes no contribution. The decisions of an individual institution to raise salaries or to adhere to one of the statements of principles lie outside the direct influence of the AAUP as an organization. The investigations are often an effective device at the local level, but their use is limited and the great bulk of local grievances of faculty is outside the AAUP's chosen area of responsibility. The AAUP is a useful ally in academic atrocity cases involving academic freedom or tenure problems, but it has not been staffed or organized to deal with routine administration-faculty conflict. The faculty of an institution that has an effective system of internal governance, through either a senate or a faculty association, can make use of the AAUP as a fire brigade or a form of disaster insurance. For many campuses this has been and may continue to be a workable alternative to a more formal system of adversary representation.

The growing number of states adopting laws that encourage public-employee bargaining and the decision of the National Labor Relations Board to extend its jurisdiction to cover institutions of higher education above a low minimum size brought the professional association representation system under pressure from the traditional union approach to the representation of occupational interests.

The Trade Union Model The American Federation of Teachers, affiliated with the AFL-CIO, is the obvious example of a trade union of teachers, but some rivals for the role of bargaining agent have appeared recently. The hallmarks of the trade union approach are the recognition of one organization as the exclusive representative of the members of the bargaining unit; explicit adversary relations; exclusion of administrators from membership; formal bargaining over issues; detailed, legally binding written contracts; formal grievance procedures with binding arbitration of disputes by outside arbitrators; and the use of strikes or other economic pressure to resolve impasses. Unions do not deny the existence of a substantial element of community of interest between administration and faculty, but they regard conflicts of interest as not only inevitable but potentially dominant in the relationship. They believe, therefore, in developing a decision-making system that accepts the possibility, if not the probability, of conflict and is organized to deal with it as the natural state of affairs.

One way of describing academic unions is by comparing them with other forms of faculty organization. This has the advantage of emphasizing the process of evolution by which many of the unionized campuses have reached their present stage of organization. At the campus level, unions resemble senates in that they emphasize local organization, concentrate on local issues, and regard any matter that is of interest to their membership as within their jurisdiction. At the same time they resemble the professional associations in that they claim a national, or even an international, constituency. Historically the AAUP and the NEA have been membership organizations whose greatest strength resided in the national or the state offices and whose local campus branches were relatively undeveloped. The division of activity with the AFT has been much more balanced, with the local and lower-level units often the source of much of the union's activism.

Their concern with local day-to-day problems of their members forces unions to have a more elaborate structure, a larger number of full-time staff, and, on the average, a larger absolute amount and probably a larger proportion of organization effort expended at the grass roots. They have a lower organizational center of gravity than does the typical professional association.

This is not to assert that large and active local associations do not exist in professional associations such as the AAUP or, for that matter, the American Medical Association. As a matter of definition, unless a professional association develops a system of local branches concerned with local conditions of practice or employment, which enter into formal negotiations and which conclude agreements with employers or groups of clients covering remuneration and other conditions of work, it has not made the transition to union status.

These organizational distinctions are often overstressed, but they are helpful in illuminating the dynamics of change in the structure of employee representation in colleges and universities (and in corporations and government agencies, for that matter). In the sectors of the academic world where administration-faculty conflict is serious, the associations and the unions tend to converge toward a common structural form, a common functional purpose, a common set of techniques, and a common set of tactics. The product of the convergence is the academic union.

RECAPITU-LATION The basic theme of this chapter is that the unionization of faculty at some 330 colleges and universities is part of a larger movement toward restructuring the system of faculty participation in campus governance. Participation in general is becoming more formal and structured, and unionism is the most formal and structured version of the process, lying at one extreme of the governance continuum. The analysis supporting this view is summarized as follows:

1 The internal changes that affected the faculties most were, first, the new managerialism that arose in response to the need for better coordination of policy and more efficiency in the use of resources, and second, the challenge to the traditional approaches to governance in which the faculty had been dominant to become more responsive to other sections of the institution's "citizenry," especially the other professional staff and the students. With new, more aggressive administrations, new demands for accountability, and new claimants to participation in decision making, many faculties felt a need for stronger, more direct representation of their occupational interests.

2 The methods used to meet this need take a number of forms, depending on the already existing system and on the level of administration-faculty conflict. In many institutions the creation or the strengthening of faculty senates may meet the need. In others independent local associations arise to deal with the institution's governing board and the legislature as an entity working from outside the official institutional structure. The professional associations have increased the level of their activity in their traditional areas of interest and have embarked on new types of more direct and continuous representation of local faculty interests. In a growing number of institutions faculty are choosing to be represented by academic unions, in the process adopting a style of representation that represents a sharp break with the past.

3 The new organizational forms and the new roles for old forms are best viewed as alternative methods of participation in governance. The more than 2,800 institutions of higher education run the gamut from complete administrative domination to almost equally complete faculty dominance in the making of decisions. The AAUP governance survey emphasizes the variety of arrangements that exist, the large number of institutions in which, on the average, faculty have little effective voice in governance, and the relatively low degree of participation in decisions on subjects outside of academic matters, narrowly defined.

4 However American colleges and universities were distributed along the governance continuum from individual bargaining to formal contractual arrangements with national organizations at the beginning of the 1960s, it is certain that there was a general shift toward the formal bargaining end of the spectrum. On the average more bargaining was taking place, whatever the form of representation, and by 1974 faculties in one of every eight institutions, including one of every five faculty members, had chosen to be represented by academic unions.

The remainder of this book concentrates on analyzing this newest and most challenging form of faculty participation in university governance.

3. Faculty Unions: Patterns of Organization

In a mood of moderate exuberance apparently induced by the victory of the unions in two elections of the City University of New York in 1969, Myron Lieberman, a member of the CUNY staff, used the battle cry of "Professors Unite!" as the title for an article that attracted a good deal of attention. At the time of the CUNY elections more than 100 institutions of higher education, most of them two-year institutions, had recognized unions of faculty members. By late 1974 there were 331 recognized bargaining agents in higher education as a whole, 132 of them in four-year colleges and universities. The bargaining agents represented about 92,000 faculty and professional staff, which means that about 20 percent of all full-time regular faculty and 11 percent of all professional staff combined were represented by unions.

Unions first penetrated the higher education sector in 1963, so we have now had a decade of experience with faculty unionism, although most of the early experience was in two-year colleges and fewer than 4,000 faculty were involved prior to 1969. The duration and expansion of the organized sector permit an analysis of the internal characteristics of the movement.

DIMENSIONS OF SUPPORT FOR UNIONISM It appears that the first institution of higher education to be organized was the Milwaukee Technical Institute in 1963, a two-year institution in a district that included elementary and secondary schools as well. The original bargaining representative was a local association of faculty members. The first four-year institution to be organized was the United States Merchant Marine Academy, organized in 1966 by the AFT. The Academy is a federal institution, and its organization for collective bargaining resulted from the promulgation of Federal Executive

Order 10988. In spite of these early manifestations of unionism, faculty unionism did not attract substantial public attention until it expanded in the university sector, winning in the giant CUNY system, in Central Michigan University, and in Southeastern Massachusetts University in 1968–69.

There are a number of ways in which the incidence of faculty unionism could be analyzed. One way would be to concentrate on the membership of the organizations that claim to represent faculty. By this measure, in 1974 the American Federation of Teachers had about 30,000 members in higher education located in more than 200 locals. The American Association of University Professors had about 75,000 members and more than 1,200 chapters. In addition, there were thousands of faculty who were members of civil service associations in the various states and others who were members of local faculty associations. These data are an interesting index of the prevalence of union membership, but they do not tell much about the frequency of collective bargaining as a process. In fact, large segments of the AAUP, and to a lesser extent of the NEA membership, are probably unenthusiastic about the competition of their organizations for recognition as bargaining agents.

Another widely used approach to evaluating union support among faculty has been the use of data from attitude surveys. A number of these have been conducted by individual investigators at single institutions, but the most elaborate and exhaustive analysis was undertaken by Everett Ladd and Seymour Lipset for higher education as a whole (1973).[1]

The Ladd and Lipset study utilized the attitude data from the 1969 Carnegie Commission *National Survey of Faculty and Student Opinion*. The response to this survey indicated that in 1969 about 59 percent of all faculty supported unionism, as indicated by their disagreement with the statement, "Collective bargaining by faculty members has no place in a college or university" (Ladd and Lipset, 1973). The same question was asked in a follow-up survey by the American Council on Education during 1972–73 (Bayer, 1973). At that time the percentage supporting unionism had risen to 66 percent overall, ranging from a low of

[1]For an interesting example of an attitude survey closely related to the bargaining election in an organized institution, see J. Seidman, L. Kelley, and A. Edge (1974).

53 percent among male faculty members in universities to a high of 71 percent among men on community college faculties. Ladd and Lipset sum up their analysis of the data by concluding that there were "two independent sources" of support for unionism among faculty: one based on a class interest and the other based on ideology:

Faculty employed in the lower tier of academe—in terms of scholarly benefits, financial resources, and economic benefits—and those who are in the lower ranks, lack tenure, and who are younger are much more likely to favor organized collective action. . . . Those who perceive themselves on the political left (on both community and campus issues) . . . are more likely to endorse collective bargaining and faculty strikes and to view increased unionization as a good thing. (p. 16)

The collective bargaining question quoted above is one of two survey questions commonly used to measure faculty attitudes toward unionism. The other question used to evaluate faculty sentiment was phrased, "Do you feel that there are circumstances in which a strike would be a legitimate means of collective action for faculty members?" (CCHE, 1969). The proportions responding "definitely yes" or "probably yes" to this question were lower, 46 percent overall in 1969 (it was not asked in 1973).

The answers to these questions undoubtedly reveal a good deal about faculty attitudes toward two of the characteristic elements of unionism—collective bargaining and strikes—but unfortunately there was no direct question about support for unionism on their own campuses. The responses to the questions asked do not reveal whether the individual responding would vote to be represented by a union in his own institution. Faculty members could almost be regarded as professionally trained to express at least a qualified disagreement with a categorical statement that bargaining had no (none at all?) place in a (any?) college or (any?) university (under any circumstances?). A decent respect for the heterogeneity of conditions in higher education and for the unpredictability of the future almost certainly led a substantial fraction of faculty members to "strongly disagree" or to "disagree with reservations" to the quoted statement on the legitimacy of strikes. Only an inexperienced or incurably optimistic union representative would launch an organization drive on a particular campus on the basis of evidence no stronger than this.

The relationships revealed by the Ladd and Lipset analysis provide a valuable picture of faculty attitudes as correlates of a large number of variables and are undoubtedly of considerable significance for the future of faculty unionism in the long run. Not only are the attitudes subject to change as the situation at an institution changes, but questions considered in the abstract as matters of principle may be answered differently in a concrete situation when actual choices affecting the individual have to be made among imperfect real-life alternatives. The Ladd and Lipset data, for example, show that 56 percent of the faculty members in four-year institutions supported unionism in 1969, and this figure rose to well over 60 percent in 1972. In spite of this, only about 14 percent of the faculty in four-year institutions were represented by unions in 1974, and many of that number undoubtedly had voted against representation in their own bargaining elections. Again, 53 percent of the faculty at institutions classified as "elite" by Ladd and Lipset expressed support for collective bargaining in 1969, but in 1974 only one of the total of 37 (Brooklyn Polytechnic Institute) had been organized. Finally, although in the 1969 survey public and private college faculty showed the same level of support for the legitimacy of the strike (46 percent), very few private institutions had been organized by 1974. The failure of the opinion data to predict behavior probably results in part from the ambivalence Ladd and Lipset found among the liberal-to-radical faculty at prestigious institutions: these groups support collective action in principle while apparently holding individualistic, meritocratic beliefs about the way affairs ought to be arranged at their own institutions. Union activists in these universities find it difficult to convert favorable generalized sentiments into votes in actual bargaining elections.

In this chapter the incidence of unionism will be analyzed primarily by concentration on the population of organized institutions. This means that more emphasis will be given to structural, functional, and environmental variables than to attitudinal data. An institution of higher education will be considered unionized if an employee organization has been formally recognized by the administration as the exclusive bargaining agent for a group including all or part of its faculty.[2] Using recognition instead of the execution of a collective bargaining contract as the critical act keeps the data timely because the negotiation of a contract after recognition is typically a long, drawn-out affair. Except for the time lag, data for contract coverage should be identical with recognition data.

Since the election district is often not the institution but the "bargaining unit," this unit is in many ways the logical element of analysis. A bargaining unit is a legal concept that refers to the administrative area covered by a single negotiation and the constituency in which the question of representation is actually decided. Bargaining unit determination is a complex proceeding that will be discussed later; at this point it is sufficient to say that the boundaries are set through an administrative process primarily on the basis of a showing of a "community of interest" among the institutional staff included.

Bargaining units have a geographical and an occupational component. They may be made up of the faculty of a single element of a campus such as the law school, of all the faculty at a single campus location, of the several campuses of a multicampus institution, or of the several institutions of an institutional system. Occupationally the unit may be a relatively pure unit of full-time teaching faculty or one that includes many varieties of support staff. In order to make meaningful statements about the incidence of bargaining in terms of numbers of persons covered, it is necessary to estimate the number of faculty covered and the size of the eligible population when comparisons are made. Figures like these are difficult to estimate accurately and are usually only roughly comparable among institutions, primarily because they involve questions of whether professional staff and part-time teachers are included in specific instances.

Occasionally a single institution will contain more than one academic professional bargaining unit; more commonly single

[2]A tendency for law schools to win recognition as separate units creates something of a problem because in most cases they are small proportions of all faculty and often no other unit is recognized. Unless otherwise stated, if the law school is the only element of the university that has chosen a bargaining agent, the institution as a whole will be considered unorganized. Examples are Syracuse and Fordham universities, where the faculty as a whole rejected organization, but the law school elected an independent faculty association as its representative. Similarly, if only teaching or research assistants have organized, the institution is not considered unionized.

bargaining units will include more than one institution. Because most interest attaches to the institutions, the bulk of our data refer to institutions rather than bargaining units. The problems of defining institutions were covered in Chapter 1, but it might be noted that there are about twice as many organized institutions as bargaining units. Unless otherwise stated, the numbers of "faculty" reported refer to all members of the bargaining unit, even though the units include a substantial number of nonteaching professionals.

GROWTH TRENDS OF FACULTY UNIONISM The years 1973 and 1974 saw relatively slow growth in faculty unionism, particularly in the community colleges. The pattern of growth has been traced back to 1966, the year the first four-year colleges were organized, and the data are presented in Table 5, separately for all institutions and for four-year institutions. The picture presented is one of steady growth with substantial variations in the annual growth rate. There are two major discontinuities in the data: one in 1969, when the organization of CUNY added 20 institutions and about 15,000 individuals to the roster, and another in 1971, when the addition of SUNY raised the totals by 26 and 15,000, respectively. Even allowing for these examples of the "lumpiness" of growth in the earlier years, 1973 represented a "growth recession," with only

TABLE 5
Unionization in institutions of higher education, 1966–1974

	Total institutions	Total faculty	Four-year institutions	Four-year faculty
1966	23	5,200	1	200
1967	37	7,000	2	300
1968	70	14,300	10	3,300
1969	138	36,100	26	16,100
1970	177	47,300	40	23,400
1971	245	72,400	84	45,400
1972	285	84,300	102	54,600
1973	310	87,700	121	57,400
1974	331	92,300	132	60,600

NOTE: Data are for all professional staff and include five institutions with only professional schools and two with only teaching assistants organized. Figures are as of December 31. (Data revised February 1975 from earlier published estimates.)

25 institutions and 3,400 professional staff added. This was the smallest absolute growth since 1967, a year in which most faculty, to say nothing of the general public, were hardly aware that a faculty unionism movement existed. The slowdown was particularly apparent in the most mature sector, the community colleges, where only six institutions with 600 faculty were organized. In 1974 the slowdown continued with 21 institutions and 3,600 staff organized. Although 1975 looks better, the overall record seems to justify use of the term *creeping unionism* to characterize the trend.

The situation portrayed in Table 5 can be put into perspective by a calculation of the percentage of the population of institutions and faculty that is organized. About one of every eight institutions of higher education is organized, including about 6 percent of the four-year and 25 percent of the two-year institutions. The figures for coverage of "faculty" in the table really refer to all professional staff in the bargaining units. The bargaining penetration ratio for that group is about 11 percent. Estimates of the number of full-time regular faculty represented by unions have also been made. In this instance the ratio of faculty organized to all full-time faculty is about 21 percent. This ratio is higher than that for all professional staff because the major research universities with a large complement of support professionals have a low degree of organization.[3]

THE ANATOMY OF UNIONISM
Turning from the pattern of growth over time to a cross-sectional view, Table 6 is something of a master chart of the status of union organization as of mid-1974. Several conclusions stand out:

Faculty unionism is a phenomenon of public higher education, even though four years have elapsed since the National Labor Relations Board assumed jurisdiction over most of the private colleges and universities. Ninety percent of all organized full-time teaching faculty are in public institutions, although they account for only two-thirds of all faculty. An even larger percentage of all organized staff is in public units. Measured in terms of institutions, only 2 percent of all private institutions

[3]Data in this section are taken from estimates of the USOE, *Digest of Educational Statistics* (1970). Figures for full-time teaching staff were obtained from Parker (1972) and the American Association of Junior Colleges (1971).

	Public		Private
TABLE 6 *Numbers of institutions and instructional staff with faculty unions, Spring 1974, by level, control, and type of state law*	*Four-year*	*Two-year*	*Four-year*
Comprehensive law			
New York	32-22,500	40- 9,800	12-3,300
Michigan	6- 3,600	26- 4,100	1- 100
New Jersey	11- 5,800	13- 1,500	4-1,100
Pennsylvania	16- 5,500	9- 1,300	1- 100
Minnesota	—	18- 1,100	—
Hawaii	2- 1,600	6- 1,000	—
Oregon	1- 200	4- 800	—
D.C.	—	1- 200	—
TOTAL	68-39,200	117-19,800	18-4,600
Inclusive law			
Massachusetts	9- 1,600	3- 300	4- 100*
Rhode Island	2- 1,000	1- 300	2- 200
Nebraska	4- 500	—	—
Delaware	1- 700	—	—
Vermont	3- 300	1- 100	—
TOTAL	19- 4,100	5- 700	6- 300
Selective law			
Washington	—	24- 3,500	—
Wisconsin	—	16- 2,200	1- 100
Maine	—	5- 200	—
Maryland	1- 500	1- 200	—
New Hampshire	—	—	2- 200
North Dakota	—	—	1- 100
Connecticut	—	—	1- 400
TOTAL	1- 500	46- 6,100	5- 800
Meet and confer law			
Florida	—	1- 100	—
Kansas	—	8- 500	—
TOTAL		9- 600	

TABLE 6 (continued)	Public		Private
	Four-year	Two-year	Four-year
No law—favorable			
Illinois	—	15- 2,600	1- *
No law—unfavorable			
Colorado	—	1- 100	2- 200
Ohio	1- 600	—	1- 200
Iowa	—	—	1- 100
TOTAL	1- 600	1- 100	4- 500
GRAND TOTAL	89-44,400	193-29,900	34-6,200

*Massachusetts and Illinois have 4 organized, private, two-year institutions, each with less than 50 faculty members. Data refer to instructional staff in 1973. Separate professional-school and graduate-student-only units are not included. Note that the figures in Table 5 include all professional staff and all institutions, including those with only professional school and graduate students organized.

are organized, while about 20 percent of the public institutions have chosen bargaining agents.

The slow rate of growth in the private sector is particularly surprising because the existence of a public-sector bargaining law is of vital importance to union growth in public higher education. In the private sector the prototype of the supportive labor law, the National Labor Relations Act, which covers two-thirds of all the institutions of higher education, has produced organization in only about 10 percent of the nation's private institutions in four years. Since the NLRB took jurisdiction over higher education in 1970, about five times as many public as private institutions have opted for collective bargaining, even though hundreds of public institutions are in states without bargaining laws.

Part of the difference in organizational levels is accounted for by the situation in the community colleges. These are the most highly organized sectors of higher education, and there are three times as many public as private two-year colleges. Even with the community colleges eliminated from the data, however, the concentration of organization in public institutions is extraordinary. Seventy percent of all organized institutions, accounting for 83 percent of faculty, are in four-year colleges in the public sector, although only 27 percent of all institutions and 55 percent of all the faculty are in these institutions.

There is little hard evidence to explain why the private institutions have been slow to organize. A number of possible explanations will be advanced in later sections.

The future of faculty bargaining lies in the four-year institutions. Although the community colleges got an early start in collective bargaining and are sometimes thought to dominate the movement, most of the organized faculty population is in the four-year colleges and universities. Not only is the organized population in four-year colleges larger now, but organization is growing faster, and the potential eligible population is much larger. Except in a few states, notably California, community colleges have relatively small numbers of full-time faculty. Since 1969, the year of the big breakthrough, more four-year than two-year institutions have been organized, and these institutions have included 3½ times as many faculty members. In 1974, although there were more two-year institutions organized, 70 percent of all organized faculty were in four-year colleges.

In addition, although there is a natural tendency to think of institutions of higher education as arranged in a pyramid, with the community colleges as the broad base, in fact the pyramid is inverted, with most faculty in the universities, the next largest number in the four-year colleges, and the fewest in the two-year colleges. Although the proportion is probably growing, in 1969 less than one-sixth of all faculty were in the two-year institutions.[4]

Faculty unionism is highly concentrated in a few states. New York State is the faculty collective-bargaining center of the nation. In large part this is because of the Taylor Act, the New York public employee bargaining law enacted in 1967. Over 90 percent of all the public employees in New York are organized, and the public higher education sector is almost completely

[4]The figures cited are for full-time faculty. Where two-year colleges are included in comprehensive systems with other levels, they have been taken out and counted separately. U.S. National Center for Educational Statistics (1970, pp. 4–7).

unionized. As a result, almost one-third of all the organized institutions and almost one-half of all the academic staff represented by unions are in New York. SUNY and CUNY alone account for about 40 percent of all the faculty in bargaining units.

The other states with large numbers of union faculty are Michigan, New Jersey, and Pennsylvania. Together with New York these three states account for about three-fourths of all the higher education staff in bargaining units. The other quarter is spread over 20 other states. The remarkably high concentration of faculty unionism in a few states, coupled with the fact that most states have little or no organizing activity, makes it clear that the incidence of faculty unionism must be different from that of unionism generally. Moreover, the geographical distribution of faculty organization obviously does not correspond to the distribution of faculty members among the states. The most important single factor that explains the pattern of unionization is the character of state public-employee bargaining laws.

INSTITUTIONAL CORRELATES OF FACULTY UNIONISM *The law and the unions* In Chapter 1 the growth of public-employee unionism was presented as a major factor in the growth of faculty unions. We noted that 40 states had enacted some form of negotiation law for at least some of their public employees and that a rapid upsurge of union growth had occurred.

An analysis of the state laws suggested that a six-way classification of the legal environment in each state would be feasible and helpful. The six categories are:

1 Comprehensive law—a single law covers all public employees and mandates collective bargaining.

2 Inclusive education law—a separate law provides for collective bargaining for educational personnel, including all of higher education.

3 Selective education law—a separate law covers educational personnel but excludes four-year institutions.

4 Meet and confer laws—either a comprehensive or an inclusive law exists that includes higher education, but it is a weak law limited to requiring the parties to "meet and confer" rather than to bargain collectively.

5 No law—favorable—refers to a situation in which there is no applica-

ble law, but there have been court decisions favorable to the establishment of negotiating procedures.

6 No law—unfavorable—refers to the situation in which there is neither a law nor favorable court decisions.

The ranking represents, in a general way, a progression from the most to the least supportive legal climate for public employee bargaining.

As one would expect, the relationship between the legal environment of public negotiations and organization is clearcut. Table 7 shows the situation as it exists in each of the 24 states in which at least one faculty union has won recognition. Almost two-thirds of all organized public institutions are to be found in the 8 states with comprehensive bargaining laws. The concentration of faculty members is even greater, since these institutions account for about three-fourths of all the organized faculty. One of the interesting points brought out by Table 7 is that the potential for union organization in these states has been pretty well exhausted, with three-quarters of all the public institutions already organized. Of the 8 states with comprehensive laws only Oregon has less than 40 percent of public institutions organized, and that is because Oregon's comprehensive law only went into effect in October 1973.

Comprehensive laws covering all public employees in the state seem to be more effective in spurring organization among faculty members in higher education than do the separate education statutes of either the inclusive or the selective types. About half of the public institutions in the states with separate education laws have been organized to date. The other three types of legal situations are less supportive, and each has a degree of organization lower than the states with either comprehensive or separate education bargaining laws. The seven states in the three lowest categories together provide only about one in ten of the public institutions in the country that are organized. The most interesting state in the lower half of the categories by degree of organization is Illinois, a state without a bargaining law in which 28 percent of the public organizations have organized. All 14 of the organized institutions are two-year institutions. Half of all the faculty involved are in the Chicago City Colleges, a seven-campus institution organized by the AFT in 1966 and a storm center of bargaining activity

TABLE 7 *Organized public institutions and faculty by type of state legal environment*

		Public institutions			
	*Number of states**	*Organized*	*Percentage of total†*	*Total*	*Full-time teaching staff in units*
Comprehensive law	8	185	78	236	47,100
Inclusive law	5	24	59	41	4,500
Selective law	4	47	53	88	5,000
Meet and confer law	2	9	14	64	500
No law—favorable	1	15	30	50	2,600
No law—unfavorable	2	2	4	53	500
TOTAL U.S.	22	282			60,200

*Includes only those states with at least one exclusive recognized bargaining agent of faculty in an institution of public higher education.

†Percentage of organized public institutions in each category.

KEY:

Comprehensive bargaining law: Statute obligates all public employers (state, local, and public school) to bargain in good faith in an attempt to reach agreement and requires exclusive recognition by employers of faculty representatives. (District of Columbia, Hawaii, Michigan, Minnesota, New Jersey, New York, Oregon, and Pennsylvania)

Inclusive bargaining law: Separate statutes obligate state, local, and public school employers to bargain in good faith in an attempt to reach agreement and requires exclusive recognition by employers of faculty representatives. Includes faculty of four-year institutions, either as state employees under the state law or under the education law. (Delaware, Massachusetts, Nebraska, Rhode Island, and Vermont)

Selective bargaining law: Statute obligates only public school employers to bargain in good faith with faculty representatives. Excludes faculty of four-year institutions. (Connecticut, Maine, Montana, Washington, and Wisconsin)

Meet and confer law: Statute obligates public employer to meet and confer with employee representatives. Exclusive recognition by employers of faculty representatives is not required and may not be permitted. In this classification the emphasis shifts from the coverage of the laws as above to the degree of support for bargaining. All provide a low degree of support. (Florida and Kansas)

No law—favorable: No statutory provision for collective bargaining for public higher education. Court rulings or attorney general opinions permit organization or negotiations by some or all employees in higher education. (Illinois)

No law—unfavorable: No collective bargaining statute covering public education or higher education. (Colorado and Ohio)

since that time. The substantial level of organization in Illinois is a reminder that, in the absence of positive legal barriers to recognition, a union can win bargaining rights on its own by direct action.

The concentration of organization in states with bargaining laws is further illustrated by the fact that about 90 percent of all the organized institutions and of the organized faculty are found in the states with the three strong types of bargaining law, although only about 20 percent of all institutions and all faculty are located in them. Finally, except for Illinois, not only are faculty bargaining units clustered in states with strong laws, but there are very few states with supportive laws in which organization has not occurred.[5]

The overwhelming importance of the legal status of public-employee bargaining for faculty organization has great significance for the future of the movement. The effectiveness of the strong laws in encouraging unionization means that the probable passage of such legislation in a substantial number of states in the near future is likely to produce a new surge of organization in the next two years.[6] If California, the sleeping giant of faculty unionism, where an inclusive bargaining law was vetoed by former Governor Ronald Reagan in 1973, should enact a favorable law, the impact could be substantial. A clean sweep of California higher education would add about 40 percent to the present total of organized faculty. This is unlikely to occur in the short run, but the state college system would probably organize quickly, as would substantial portions of the gargantuan community college system (Aussieker, 1974; Garbarino, 1974b; Walker, 1974). An educated guess is that 25,000 to 30,000 persons could be added to the total of organized faculty within a year of the passage of a supportive law in California.

There is a very active labor lobby pressing for a federal public-employee bargaining law with, as one of its major elements, provision for the Coalition of American Public Employees—an alliance of the American Federation of State, County, and Municipal Employees, the National Education Association, and the International Order of Fire Fighters. It is unlikely that such a law will be enacted in the near future.

---

[5]As of Spring 1974 one state with a comprehensive law, Oregon, had no organization, but its law was changed from a "meet and confer" law only in October 1973. Two states with inclusive laws, Alaska and New Hampshire, with a total of five public institutions, had no organization. Three states with selective laws, Idaho, Nevada, and Oklahoma, with a total of eighteen public two-year institutions, had no organization.

[6]The *Chronicle of Higher Education* reported that 28 states were considering new legislation (March 6, 1974, p. 1).

In Chapter 1 we predicted that changes in the structure of higher education were likely to increase the desire of faculty members for some form of organizational representation. Five different types of institutional structure were identified: the comprehensive system including all levels of institutions; the segmented systems that divide into institutional and multicampus versions, both of which are limited to either two- or four-year institutions; the main-branch institutions made up of administratively dominant main campuses with satellite branches; and the single-campus institutions.

When the pattern of faculty organization is related to the existing structural types, as in Table 8, two areas of concentration stand out. Unionism is found to be concentrated at both ends of the distribution—among the comprehensive systems on the one hand and among the single-campus institutions on the other. Although more than two-thirds of all organized units are located at single-campus institutions, the very large number of unorganized private institutions holds the extent of organization for that group as a whole at 10 percent. At the other end of the distribution the large SUNY and CUNY complexes assure that about half of the institutions in comprehensive systems are counted as organized. Although fewer than 5 percent of all institutions are included in comprehensive systems, these account for one-sixth of all organized institutions. Segmented systems are also somewhat more organized than their proportion in the total population would suggest.

The fact that more than 70 percent of all unionized institutions are single-campus institutions sounds impressive until one realizes that almost 90 percent of all institutions fall into that category.

The three organized comprehensive systems are SUNY and CUNY in New York State and the University of Hawaii, both in states with comprehensive laws and a very high percentage of union organization among employees in both the public and the private sector. With the familiar exception of Oregon, the other comprehensive systems are all in states with legal environments that do not encourage unionization. Although the three organized comprehensive systems deserve further analysis, their status is obviously linked to the legal environment in their states. The great majority of organized single-campus

TABLE 8 *All institutions, all organized institutions, and degree of organization by type of institutional structure*

	All institutions		All organized institutions		
	Number	*Percentage of total*	*Number†*	*Percentage of total*	*Percentage organized*
Comprehensive systems*	109	4.2	54	17.8	49.5
Segmented systems	135	5.3	22	7.2	16.3
Institutional systems	(110)	(4.3)	(15)	(4.9)	13.6
Multicampus systems	(25)	(1.0)	(7)	(2.3)	28.0
Main-branch institutions	74	2.9	4	1.3	5.4
Single-campus institutions	2,240	87.6	224	73.7	10.0
TOTAL	2,558	100.0	304	100.0	11.8

*The U.S. Office of Education includes 30 New York community colleges outside New York City as part of the SUNY system, but they are separate single-campus bargaining units in fact and the 26 organized institutions have been so classified.

†Excludes 5 organized Maine vocational-technical institutes, 5 organized Wisconsin vocational-technical institutes, and 2 organized Washington community colleges not listed in the 1970–71 *Directory* of the USOE.

KEY:

Comprehensive institutional system: A complex of two or more institutions offering different levels of programs (for example, two-year, four-year, doctorate), each separately organized as independently complete, under the control or supervision of a single administrative body (for example, SUNY).

Segmented institutional system: A complex of two more institutions offering the same level of programs (for example, two-year, four-year, doctorate), each separately organized or independently complete, under the control or supervision of a single administrative body (for example, the Massachusetts State College system).

Multicampus institution: An organization bearing resemblance to an institutional system but unequivocally designated as a single institution having two or more campuses to a central administration (for example, the University of California).

Main-branch institution: An institution having a main campus with one or more branch campuses, not seminaries or military installations, attached to it (for example, Rutgers University).

SOURCE: U.S. Office of Education, *Directory, 1970–1971.*

institutions are also in states with supportive laws. It is impossible to escape the conclusion that, at least for public institutions, the type of applicable collective-bargaining legislation in the various states so dominates the situation that it is difficult to find other variables that have a significant independent effect. The overwhelming importance of a legal climate favorable to faculty unionism is one-half of the law-unionism relationship; the other half is the negligible effect that the extension of the National Labor Relations Act to private institutions has had.

Four years after the National Labor Relations Board extended the protection of the National Labor Relations Act to the private sector of higher education, 98 percent of the private institutions remain unorganized. In addition, 26, or about 2 of every 5, of the bargaining elections held in private institutions through mid-1974 resulted in victories for the "no agent" choice. In the more than 200 bargaining agent elections in public institutions, "no agent" was the winner only three times. So few private institutions are organized that no significant analysis of the organized group can be made, but certain tentative positive or negative conclusions can be reached by inclusion in the analysis tests of whether the private colleges differ from public institutions in ways that suggest support for various hypotheses.

Institutional change   One of the types of structural institutional change that might have been expected to encourage faculty unionization was the creation of larger and more complex administrative units by the conversion of single campuses into multicampus institutions or by the gathering of sets of independent institutions into larger systems, including, on occasion, the mingling of two-year colleges with four-year colleges and with graduate centers. It was noted at that time that the number of comprehensive systems rose from 6 to 12 in the 1960s, while the number of institutions included in such systems more than tripled (see Table 1). Overall, between 1962–63 and 1970–71 the number of multicampus institutions almost tripled, and the total number of campuses that were parts of multicampus institutions increased from 304 to 598. By the latter year more than 1 of every 5 campuses were part of a multicampus institution, up from 13 percent in the earlier year. According to the source used in developing Table 8, there were only 34 private multicampus institutions in 1970–71, so that the very large expansion in the number of multicampus institutions was almost entirely concentrated in the public sector of higher education. Even without adjustments for the strong influence of various legal environments, Table 8 shows that three times as many public institutions in comprehensive and segmented systems are organized as their proportion in the population would suggest.

In the main-branch institutions, the only complex institutional type with a significant number of private institutions represented, 20 percent of the private universities included are organized. It seems clear that one reason for the lack of organization in the private sector is the relatively simple organizational structure of the great majority of these institutions and the organizational stability that they have enjoyed during a period of proliferating multicampus institutions in the public sector.

Another type of institutional change that was considered significant was functional change, measured by changes in the level of the degrees granted and in the variety of programs offered. The usual changes that marked the 1960s were the additions of more types and higher levels of degrees and the addition of liberal arts and general programs. According to the Hodgkinson study (1971), about 40 percent of all institutions of higher education made some functional change of this sort between 1962 and 1966, and many more must have been made since then. Unfortunately, that study did not distinguish between public and private institutions. General knowledge suggests that such changes must have been centered in the public sector. There are no counterparts in the private sector to the wholesale transformations of former state teachers colleges to general liberal arts colleges such as occurred in New York, New Jersey, Massachusetts, Pennsylvania, and Michigan, of the states with high levels of faculty unionization, and in California, Illinois, Texas, Ohio, and Wisconsin, of the states with little faculty unionism to date. Another indication of functional change is the expansion in the number of institutions granting the Ph.D. degree, most of which took place in public institutions. As noted earlier, changes of this sort create stresses within and between institutions as they produce changes in the allocation of faculty and students by academic discipline; in the standards of recruitment, retention, pay, and promotion; and in the relations with the various constituencies with which the college has external ties.

In states with strong bargaining laws it is in these "emerging" colleges and universities that support for unions has tended to appear first, and in such states unionism appears to be concentrated in this range of institutions. But, again, this is an aspect of institutional change that private institutions have experienced to a much lesser degree than public institutions, and this may be another element in the explanation of the differing patterns of organization.

Although the data prevent firm conclusions from being drawn, there is at least circumstantial evidence that differences in the administrative structure of the public and the private sectors is one of the reasons for the lack of organization in the private sector.

Governance and unionism   In 1967 a pioneering study of "faculty discontent" sponsored by the American Association for Higher Education concluded that "the main sources of discontent are the faculty's desire to participate in the determination of those policies that affect its professional status and performance and in the establishment of complex, statewide systems of higher education that have decreased local control over important campus issues" (p. 1). In short, the main sources of discontent were governance issues. Carr and Van Eyck (1973) analyzed the 1969 Carnegie survey of faculty attitudes to test the relation between various indices of dissatisfaction with conditions at institutions and the support for bargaining. They concluded that faculty who supported bargaining were more likely to be dissatisfied with such aspects of their campus situation as the power of senior professors, the effectiveness of the faculty senate, and the autocratic or democratic nature of departmental governance. This suggests that differences in the level of participation in institutional governance might account for differences in the propensities of faculties to organize in different sectors of higher education.

The AAUP governance survey reviewed in Chapter 2 can be used to measure participation levels in institutions ("Report of the Survey Subcommittee of Committee T," 1971, pp. 68–124). The AAUP survey quantified the participation of faculty in governance with regard to 31 different types of decisions. The responses were used to calculate a summary index figure for each institution. For the population as a whole the median of the unweighted scores for the individual institutions was in the interval 275 to 299, a level that fell just below the numerical value assigned to the type of participation denoted "consultation."[7] When the institutions were classified by type of institution and control, participation in governance was found to be greatest in the private universities, followed closely by the private liberal arts colleges and emerging universities. The public universities were third, with the public liberal arts colleges and emerging universities substantially lower and well below the overall median score. Except for a small number of technical schools, the two-year colleges had the lowest score.

The substantial differences between the public and the private institutions in the level of faculty participation in governance as measured by the AAUP survey indicate that a higher degree of effective involvement in governance in private institutions may be one of the factors that explains their low level of union organization.

The clear-cut differential between public and private institutions in faculty participation in governance suggested that it would be useful to test the hypothesis that unionization and participation in governance are inversely related. The national office of the AAUP assisted us by calculating governance scores for the four-year and the two-year institutions that had been organized by the fall of 1973. Among the institutions for which scores were available there were 80 four-year and 43 two-year institutions. Unfortunately for the hypothesis that unionism and participation were inversely related, the median participation scores for the organized four-year and two-year colleges were both in the 300 to 324 interval and higher than the median scores for the population as a whole. The differential was particularly marked for the two-year colleges.[8]

There are at least two possible reasons why the reported governance score for organized institutions exceeded the scores for the sample as a whole. The first is that the important variable may not be the actual degree of participation in governance as measured by the AAUP survey but the gap between

[7]The definition of the five forms of faculty participation are given in Chapter 2; briefly they are "no participation," "discussion," "consultation," "joint action," and "faculty determination." The scale ran from 100 to 500 in multiples of 100, with "consultation" scored as 300.

[8]A possible reason for this discrepancy in the two-year sector is that a substantial number of the two-year colleges were already organized at the time of the survey in 1969–70. Only a handful of the four-year colleges in the survey had been organized and those only in the preceding year. The data for this comparison were provided by Maryse Eymonerie of the AAUP.

what the faculty thinks the appropriate level should be and what it is in fact. The factor would be particularly important in the substantial number of organized institutions in which institutional change of either the structural or functional type has occurred. A state college or a community college faculty which has been included in an institutional system with universities or other institutions enjoying what they perceived as higher levels of governance participation might be dissatisfied with their present level of governance because their standard of reference is that of the university segment of the system. Similarly, a state college that has been transformed from primarily a teacher-training institution to a general liberal arts college typically adds a large number of faculty in the arts, the humanities, the social sciences, and the physical and natural sciences. They may also add faculty in such professional schools as business and engineering. The new faculty members are almost certain to be considerably younger than the faculty in the preexpansion period. It has been well established that the arts, humanities, and social science faculties are much more likely to support unionism than other groups and that younger faculty in all fields are more activist in their support for organization (Carr and Van Eyck, 1973, pp. 44–49; Ladd and Lipset, 1973, pp. 27, 39). Once again, the expectations of the faculty that chose unionization as to the appropriate level of governance participation may be higher than the levels that characterize the "emerging" institutions as a whole.[9]

The other major explanation of why the organized institutions seem to have higher levels of governance participation than the average is that organization often appears to be defensive and anticipatory. The existing level of participation may be higher than average, but changes in structure, in function, or in the philosophy and techniques of administration may appear to threaten the historical relationships. Activities such as program budgeting, work load measurement, comparative cost effectiveness studies, legislatively mandated teaching loads, and threats to tenure or sabbatical systems, when added to the changes in

[9]Support for this version of the "relative deprivation" explanation of the incidence of unionization is provided by the two-year colleges. Although they have the lowest actual participation in governance, the Carr and Van Eyck data show that they are the sector most satisfied with their governance arrangements, suggesting that their expectations are correspondingly low.

structure and function already discussed, may cause even a faculty with a historically high level of participation of the traditional versions to move to what they hope will be an even stronger organizational form in order to protect their position.[10]

To sum up, the survey of the relations between governance and unionism suggests two major conclusions:

1 Faculty participation in governance is clearly higher in private than in public institutions on the average. This may explain some part of the relative lack of organization in the private sector, particularly since the stresses that institutional change, both actual and anticipated, place on the governance system are much stronger in the public sector.

2 It appears clear that, on the average, the institutions that have unionized had higher levels of participation in governance than the institutional population as a whole. Their unionization may have been the result of a "leveling up" of expectations of lower-level institutions in consolidated systems or in "emerging" institutions. Alternatively, unionism may result from expectations about the proper level of participation that were even greater than the existing above-average level. Unionism may have been a defensive reaction to an actual or expected attack on an existing effective governance system. All of these hypotheses would be more applicable to public than to private systems.

Other possible explanations　One factor that might be thought to distinguish public from private institutions and to be related to unionism is salary levels of faculty. Salary disadvantages might lead public organizations to organize more readily. Unfortunately for this theory, in 1968–69, the year prior to the wave of organization, the average salary for the public four-year institutions in the AAUP survey of that year was substantially higher than the average for the private four-year institutions. Fifty-three of the 427 institutions in the survey have been unionized

[10]It might be thought that the relatively high level of governance found in organized institutions prior to organization is the effect of unionization's being concentrated in states with supportive laws and also with above-average levels of governance. This does not appear to be true; the most highly organized geographical section is the Middle Atlantic region, which had a median governance score of 300, below the average of the unionized institutions as a whole. The only geographical region with an average score equal to that of the organized group was the eastern North Central states, but here only Michigan has a high concentration of unionization ("Report of the Survey Subcommittee T," 1971, p. 2).

since 1968–69. The 42 public institutions and the 11 private institutions that chose unionization had approximately the same average salaries as the other public and private four-year institutions, respectively (AAUP, 1969, pp. 192–253).

It may be that the lower average salaries in private colleges are related to an explanation of low organization in the private sector in a different way. The well-known (particularly to their faculties) financial difficulties of the private colleges and universities and the lack of a tax-based source of funding may have discouraged faculties from seeing unions as an effective lever for financial gain. With tuition as a major source of income, with widening differentials between public and private charges, and with enrollment shifting to the public sector, unionization may have been seen as having little potential for increasing salaries or winning other types of cost-raising benefits. This belief may have been reinforced by the smaller size, simpler organizational structure, and higher level of participation in governance at the average private institution. Financial stringency may not lead faculties to exert bargaining pressure but, instead, may actually discourage conflict and encourage cooperation in a common drive for survival.

A final explanation for the low level of organization in private institutions has been suggested in interviews with a number of union representatives. Although the National Labor Relations Act provides comprehensive protection from punitive actions against union activists by employers, in a college setting discrimination because of union activity may be harder to detect and to prove than in an industrial plant. Private institutions often are without written, publicly stated personnel rules and procedures and without formal salary scales or salary administration practices. Informal personal administrative-faculty relationships are often the rule. Under these circumstances faculty members may be reluctant to take a leadership role in organizing, bargaining, or even openly supporting an outside union. AFT organizers in particular claim that fear of reprisal has a "chilling effect" in higher education organizing campaigns that is likely to be more important in the private institutions that do not have the civil service type of personnel system.

THE QUALITY CONUNDRUM

Few observers of the growth of faculty unionism have not at some point entertained the suspicion that the propensity of faculty to organize is inversely related to the quality of the institution involved.[11] The identification and measurement of characteristics of an institution that determine its "quality" are formidable tasks that no one has accomplished very satisfactorily. One method is to survey a group of persons presumed to be knowledgeable about institutions of higher education, such as deans, chairmen, or a sample of faculty, and ask them to rank departments or schools (Cartter, 1966). But few faculty are likely to know more about other institutions than the reputation of their faculty members or, occasionally, of their outstanding graduate students. These rankings are essentially prestige rankings of faculties. Because only a small percentage of faculty in any field is widely known even to their colleagues, this sort of ranking seldom encompasses more than a few dozen institutions at the most.

Attempts to provide more comprehensive ratings for large populations of institutions have been made, based on a variety of factors, some of which are subjective and vaguely specified (Gourman, 1967; *The College-Rater*, 1967). Some of the more objective items used are number of volumes in the libraries, expenditures per student, faculty salaries, and test scores of students. Some of the more subjective are the "effectiveness" of administrations and faculty "morale." The shortcomings of this approach are obvious and serious, but they can be mitigated by the use of only a few large quality categories.

Martin Trow (1972) classified the institutions included in the Carnegie survey by type of institution and by quality category by using a combination of the Gourman and the *College-Rater* scores. We have somewhat modified Trow's basic approach to make an analysis of the relation between quality and unionization as of mid-1974.[12]

The results of our analysis are summarized in Table 9. The pattern of unionization by quality category is not overwhelm-

[11]For discussions of this relationship see Aussieker and Garbarino (1973) and Ladd and Lipset (1973). Criticisms of the Aussieker and Garbarino paper can be found in Fearn (1974) and Gold (1974), along with the authors' replies.

[12]The modifications were: 1. we adhered strictly to the classification by Gourman and *College-Rater* scores as described in the text of the Carnegie Commission (Trow, 1972); and 2. we updated the classification by type of institution, using the U.S. Office of Education, *Directory, 1972–73*.

TABLE 9 *Unionized institutions as a proportion of all four-year institutions by quality, control, and legal environment*

Quality	Public (C)		Public (O)		Private	
	Percentage	N	Percentage	N	Percentage	N
Universities						
High	0	2	0	6	0	21
Medium	56	9	0	23	0	12
Low	67	6	4	53	11	27
Colleges						
High	100	3	0	16	1	67
Medium	56	16	0	37	5	183
Low	79	56	5	161	1	738

NOTE: *Public (C)* and *Public (O)* refer to public institutions in states with comprehensive and "other" bargaining laws, respectively. Unionization data as of mid-1974. Institutions with only law school graduate student units are regarded as unorganized. Quality: based on Gourman (1967) and *College Rater* (1967) scores. Assignment to classifications as university or colleges on basis of information in the U.S. Office of Education, *Directory, 1972–73.* See also Trow (1972).

ing, but there appears to be a clear-cut tendency for unionization to be concentrated in the institutions that are in the lower tiers of the quality distribution. There is no question about this tendency among the universities. The contrary evidence in the college sector of the table is the result of the small number of institutions that have been unionized and that must be spread over the cells in the table.

The most important aberration is the 100 percent unionization score among the high-quality public colleges in states with comprehensive laws and the negligible proportion of unionized low-quality private colleges.

Although the evidence in the college sector of the table is not uniformly supportive of the hypothesis, it is nevertheless consistent with the assumption that whatever is measured by the quality indices is inversely related to the propensity to organize. This is true in spite of the fact that the unionized institutions with the highest quality ratings are dominated by SUNY and CUNY campuses. Of the five medium-quality universities in the medium university category that are unionized, two are parts of SUNY and one is a CUNY campus (SUNY Buffalo,

SUNY Stony Brook, and CUNY's City College of New York—the other two are Rutgers and Wayne State). Three of the four top-quality colleges that are organized are the Baruch, Hunter, and Brooklyn colleges of the CUNY system. The other is the independent Brooklyn Polytechnic Institute. The SUNY and CUNY units opted for unionism in systemwide elections, and, although there is evidence that the CUNY colleges each voted separately for unionism, had there been a series of independent elections the results might have been different.[13] The SUNY election results by campus are unavailable, but the Buffalo and Stony Brook University centers have consistently enrolled proportions of their eligible faculty in the academic union that are well below the average for the system as a whole. In short, not only is the number of observations too small for rigorous analysis, but the observations do not always represent independent institutions.

Lois Swirsky Gold (1974) criticizes both the concept of quality as a variable and the conclusion that unionism is concentrated in the lower tier of the quality or prestige distribution. She rightfully stresses the difficulty of testing this proposition conclusively with the relatively small number of organized institutions available in tabulations such as those in Table 9. It is unfortunate that discussions of institutional quality are so nebulous in character and that they inevitably take on a pejorative character. It is entirely possible that quality as a variable is a proxy for such variables as research orientation, salary, or governance structure. Two of these variables, however—salary and participation in governance—have been shown earlier in this section to be unrelated to unionization in any simple way.

It is possible that, as the number of organized universities grows, more sophisticated analytical techniques can be applied and quality will either be shown to be irrelevant or the true variables that it currently masks will be exposed. At the moment, however, the available evidence supports the proposition that higher-quality institutions are less likely to unionize. In addition, at this stage of the movement to faculty unionism it is hard to believe that it is not of some significance that

[13]For the results of the CUNY election by campus see "Election Analysis" (1969). Statements about union memberhip in SUNY are based on data provided by Lawrence De Lucia (1974), president of the SUNY union.

under the Michigan law there has been no organization campaign attempted at the University of Michigan and that the campaign the unions felt justified in undertaking at Michigan State resulted in a victory for "no agent," while unions won elections at Saginaw Valley and Ferris State colleges, and at Central, Eastern, Oakland, and Wayne State universities (Northern Michigan in the latter group also rejected unionism). Similarly, in Massachusetts unionism won victories at Southeastern Massachusetts University and eight state colleges but lost at the University of Massachusetts. A similar quality-unionization pattern seems to be observable in Pennsylvania, and we predict will also appear in Minnesota and Washington.

Economists have made very good use of the deceptively simple axiom that "a rich man is a poor man with money," but we suspect that the quality variable is not simply a proxy for some combinations of affluence and faculty power. Some personal characteristics of faculty are likely to turn out to be significant in the final analysis.

It may be useful to imagine the existence of a low-quality university, Back Bay University, located in Cambridge. Is it likely that an increase in salary levels, a much more collegial governance system, a more selective admission policy, and more research money would convert it to a Harvard as far as faculty attitudes are concerned? Some readers might be tempted to respond that, given time and the ability to recruit the new faculty that these new employment conditions would attract, the transformation would be accomplished. But this response clearly indicates that there must be something to the notion of faculty quality measured in terms of personal attributes. We do not know whether the new Back Bay University would be more or less likely to organize than the old after the transformation was complete. The analysis of this chapter suggests, however, that if a Back Bay University existed and a program to accomplish the transformation of the institution were announced, then the original faculty would form a union overnight.

As a practical matter the question of the relationship between institutional or faculty quality and unionism may well turn out to be a question of timing. If faculty quality is related to personal attitudes and opinions, these are themselves subject to change as the objective situation in particular institutions changes. As a prediction it seems probable that most of the prestigious public universities will adopt some form of overt faculty bargaining under the pressure of events over the next decade.

SUMMARY In this chapter we have tried to identify factors explaining the incidence of unions in particular institutions. The conclusions can be expressed in a series of propositions:

Faculty opinions about unionization are a poor predictor of the propensity to organize. It is not that opinion data are irrelevant but that the attributes associated with differences do not permit us to discriminate well between institutions. The current weakness of such data is illustrated by the fact that there appears to be little difference in attitudes or opinions between public and private universities, but the differences in levels of organization at these two types of institutions are overwhelming. Similarly, although faculty support for unions in Ladd and Lipset's "elite" institutions is somewhat below that found in less prestigious institutions, more than half of their faculty support bargaining, and yet there is virtually no organization in the group.

Bayer (1973, p. 30), found that two-thirds of all faculty supported bargaining, but he also discovered that, when the responses were broken down by sex and level of institution, the degree of support ranged only from 75 to 61 percent. The differences that opinion data reveal between young and old, tenured and nontenured, research and teaching orientations, arts and engineering faculties, and liberals and conservatives are canceled out to a substantial extent because of the heterogeneity found among the faculty of individual institutions. The decision for or against bargaining is made within an institutional framework, and most institutions contain a complex mixture of the various groups holding divergent views. Other factors must be called upon to explain the pattern of organization.

Among public institutions of higher education the effect of the applicable state law on faculty unionism is overwhelming. In 8 states with comprehensive laws, 75 percent of the public institutions are organized, and the number is still rising. The 17 states with the stronger types of law have only about 30 percent of all public institutions, but they have about 90 percent of all the organized public institutions.

The law seems to produce its effects in two ways. One is the direct support that protection of organizational rights gives to the organizational process in public higher education. The other is the indirect support (pressure may be a better word) that is produced when other public employees in the state organize and begin to bargain for benefits.

In public higher education organization is concentrated in institutions that are part of comprehensive or segmented systems of higher education. More than half of all institutions in comprehensive systems (combining two- and four-year levels) are organized. One-sixth of all the institutions in segmented (single-level) systems have unions. Less than 10 percent of the single-campus institutions are organized.

Although quantitative data are lacking, unions appear more frequently in institutions that have experienced functional changes in degree levels and program content. The "emerging" universities are an important element in this category, which appears particularly susceptible to organization.

Although they have the backing of the nation's most supportive bargaining law with uniform application in all 50 states, the private institutions have little organization and show few signs of increasing that level. About 23 percent of all public institutions but only about 2 percent of private institutions are organized. Unless the situation changes drastically, it appears that faculty unionism will be largely a phenomenon of public higher education.

Neither salary levels nor the degree of faculty participation in governance are related to unionization in any simple, direct way. The organizations that have chosen to organize since 1969 had salary levels somewhat higher than the overall average in that year. When levels of participation in governance are studied, the now organized institutions had above-average levels of participation in 1969. In both cases the relevant variable may not be the absolute level of salary or participation but the existing level relative to the aspirations and expectations of the faculty. Another possible explanation is that uncertainty about future levels of salary and governance participation rather than the current situation may be the force leading to unionization.[14]

When public and private institutions were compared, private institutions reported lower salaries but higher levels of governance than public institutions.

There appears to be an inverse relationship between institutional quality and the tendency to organize. The evidence on this issue is not very strong, and more positive statements will have to await the patterns that may be revealed as further expansion occurs in the organized sector. The problem is compounded by the obvious interrelations between "quality" and a large number of other potentially important variables. A major problem is that there are relatively few public institutions in the top-quality university category and a very large number of private colleges in the low-quality college category, so that the public-private differential in organization influences the results at both ends of the distribution. Nevertheless, it is hard not to conclude that whatever quality scores measure, they are associated with a relative reluctance to organize.

In short, the great majority of unionized colleges and universities as of 1974 fall into one of three categories:

The educational conglomerates These are the comprehensive supersystems of higher education, which include within a single administrative unit almost every conceivable type of academic (and some nonacademic) relationships. Their internal problems are exacerbated by the necessity of developing a whole new set of inter- and intra-institutional power relationships. In any state with a supportive public-employee bargaining law it is a very good bet that these systems (or very large

[14]Fifty-three organized four-year institutions (in 1974) were identified in the 1969 AAUP salary survey. The median salary for the 11 unionized private colleges was an insignificant $13 higher than the median for 314 nonunion private institutions. The 42 public institutions had median salaries of $209 or 1.6 percent below the 70 public nonunion institutions. Robert Birnbaum (1974) made a careful study of union-nonunion salaries by a different methodology and found that institutions with collective bargaining in 1972–73 had an average $47 advantage over those without in 1968–69. Incidentally, he found that the unionized did substantially better than the nonunion institutions in salary terms over that period.

portions of them, depending on unit determinations) will be organized. It seems likely that most of the segmented systems will also organize under these conditions. Examples are numerous, but SUNY and CUNY lead all the rest.

The "emerging" institutions Many emerging institutions are part of one or the other type of supersystem, and they contribute their internal stresses to the sum total in the system. The SUNY state colleges illustrate this category. Emerging institutions often appear as separate institutions as well, for example, Central Michigan and Southeastern Massachusetts universities.

Miscellaneous category A miscellaneous category is made up of individual institutions that organize for a variety of reasons tied to special circumstances on their particular campuses, ranging from authoritarian administrations to the possibility that unionism is "contagious" and spreads by proximity, as Carr and Van Eyck have suggested. St. John's University and the divisions of Long Island University are examples of these forces.

The large number of institutions that fall into one or the other of these classifications guarantees ample room for faculty organizations to compete for representation status and to expand the areas of faculty unionism.

4. Collective Bargaining: The Parties and Their Relationships

The status of collective bargaining in four-year institutions of higher education of the early 1970s resembles the situation in the private sector of the economy in the 1930s. There has been competition between organizations for the right to represent the faculty, a competition that produced new organizations and transformed some of the existing organizations. Many of the same legal and bargaining issues arose for many of the same reasons. As in the industrial sector in the 1930s there are conflicts over the proper role of internal associations of employees, over the geographic scope of the appropriate bargaining units, over the occupational composition of the bargaining units, over the definition of supervisors and their relation to the main body of the staff, over the proper subject matter of bargaining, over the inherent prerogatives of management, and over the competence of the administrative agencies, the legislators, and the judiciary that made the decisions that shaped the system.

The industrial relations system that evolved in the private sector is flexible enough to encompass bargaining arrangements that are workable for groups as diverse as sanitation workers, musicians, cannery workers, and professional athletes. The rhetoric in which the contemporary issues in academia are discussed may be more sophisticated, but much of the substance has a familiar ring to the industrial relations specialist. This feeling of familiarity makes the specialist less attentive than he might be (and possibly should be) to the unique character of the problems of higher education. Nevertheless, the fact is that decisions made by legislators and administrative officials in the 1930s and 1940s created a new system of industrial government in the private sector. Virtually all interested parties would agree that the system has serious flaws, although they would not agree on what these flaws are.

Now a combination of legislators, administrative officials, and the judiciary is creating a new collective bargaining system, this time in the public sector. Public higher education is an integral part of the public sector, and private higher education is simultaneously being fitted into the private sector arrangements. The implementation of the Wagner Act had a major impact on the internal organization of employee relations of the industrial sector, and the higher education "establishment" is disturbed by the prospect that similar changes may be under way in colleges and universities, fearing that they will destroy or damage the unique quality of higher education.

The major competitors for faculty bargaining rights are the AAUP, the AFT, and the NEA. We also discuss the smaller organizations and the mergers and coalitions that have taken place among organizations. Issues that arise in the process of establishing collective bargaining relationships are analyzed. These include the problematical roles of the administration, department chairmen, nonteaching professionals, and students. We conclude by analyzing and comparing four models of managerial bargaining—in New York, Michigan, New Jersey, and Hawaii.

THE AMERICAN ASSOCIATION OF UNIVERSITY PROFESSORS The AAUP was established in 1913 by some of the leading figures among the faculties of American higher education and has since become the leading faculty organization, as measured by its prestige among faculty, administrators, and the general public. It has advanced the interests of the profession and articulated what former president Sanford Kadish calls "the theory of the profession" in some 25 policy statements (AAUP, 1973).

The major policy achievement of the AAUP is the promulgation of a code of internal faculty-administration relations that is impressive in scope. Most of the principles enunciated, if not all the details of procedure, have been accepted by many institutions. Perhaps the most important of these statements is the famous 1940 *Statement of Principles and Interpretative Comments on Academic Freedom and Tenure* (revised on occasion since that date). This statement has played an important part in gaining institutional acceptance of the principle of tenure over the years. The policy statements and reports of the AAUP are the products of committees of the association that attract a membership of impressive caliber. The reports are the product of mature deliberation, are temperate if somewhat magisterial in their language, and are judicious in their recommendations.

As noted in Chapter 1, a key program of the AAUP is their annual salary survey, begun in the late 1950s and described, in a masterful example of rhetorical cunning, as a "self-grading" survey. This means not only that the institutions furnish detailed information on a voluntary basis but that the AAUP has established a structure of classifications or grades of salary ranges into which the institutions fall automatically and inexorably, depending on the salary decisions of the administrations. During the period of faculty shortages the AAUP ranking had considerable importance for some administrations. The analysis of the data is workmanlike, and the status of the survey is such that about 1,300 institutions respond in a typical year and the results are widely used.

Another major professional activity of the AAUP is the conduct of investigations, in response to requests from individuals or institutions, of incidents that seem likely to threaten the corporate or individual functions of the faculty of an institution. In such cases the association's officers attempt a settlement by some form of mediation or, that failing, send a team of investigators to study the situation and produce a report. If the administration is deemed to have acted wrongfully by the norms of justice or the canons of academic behavior, it may be placed on the AAUP's censured-institution list. The work load from this type of complaint has risen rapidly. The number of cases closed after successful mediation by the AAUP staff went up from between 30 and 40 in 1969 to 127 in 1973 ("Report of Committee A, 1972–73," 1973, p. 150), and the number of censured institutions reached an all-time high in 1974.

This range of activities is referred to as the "fundamental program" of the AAUP. They preceded the AAUP's entrance into bargaining relationships, and many of the members fear that their success will be compromised by the association's new role as a bargaining agent. An institution is not likely to take very seriously a solemn act of "censure" if that act is performed by its collective bargaining adversary. The AAUP was successful in the past in persuading institutions to adhere to its statements of principle and follow its recommendations by reason, compromise, and joint discussion backed up only by the threat of adverse publicity rather than by bargaining and threats of strikes.

The AAUP and collective bargaining The AAUP first considered what its stance toward collection bargaining should be in 1964 in response to a "display of interest in bargaining by faculty members in the City University of New York."[1] The result was its adoption of the position that, if bargaining was thought to be necessary, the college faculty itself (presumably through its separate internal organization) was the most appropriate representative. At this stage the AAUP appeared to see itself as the external arm of the faculty senate system. In 1966 the association recognized the possibility that under "extraordinary circumstances" an AAUP chapter might become an official bargaining agent. Restrictions were further loosened in 1968 and 1969, with the last position being that where "conditions of effective faculty participation in college or university government do not exist, the local chapter may offer itself as the faculty's representative."

In October 1971 the governing body of the AAUP approved, by a vote of 22 to 11, a statement that "the Association will pursue collective bargaining, as a major additional way of realizing the Association's goals in higher education." Their action was ratified at the 1972 annual meeting by a ratio of 7 to 1.

The AAUP's participation in bargaining has been marked by ironic developments. For example, the first AAUP chapter to be recognized as a bargaining agent was the Belleville Area College in 1967. Belleville is a two-year college in a state with no bargaining law (Illinois), and the AAUP has been able to secure bargaining rights in only two other two-year units since 1967. Another ironic development is that the AAUP, regarded as the most "establishment"-oriented of the organizations, found its local chapter calling a strike at Oakland University in 1971, the

[1]The primary source for this section is the *AAUP Bulletin* (March 1972), which contains a report of the AAUP Council's proposed policy statement on collective bargaining, a review and an explanation of their position, a supporting argument by Carl Stevens, and a statement in opposition by Sanford H. Kadish, William W. Van Alstyne, and Robert K. Webb.

TABLE 13 *Student involvement with collective bargaining*

Type of relationship	*Type of action*
End-run bargaining	
Chicago City Colleges (1972)	Injunctions secured by students in faculty strike.
Allegheny Community College, Pa. (1972)	Injunctions secured by students in faculty strike.
Community College of Philadelphia (1972)	Injunctions secured by students in faculty strike.
CUNY (1972)	Appeals to Board of Higher Education and PERB.
Lake Michigan Community College (1973)	Support for trustee recall, appeals to legislators.
California: university and state colleges (1973)	Lobbying to influence provisions of bargaining law.
Washington: all sectors (1973)	Lobbying to influence provisions of bargaining law.
Coalition bargaining	
Ulster Community College, N.Y.	Student boycott of classes during faculty-administration negotiations.
Chicago City Colleges (1972)	Observers in negotiations.
Ferris State University (1973)	Student on administration team.
Tripartite bargaining	
Boston, Worcester, Fitchburg, and North Adams State Colleges, Mass. (1971–73)	Students participated in negotiations, voted to ratify some provisions.
CUNY (1973)	Students presented demands to both parties.
Southeastern Massachusetts (1973)	Students negotiated with both parties.
Richard Stockton State College, N.J. (1973)	Student and faculty unions negotiated a contract.
*Direct bargaining by employed students**	
University of California—Berkeley (1964–present)	Teaching assistants.
University of Indiana—Bloomington (1969)	Teaching assistants.
Stanford University (1969)	Teaching assistants.
University of Colorado (1970)	Teaching assistants.
University of Washington (1970)	Teaching assistants.
University of Wisconsin (1970)	Teaching assistants.
Harvard University (1972)	Teaching assistants.
University of Michigan (1974)	Teaching assistants.

*Includes known instances of bargaining, not necessarily continuous bargaining or bargaining involving formal recognition; excludes cases in which students are part of a faculty unit, as at Rutgers or CUNY.

SOURCE: Newspaper reports and bargaining unit survey.

senate also appealed to the state's Public Employee Relations Board for inclusion as a third party in negotiations. They attempted to bring suit to be included in negotiations, arguing that they might be considered either as equivalent to employers of the faculty or as the representatives of the consumers of higher education in New York City. Unsuccessful in these attempts, they petitioned, without effect, the Cost of Living Council (which had to approve the settlement) to reduce the pay increases granted in the contract.

Perhaps the most successful instances in which students as third parties have appealed to fourth parties to influence events are their uses of the injunctive powers of the courts in faculty strikes. Four weeks after the 1972 negotiations between the Chicago City Colleges and Local 1600 of the Cook County College Teachers Union ended in a strike, student groups obtained an injunction against the strike. Two of the seven student body presidents had been observers in the negotiations, and six of the seven supported the petition for an injunction. Cook County Circuit Judge Nathan Cohen ordered further negotiations to be held in court under his supervision, and he eventually resolved the final five disputed issues himself. The parties were reported to be less than satisfied with the result, and in 1974, after a one-day strike and a threat of another injunction, they reached a settlement on their own.

Students have also secured court injunctions against faculty strikes in the community colleges in Pittsburgh and Philadelphia. The intriguing possibilities of the widespread use of the injunction in faculty strikes would seem to depend on the legality of public-employee strikes and the impasse procedures provided in relevant state law.

At Lake Michigan College, a community college in southwestern Michigan, students actively supported the faculty position during a lengthy strike in which most of the faculty members were fired by the college board of trustees. The students circulated petitions calling for the recall of board members, lobbied their state and national representatives to get them to intervene, and made a trip to New York to try to get support from the communication media. These efforts seem to have had little effect.

Students have been more successful in other versions of end-run bargaining involving lobbying in the state legislatures. As the only organized group purporting to speak for the new youth vote, student lobbyists have been particularly effective in state legislatures, where their concern with such issues as faculty work load, possible overemphasis on research, and more responsive administrations has struck a sympathetic chord with many legislators. In addition to the national student lobbying activity, state groups have lobbied in California, Washington, New York, Wisconsin, Texas, and Michigan. In California and Washington the student lobbyists have had their greatest successes during the development of bargaining bills to cover faculty negotiations. In Washington the type and extent of student participation in bargaining was an issue on which a coalition of administration, faculty, and public officials foundered after coming close to agreement on a collective bargaining bill. In addition to a role in general bargaining, one group of students wanted the recognition of their own right to bargain collectively as principals.

In California the student lobbyists from the university and the state college systems were able to obtain the right of student representatives to sit in as observers in bargaining sessions in higher education and to compile an "educational impact study" of any contract written into a bill that passed both houses but was vetoed by Governor Reagan in Fall 1973.

In New York the student lobbyists have tried without success to get legislation passed to limit the scope of higher education bargaining to economic matters.

Coalition bargaining　Coalition bargaining occurs when students align themselves directly with one or the other of the principals in negotiations. If the CUNY Student Senate had been successful in getting representation on the Board of Higher Education's bargaining team, that would have been an example of coalition formation. When students bargain directly with the administration on their own behalf, they often join in coalitions with other unions and student organizations. One example is to be found in Wisconsin, where during their 1970 strike the Teaching Assistants Association had the support of the AFT, the Teamsters, and the State County and Municipal Employees Union (Sherman and Loeffler, 1971).

In the early stages of the faculty union movement, it appeared that activist student groups (virtually the only kind existing) and the new faculty unions were natural allies against the administration. During the 1968–69 strikes at San Francisco State, for example, student groups and some faculty unions supported the same goals. As the faculty unions gained status as bargaining agents, and economics and job security came to supersede ideology as rallying points, the incipient faculty-student coalition broke down.

The 1972 Chicago City Colleges negotiations illustrate some of the problems of establishing coalitions. After the union presented the administration with a set of demands, students asked to sit in as observers.. In three previous strikes students had supported the union in successful, but limited, coalition style. The union, therefore, supported the student request, and the board agreed. At the next meeting the union proposed a new set of demands, including some tailored to appeal to students. The board expressed surprise and insisted on reintroducing the set of demands originally presented, reading each in turn and inquiring how each would benefit the students. Provisions in the current contract that could be interpreted as threatening student interests were pointed out. Relations between the parties cooled, with the union refusing to appear for subsequent meetings and the administration continuing to make its case to the students. It was during the strike that followed that students secured the injunction that led to Judge Cohen's intervention.

Whether student-faculty or student-administration coalitions are feasible seems likely to depend on the disputed issues. The students are likely to be allies of the administration when the issue is something like the evaluation of teaching or faculty work load. When such issues as political activism or tuition in public colleges are at stake, the faculty and the students may be allies. The shifting nature of these alliances continues to limit cooperation, makes for an uneasy relationship, and is likely to produce something more like a form of tripartite bargaining.

Tripartite bargaining Tripartite bargaining refers to a situation in which three (or more) parties engage in negotiations. In its pure form the parties would negotiate together simultaneously. Tripartite bargaining is usually unstable, tending to turn into a succession of coalition bargaining situations as negotiations progress from issue to issue.

Student leaders and their legislative supporters often seem to feel that tripartite bargaining is the best model for higher education. The students (and some legislators) see the students as consumers of higher education, pure of heart as compared with the vested interests of faculty members and administrators, participating in negotiations and judiciously tilting the balance first one way and then the other to advance the consumer interest on each disputed issue.

The closest approximations to tripartite bargaining of this type are the arrangements in some of the Massachusetts state colleges. The major proponent of this approach in Massachusetts is Donald Walters, the deputy director of the system and the administration spokesman (Begin, 1973). Students participate in the negotiations and are free to enter into the discussions. They do not have a role in decisions on faculty-administration issues, but the agreements include provisions for student participation in department and college affairs. These provisions are reached in consultation with the students in the negotiations and are submitted to the students in the college for ratification.

To some extent each of the parties originally brought the students into negotiations in the hope that they would become allies. A stronger reason for this development is that the colleges had no real tradition of orthodox governance at the time of unionization, and the parties, particularly Walters, saw this as a means of simultaneously creating an integrated governance system and a bargaining system. The experiment was greatly facilitated by the fact that the Massachusetts bargaining law prohibited bargaining about salaries, making governance the main topic of negotiations. Both of the principals are reported to be increasingly dubious about the system. In 1973 Massachusetts's law was changed to permit negotiation on salaries, and this is likely to exacerbate the differences between the participants, so that the future of even this weak form of tripartite bargaining is in doubt.

Tripartite bargaining in which student representatives really participate actively and independently probably creates more problems than it solves. The usual problems of student participation exist—it is very difficult to get student leaders who are representative of and responsive to the concerns of the large majority of the student body, and the leaders want to influence decisions important to others without cost to themselves and without bearing responsibility for the results. The student leadership is equipped to accept concessions but not to commit their constituency to anything in return as union leaders do in signing a contract. More important, the students are likely to be simultaneously dealing as principals with the administration and the faculty on various other matters when functioning as third parties in faculty-administration negotiations. As a result they are in a position to use their leverage in the union negotiations to win concessions in the other areas. The conversion of bilateral bargaining into tripartite bargaining makes a difficult problem less tractable and reduces the likelihood that a mutually tolerable and stable arrangement will be worked out between faculty and administration.

Another form of tripartite bargaining, which is likely to be the most common as well as the most appropriate form, might be called *trilateral bargaining,* because it will consist of bilateral bargaining between faculty and administration, and students and administration, with limited cross-bargaining between faculty and students. It makes the administration the key element in the relationship, and in many matters of the greatest concern to students this is as it should be. The level of tuition for students and of salaries for faculty, for example, is a matter of educational and financial policy, at least in public education, and the level of each should be decided independently by the legislature and the executive branch and not by negotiation between faculty and students. The same is true of financial aid, faculty work load, and many other matters.

An example of trilateral bargaining of the type described above is reported to exist at Stockton State College, a new liberal arts college included in the New Jersey state college system. A mixed senate system, with its membership chosen in what has been described as a "highly unorthodox" procedure, may be in the process of replacement by a bargaining system (Hodgkinson, 1973a).[23] The faculty has chosen an AFT bargain-

[23]According to Hodgkinson, "representatives were selected by lottery from the large number of volunteer candidates turning in petitions carrying the names of ten supporters" (p. 93). This seems less like a system of representation for making decisions than a form of group therapy. The arrangement is being modified.

ing agent; and a union of students has been formed. The faculty union is a party to the AFT contract with the system. It has negotiated a separate contract with the student union guaranteeing certain student rights and calling for student support of faculty strikes. The student union is also attempting to establish a direct bargaining relationship with the college. Stockton appears to be an example of the difficulty that mixed senates have in dealing with problems that are really important to the separate groups represented and of the pressures on the latter to seek other bilateral ways of dealing with these problems in a crisis (Garbarino, 1971).

Finally, it is important to stress that there is as yet little evidence that faculty unionism has had any significant independent effect on the students' position. Students gained substantial amounts of power in higher education during the 1960s, even though students were then in surplus and faculty in short supply. For the next decade the situation will be exactly reversed, and student power is likely to be more evident. A good case can be made that the degree of influence held by the rank and file of students as distinct from professional student leaders has already become excessive. The influence of students is illustrated by the current competition of institutions for enrollment and of departments, programs, and faculty within the institutions for students. Faculty are advertising their courses in student newspapers, grades are being inflated or abolished, required courses eliminated, course work loads lowered, and credit given for a wide range of "life experiences." Under the circumstances the efforts of organized student leadership to picture the ordinary student as threatened by a regime of arbitrary authority, subjected to onerous requirements, and working in a harsh and unresponsive faculty relationship newly reinforced by the power of the faculty unions are highly misleading.

THE ELUSIVE EMPLOYER In a sense the diffusion of managerial authority in the public sector is an integral part of the environment that produces multilateral bargaining. In public higher education the division of authority among the administrative officials of the campus, the boards of trustees, the executive offices of the governors, and the state legislatures simultaneously complicates the bargaining process and creates the opportunity for multilateral maneuvering by the faculty bargaining agent.

Before analyzing the ways in which identifying the employer has been handled in negotiations, we must make two more general points.

First, in public higher education diffusion of authority has always existed, and the multilateral approach to influencing decisions predated faculty unionism. In Chapter 1 the historic role of internal faculty associations as lobbying and consultative bodies was described. These associations employed discreet versions of end-run bargaining: engaging in discussions with local administrations, appearing and speaking at board meetings, and then testifying before legislative committees and, on occasion, working at electoral politics.

The new faculty unions are aggressive practitioners of the same art. One view of the move to legalize public-employee bargaining in the states sees it as an attempt by the legislatures to move decisions on personnel issues from the halls of the capitol to the bargaining table. If this is true, the lawmakers have certainly been disappointed in most cases. Given the nature of the negotiations in higher education and the character of the organizations, lobbying and electoral politics are an integral and perhaps a growing part of the process. In fact, one of the central elements in the competition in representation elections is the relative effectiveness of the various alliances that the rival organizations provide with organized labor, with organized education, with the higher education establishment, or with organized fellow state employees. Collective bargaining in public employment is not an alternative to political action but a complement to it.

Second, it is sometimes claimed that the nature of the administrative structure of higher education is such that collective bargaining cannot reach the vital decision centers that control the budget. There are limits to what can be done to win economic gains without dealing with the source of funds, but even if the possibilities were negligible, there are many important noneconomic issues that are clearly within the control of university administrations. Examples are promotions, nonretention decisions, work load and scheduling of assignments, and governance. Because there is usually some budgetary flexibility as well as some budgetary slack, an aggressive claimant can often shift resources in its direction. Any observant faculty member has seen this happen in recent years if he follows the fortunes of the crafts and the maintenance workers in his institution.

In short, the diffusion of authority puts a premium on maintaining a flexible lobbying capability so as to develop a mutually reinforcing system of bargaining and political action. At the same time the diffusion of power in the administrative hierarchy need not prevent important concessions from being won through bargaining at the various levels of the governing structure.

MANAGERIAL BARGAINING MODELS The public bargaining laws of the various states are implemented by a variety of methods, so that the conduct of negotiations differs from state to state. Two examples of distinctly different approaches are provided by New York and Michigan.

The New York Model In New York State, the public-employee bargaining law, the Taylor Act, is implemented, as far as negotiations are concerned, through the governor's Office of Employee Relations (OER). Negotiations with state employees, including SUNY, are conducted through the OER, and contracts are signed by representatives of both the OER and the university. Within the university system this approach originally produced considerable concern about the independence of the university and its ability to determine its own employee relations policy. As far as the central administration is concerned, this anxiety seems to have been replaced by a cautious optimism. The optimism results from the unexpected budgetary advantage that the procedure has produced and from the effectiveness of an elaborate system of consultation with the separate campuses and with statewide administration that was followed before and during negotiations.

The New York system in practice has had the effect of separating the question of the annual salary adjustment from the budgetary process as a whole. Salary negotiations took place annually during the first contract, and they were handled without reference to the overall university budget. After the economic issues were settled, the governor undertook to, as the contract phrases it, "prepare, secure introduction and recommend passage of appropriate legislation in order to provide the benefits." During the first contract a combination of protracted negotiations and legislative inaction led to long delays in implementing the annual increases in salary. The new two-year agreement negotiated in 1974 had legislative funding approved prior to the legislature's adjournment for the summer but before the tentative agreement was ratified by the union membership. The funds were provided contingent on the approval of the contract, a technique that put considerable pressure on the membership to ratify the settlement.

The new two-year settlement departs from past practice by abandoning the annual reopening on salaries and writing the second-year increase into the current contract. The advance scheduling of a 7 percent increase for 1975 (7¼ percent was granted in 1974) could be a problem for the governor and the university, as such advance commitments have proved to be in some of the Michigan universities. This advance scheduling eliminates one of the important differences in practice between the two states.

The New York system seems to have worked well to date with the exception of the long delays in 1972 and 1973 in settling the salary problem. The university administration finds the separation of salary negotiation and funding from the overall budgetary process a useful arrangement. It may remove the SUNY administrators one step from the negotiating table, but it also may remove the legislature one step from coupling action on the budget with action on academic salary matters.

Aside from the separation of salary matters from the total budget considerations, the essence of the New York system is the centralization of bargaining in the executive branch, where other state salary policies are also established, and the consequent acceptance by the executive of the responsibility of taking the initiative in dealing with the legislature in the funding process.

The Michigan Model   The Michigan bargaining system is different from the New York model primarily because of the decentralized nature of the system of higher education. The two major organized public universities in Michigan that have had substantial experience with faculty unionism are Central Michigan and Oakland, which signed their first contracts in 1970 and 1971, respectively.

The Michigan institutions have separate governing boards, prepare separate budgets, and have considerable control over their internal budget allocations and, to some extent, their tuition charges. Each institution is on its own in bargaining with its unions, including faculty unions. The responsibility for meeting the costs of settlement lies with the university administration, and the money comes out of overall administrative budgets. These budgets are reviewed by the executive office, which prepares an executive budget for submission to the legislature. The money for funding pay increases in the universities' budgets is not specifically identified as such, and there need be no relationship between the new salary budgets provided by the state and the increases the universities have committed themselves to pay through collective bargaining. In general both Central Michigan and Oakland have granted increases during bargaining in excess of the amounts implicit in their state budgets. This has squeezed the budget allocations for other items, such as contingency funds, maintenance, and equipment. Unusual as it may seem to some faculty members, there have even been reports that faculty increases have diverted money from other nonacademic groups, although in general the institutions have tried to give equivalent raises to the nonacademic unions.

The two institutions with the longest record of bargaining, CMU and Oakland, have followed different patterns of development. CMU replaced its initial one-year agreement for 1970–71 with a three-year agreement with specified annual increases of 7.5 to 8.0 percent each year. The gap between the bargained and state-funded increases in the last year of the contract was substantial and the subject of some adverse comment in the legislature. CMU may try to shift to long-term contracts with annual reopenings on salaries.

Oakland's experience shows that CMU's problems are not entirely the result of a three-year agreement with increases scheduled in advance. Oakland has had annual contracts since its first one was negotiated in 1971. That negotiation produced the first (and so far the only) four-year faculty strike. Since that time, annual agreements have produced increases that are reported to be as high as the CMU settlements, at least until the 1973–74 contract. In that year the salary dispute was submitted to binding "last-offer" arbitration, and the result was somewhat below the CMU scheduled increase.[24]

The Michigan model seems to be an unstable one. It is unlikely that some sort of overall coordination of bargaining, formal or informal, can be avoided. Wayne State negotiated its first contract in May 1973, and the AAUP was declared the bargaining agent at Eastern Michigan University in Spring 1974 after a lengthy court battle. Two of the three research universities—Michigan State and the University of Michigan—are unorganized, and three of the six regional universities—Western, Northern, and Michigan Technological—are unorganized. Leaving the state college system aside for the moment, the possibility would seem to be small that divergent compensation patterns will be permitted to develop among the faculties in the research and the regional university sectors and between the universities and other state employees without some form of executive or legislative intervention.

The New Jersey Model

New Jersey is the other state that has had relatively lengthy experience with salary bargaining, and its system is closer to the New York than to the Michigan model.[25] Percentage salary increases have been kept in line as among Rutgers as the state university, the state colleges, and the other state employees. The Rutgers administrative budget is prepared well before bargaining has been concluded, and it contains a provision for salary increases. Although there has been no separate salary-increase funding, the close, and hardly accidental, correspondence that has been achieved between the negotiated and the budgeted increases has eliminated problems that might otherwise be caused by the fact that the salary increases are often budgeted months before the official negotiations are concluded.

Although New Jersey, like New York, has an executive Office of Employee Relations and this office is a party to the Rutgers

---

[24]In last-offer arbitration the parties each submit a final settlement "offer," and the arbitrator chooses one or the other. The arbitrator, Charles Rehmus, chose the union's proposal, an increase of 5.9 percent overall.

[25]Massachusetts has substantial unionism, but until recently salaries were not bargainable.

contract, to date Rutgers has been able to negotiate its own contract with liaison being maintained with the OER and the governor's Employee Relations Policy Committee. It is generally agreed that the early organization of Rutgers by the AAUP was intended to forestall the possibility that Rutgers might be included in a comprehensive bargaining unit with the state colleges. So far Rutgers has succeeded in retaining the separation, but it is being challenged from two directions. New Jersey's Chancellor of Higher Education and his office have a degree of authority over Rutgers, the precise degree being currently the subject of litigation. In addition, the most recent contract has been placed in effect although the section on scope of bargaining negotiated by the parties has not been accepted by the executive branch. The contract section on the scope of bargaining (Article IV) ends with the parenthetical statement "This Article is subject to further discussion with State Officials."

Although there have been problems with the structure of bargaining on the union side of the state college system, on the employer side bargaining has been handled by the Board of Higher Education and the Office of Employee Relations without the interorganizational problems found at Rutgers.

In spite of the success of informal methods of coordination of salary bargaining in New Jersey, it appears that other factors will produce a more explicitly integrated system of bargaining, as well as a more generally integrated system of higher education.

The Hawaii Model   Although the University of Hawaii has yet to negotiate its first contract successfully, the composition of the employer's side of the bargaining arrangements is of interest. The Hawaii public-employee bargaining law has several unusual features (Studohar, 1973). It permits strikes subject to health and safety qualifications; it mandates the agency shop for any union winning a bargaining election; it specifies the appropriate bargaining units in the law rather than leaving this issue to the Public Employee Relations Board (faculty in all higher education were placed in a single unit); and it defines "the public employer" for each unit to include representation from the governor's office. In the university unit the public employer named in the law for the purpose of negotiations is specified to be the governor, or not less than three of his designated representatives, along with not more than two members of the board of regents.[26]

Perhaps the most unusual aspect of negotiations in Hawaii was the state's contracting with an association of private sector employers, the Hawaii Employers Council, to handle the actual negotiations.

The structuring of the bargaining committee is an attempt to solve the problem of the elusive employer by making the public agency management and the governor's office part of the agreement-making process so that the resulting agreement can be assured of acceptability.

Pennsylvania appears to be developing a hybrid arrangement in which the governor's office bargains for the state college system and has taken the responsibility of funding the result. (This is apparently one explanation for this multiyear contract's provisions for substantial increases of 10 percent a year, annual increments, and fringe benefits.) Temple University is the only "state-related" university now engaging in bargaining, but on the basis of past budgetary practice these institutions will bargain in the Michigan pattern, with the responsibility for financing their settlements out of their overall budgets.

There appears to be a real danger that leaving college and university administrations to bargain settlements, with their academic and nonacademic unions, without state participation and state responsibility for funding the results, will create a chaotic situation. One problem is that the uneven bargaining strengths of the various unions may distort pay relationships among groups. Perhaps more serious is the situation in which an academic or nonacademic union is able to use its power in the legislature or the governor's office to get these officials to pressure the university and influence the terms of a settlement in a version of multilateral bargaining. The state may accept no responsibility for the budgetary consequences and leave the university to live with the results.

[26]The tentative agreement negotiated with the AFT union was notable for a proposal to introduce renewal-term appointments for new faculty to supplement the standard "up or out" tenure system. The faculty rejected the contract by a wide margin, and an election for a new bargaining agent was forced. Another major stumbling block to agreement was the status of "past practices" in the new situation.

Of the various methods of identifying the "employer," in the sense of identifying the body that can make a binding agreement, some variation of the centralized version denoted as the New York model seems likely to be most common. Massachusetts currently resembles the Michigan pattern but has only now begun to negotiate on economic issues. The Hawaii model is suited to a relatively small, simple, governmental structure, but it may well turn out to be the most threatening to university autonomy. The most interesting aspect of the New York system is the way the salary increase question has been divided from the overall budgetary process. Further experience may force a reconsideration, but to date this development appears to promise to limit the effect of collective bargaining on educational policy.

At least the trend toward more coordinated bargaining will continue if only because of the trend toward centralizing other aspects of higher education policy.

5. Collective Bargaining: Evaluating the Issues

The variety in institutional structure and function in American higher education and the variety of occupational groups in academe suggest that it should be possible to identify characteristic types of unions. Personal investigation and a review of the growing number of reports of experience at institutions[1] make it clear that at least two major functional types of faculty unionism can be distinguished. They can be described as *guild unionism* and *comprehensive unionism*. As the names imply, they are defined on the basis of their occupational composition. Measured by the numbers of units, guild unions are more common, but the comprehensive unions have more members and, by their nature, larger bargaining units. The distinction between the two types is related to their effect on the major issues in collective bargaining.

GUILD UNIONS AND COMPREHENSIVE UNIONS

One function of all faculty unions is to defend the existing position of their membership, sometimes against campus administrations and sometimes against higher levels of administrative control. In guild unions, however, the defensive element is probably more prominent in that they are usually created because of threats to the traditional position of faculty members, both as individuals and in their collective institutional role.

Guild unions are found in single-campus institutions and are composed primarily of full-time teaching faculty. The institutions themselves are relatively stable in structure and function; they may have more than one campus but, if so, they are main-

---

[1]For bibliographies of studies see the listing in Carr and Van Eyck (1973) and the bibliographies of the National Center (1974*a*).

135

branch institutions in which the main campus is the administrative and academic policy-making center. New degree programs and new curricula may have been added during the years of expansion, but the basic character of the institution has not changed substantially.

In addition to the pervasive influence of applicable public bargaining law, the most frequent common element in the unionization of these institutions is some form of crisis, actually experienced or thought to be impending. The most common type of crisis to date has been some arbitrary administrative action, particularly on personnel matters (for example, at St. John's University) or, less frequently, a threat to change institutional status in a system (for example, at Rutgers). The status of the faculty prior to unionization may have been either high or low. The important point is that whatever its previous level the maintenance of that level is thought to be in question.

In many of these institutions unionization has been a one-time explosion of activity. A threat is perceived, a set of relationships based on custom and inertia is threatened, and the faculty responds by formally organizing to demand bargaining rights to clarify their status and protect themselves from the consequences of change. After this the threat may recede or a new equilibrium may be reached, the situation stabilizes, and the pace of change slows to a walk. In the new context the old organs of governance often operate much as they did in the past, and the union functions as a watchdog of the process.

Once established, most guild unions move from the defensive to the offensive, at least in those institutions with a low level of faculty power. They regularly demand increases in economic benefits along with the rest of the occupational groups in the university and the economy, but they are also likely to press for noneconomic gains that will move the faculty closer to an ideal academic governance model in which faculty exert more influence on policy decisions.

Rutgers is an example of a primarily defensive version of the guild union, while St. John's represents an institution which organized in response to a crisis and which seems to have attained a substantially higher level of faculty participation in governance under the new arrangements (Hueppe, 1973). Faculty in both of these institutions are represented by the AAUP, and guild unionism is probably the stronghold of the association. But their choice of AAUP representation may be more an effect than a cause; conditions that produce guild unions are likely to produce attitudes favorable to the AAUP as the chosen bargaining instrument. A relatively simple administrative structure and an academic staff dominated by full-time teaching faculty oriented to the traditional academic disciplines are the natural environment of both guild unionism and of attitudes favorable to the AAUP.

Comprehensive unions may be comprehensive in either or both of two senses. They may be comprehensive in that they include different levels of institutions, such as two- and four-year colleges and universities. They may also be comprehensive in that in addition to the regular teaching faculty they include all professional staff in the institution and the nonteaching professionals (NTPs) make up a significant fraction of the total. Because guild unions also are likely to include some NTPs, the dividing line between the two types may not be precise, but an NTP proportion of 15 percent of the unit marks a rough boundary.

The definition of the appropriate bargaining unit has a great deal to do with whether a particular institution or system has a guild or a comprehensive form of academic unionism. However, except for perhaps the top 50 research institutions in the country, a decision to place all academic professionals in a single-campus institution in a single unit would probably produce a guild union by our criterion. It would be a mistake to assume that teaching faculty in all, or even most, institutions prefer narrowly based faculty units. The question of merging the two so-called faculty and lecturers' units at CUNY was submitted to a vote, and a very large fraction of the two-thirds of the total membership that voted favored merger.

It is our intention in this chapter to evaluate the impact of faculty unions on college and university governance and status equalization. One assumption underlying this analysis is that the effect of unionism on these two areas is a function of whether the union involved is a guild or a comprehensive union.

UNIONS AND GOVERNANCE

According to one compilation, as of early 1974 more than one-half of the unionized institutions of higher education were operating under contracts of less than two years' duration. For four-year institutions the corresponding fraction is more than two-thirds (National Center, 1974*b*). As a result, any assessment of the effects of faculty unions on governance is based on fragmentary evidence and, of necessity, includes a good deal of speculation.

To date, most of the discussion of the way unions relate to faculty senates and traditional governance systems has been prospective, and the conclusions have been based on experience with what are assumed to be analogous situations in private sector bargaining in the United States. In general, persons familiar with American industrial relations experience see the senate system of governance as the near equivalent of employee representation plans or "company unions," supported by American employers in the 1930s as an alternative to independent outside unions. Company support or domination of an employee organization has prevented that organization from being certified as a bargaining agent since the Wagner Act was passed in 1935. Certification of a union as exclusive bargaining agent under the law means that other employee organizations cannot represent employees in dealing with the employer. As a result, employee representation organizations either were dissolved or were converted into bona fide independent unions. The federal law gives the recognized exclusive bargaining agent monopoly over questions of wages, hours, and working conditions. The state public-employee laws have not gone quite as far as the federal law in some respects, but in general they are the same.

Most analysts assume that the senate system of governance will suffer the fate of the employee representation plans eventually, if not immediately. The existence of two at least partially parallel systems of representation of faculty interests is seen as an unstable situation, and when one system has an unassailable legal monopoly over most, if not all, important issues, it seems easy to predict the outcome.

Occasionally it is suggested that an agreed-on or natural division of authority can be observed, in which economic issues, such as salaries, are the province of the union and academic or educational issues, such as degree programs, are the responsibility of the senates. But this is usually viewed as a weak reed to depend on because of the ubiquitous nature of economics. Virtually all educational issues have potential economic consequences. A common example is that of average class size, but there are many others. The number and type of required courses, admission and grading standards, the number and type of degree programs, and the extent of reliance on full-time career faculty rather than part-time lecturers are other issues with economic overtones.

Even those who strongly believe that a separation of spheres of influence is desirable are pessimistic about the possibility of success in achieving it (Carnegie Commission, 1973*a*).

But the possibilities for a division of authority that is workable in at least some instances may be better than the pessimists/ realists have concluded. In the Carnegie Commission's governance report just cited, the well-worn phrase "shared authority" usually used in discussing governance systems in higher education is replaced by the word *codetermination*. In addition to being substantially equivalent to shared authority, codetermination has a special meaning in industrial relations as the English term used to describe the West German employee relations philosophy embodied in law since 1951.[2]

A WORKING MODEL OF CODETERMINA- TION

In the context of our discussion, the important feature of the German system of codetermination is the definition of two separate representative institutions with different functions to perform. The law provides for internal employee organizations called *work councils*. The members of the councils are elected from the plant employees with all employees eligible to vote. The councils vary in size up to 35 members, depending on the number of employees, and an elaborate system for allocating members among different occupational groups is provided. The council has jurisdiction over a variety of functions—personnel, economic (mainly internal wage administration matters), and social (mainly employee benefit and social service)—many of them subjects of collective bargaining in the United States. The councils are directed to be vehicles of cooperation and to abjure "industrial welfare." A company with several plants will have a

[2]There is a voluminous literature on codetermination in West Germany. An easily accessible description can be found in Seyfarth et al. (1969, Chap. 5). Codetermination was introduced in the coal, iron, and steel industries in 1951 and, in a somewhat milder form, in the rest of the industry in 1952. The laws have been further revised and codetermination strengthened somewhat since the publication of Seyfarth.

central works council with jurisdiction limited to multiplant issues.

After World War II, German unionism was reestablished on an industrial union basis with relatively few large unions. In most instances bargaining is conducted with associations of employers in the various industries. Unions may negotiate on a broad range of subjects, but their agreements apply to the industry as a whole—for example, the basic wage level—while the works councils are expected to handle most intraplant problems. German law does not permit unions to negotiate compulsory membership arrangements, and the unions are not obliged to represent nonmembers.

In the coal, iron, and steel industries the law provides for representatives on the company board of directors from the unions and from the works councils. The extension of this form of representation to other industries is a continuous subject of controversy. A 1971 revision of the 1952 law provided that the firms' employees (not the unions) would name one-third of the members of the boards of directors (Bergmann, 1974).

The German system thus provides a dual system of representation, with one employee organization operating at the industry or company level and another at the plant level. The law specifies the subject matter assigned to each section of representation. The two organizations have at least partially distinct constituencies. Many of the questions of employee rights that are major subjects of collective bargaining in the United States are regulated by law in Germany.

Some of the recommendations for developing a new model of collective bargaining in higher education in the United States rather than transferring the American industrial model to the colleges and universities call for something like the German two-tier system.[3] Particularly in the multicampus university systems which dominate faculty unionism, it might be possible to have one union organization that represents employee interests at the system level on general economic and policy matters, with implementation at the campus level in the hands of a works council–senate.

However, it is difficult to transplant social institutions from

---

[3]Another model, the British system of academic unionism, is described and analyzed in Chapter 7.

one national society to another. The pervasive influence of 40 years of American experience and the practices that have grown up during that period make the use of a different approach in a single sector of a single "industry" unlikely. Installing a system of codetermination like the German one would require special legal provisions defining the scope of bargaining, abandoning the concept of exclusive representation, legitimatizing employer support of employee organizations, and possibly prohibiting compulsory membership. The political conditions necessary for implementing this particular form of employee representation are not likely to exist.

Even in Germany the unions do not regard their codetermination system as stable. They are trying to extend their influence upward by securing the right to name members of boards of directors, and downward by running candidates for the works councils. Bergmann reports that the unions have had considerable success in both endeavors. Although only 31 percent of the total work force are union members, 490 of the 500 employee members of boards of directors in the coal, iron, and steel industries are union members. In the other sectors 80 percent of the 140,000 works council members and 70 percent of the 10,000 workers on boards of directors are union members.[4] These difficulties in maintaining a division of authority in an employee representation system exist even with the support of law.

Knowledge of experience such as this with dual representation systems lies behind the skepticism of industrial relations experts about the workability of dual faculty union–faculty senate systems in American higher education.

Patterns of Union-Senate Relations

The impact of the faculty unions on governance systems, particularly faculty senates, may be the topic that has attracted the most attention in discussions of academic collective bargaining. Unfortunately, definitive conclusions are impossible at this time because of the relatively short experience with bargaining and, more important, because careful, intensive studies by persons familiar with the actual operations of the governance

[4]Some indication of the possibility of union success in achieving their goals in the future is provided by the fact that more than 50 percent of the members of the German Parliament are union members. These data are from Bergmann (1974, p. 17).

systems both before and after unionization do not exist.[5] Short visits by researchers are inadequate to the task, although they can convey a good impression of the situation.

Another approach has been to collect a substantial number of negotiated contracts and to analyze provisions that appear to affect governance and senate relations, for example, methods of selecting chairmen.[6] This method of analysis is also helpful, but does not permit comparisons with the way the system functioned prior to unionization and does not reveal how the clauses are actually operating in practice.

As the experience accumulates, however, it is becoming clear that some of the earlier analyses did not do justice to the complexities of the actual situation.

The text for the present discussion is a comment by Caesar Naples (1974), one of the more experienced and perceptive participants as a negotiator for the SUNY system:

When the union feels that management is able to circumvent it by dealing with the senate over issues for which the union has firm faculty support, the union will be in a position to mount an effective bargaining table attack on collegial governance. Conversely, when management perceives the senate as a vehicle through which the union may achieve advances it was unable to achieve at the bargaining table, I believe the time for collegial governance will be past. In the meantime, however, both parties still have much to gain from the senate's continued existence. (p. 58)

Several implications can be drawn from this statement. First, university management's recognition of its interest in the potential role of the senate may improve the senate's chances for survival, at least in the short run. Certainly in higher education as a whole, faculty unionism seems to have strengthened the position of senates in at least one important way. The

[5]Some studies of existing systems are in progress, in particular one of Rutgers and the New Jersey State Colleges directed by James Begin of the Rutgers faculty and one of Pennsylvania by Kenneth Mortimer of Pennsylvania State University. A project monitoring the development of collective bargaining in California is being conducted under the author's direction. See Garbarino (1974*b*), Walker (1974), and Aussieker (1974) for preliminary reports.

[6]A computerized file of agreement provisions has been established by the National Center for the Study of Collective Bargaining at Baruch College, CUNY; it included 110 agreements in Spring 1974. Some interpretive articles have been prepared by Begin (1974), Mason (1974), and Mortimer and Lozier (1972).

unionization of University A may do a good deal to improve the position of the senate of University B. Of course, the effect on the senate of the newly organized institution itself is the immediate question, but the long-run importance of this indirect effect should not be ignored. Administration interest in the senate as a possible alternative to a union may, however, work to discredit the senate in the eyes of many faculty members.

Second, Naples's comment stresses the possibility that senates could complement union activity rather than substitute for it. The relationship between senate and union could be similar to that of senate and governing board in that the union might "share" some of its legal authority to represent faculty with the senate, either out of an attachment to separation of power as a principle or, as Naples suggests, as a tactical maneuver to gain advantages from the existence of a dual procedure.

Third, the statement reflects the usual assumption that faculty senates and academic unions are two separate entities with distinct organizational identities and possibly with divergent policies. In view of the fact that they both are assumed to be democratic institutions representing largely the same constituency, the validity of this assumption is not self-evident. In any event the emphasis on the possibility that faculty members may choose to support one or the other organization is worth noting.

This formulation can be summed up by the proposal that the relationship between senates and unions could be one of cooperation, competition, or cooptation.

The cooperative model   Cooperation is a situation in which both organizations maintain their independent identities and are both active in faculty affairs, not entirely without conflict but with neither challenging the existence or functioning of the other. Surprising as it may seem, in terms of numbers of bargaining situations the consensus of observers is that the most common relationship between unions and senates has been one of cooperation or, at a minimum, coexistence.[7]

In his study of "broadly based" senates, Hodgkinson reports

[7]Some assessments of experience in individual institutions are: SUNY, Fisk and Puffer (1973); Central Michigan, Bucklew (1973), *Chronicle of Higher Education* (November 26, 1973), and Pillotte (1973); St. John's, Hueppe (1973); Rutgers, Blaustein (1973); Youngstown State, Shipka (1974); Temple, Katz (1973); Massachusetts state colleges, Walters (1973).

"some data" showing that the existence of a collective bargaining unit on campus might "do in" the campus senate (1973*a*, p. 144). (His study does not cover the more narrowly based faculty senates.) He also reports that in several cases unions had provided support for the continued existence of senates. Aussieker (1974) found that, where collective negotiations are carried out in California community colleges under a meet-and-confer law, by far the most common relationship is cooperation. There has been no report of the elimination of a senate anywhere following the establishment of collective bargaining. (The New York legislature cut off the funding of the SUNY senate when it became directly active in promoting bargaining, but the university administration continued senates from other funds with no repercussions.) Unionization clearly has created more senates than it has eliminated, although it may have reduced the role of some senates in some types of decisions.

The most important qualifications to this conclusion unfortunately may turn out to be critical. Cooperation to date has been the dominant style on the single campus or at main-branch institutions where guild unionism is the rule. Senates and unions are least cooperative and most competitive in the bargaining units of large, complex, institutional systems with comprehensive unions; these units include a majority of all unionized faculty members. This is in part a result of the generally higher degree of conflict that appears to exist in these institutions in a context of large-scale changes in governance structures, an extended administrative hierarchy, and a more heterogeneous set of interest groups. As a result, institutionwide mechanisms for decision making on both employer and faculty sides are likely to be new and unseasoned. Even in these systems the relations between local campus senates and the local branches of the union are often cooperative.

One reason for the differences between guild and comprehensive union experiences is that the constituencies of the senate and the union naturally coincide in guild unions, whereas in comprehensive groups the union is more broadly based.

A factor that has made cooperation work is a natural division of labor suggested by the AAUP governance survey results (see Chapter 2). Senates clearly are most active in academic matters, followed by personnel matters, and finally administrative matters. Unions have concentrated on the last two areas, with little attention to academic affairs.

Where guild unions exist, there is often a common membership and an overlapping group of leaders and activist members, and there is usually agreement on an agenda of problems and a willingness to accept a division of responsibility. A faculty senate and the members of a professional staff bargaining unit are much more likely to differ on the goals of the organization, their relative urgency, and the methods to be employed in their pursuit. In institutions where these kinds of problems exist, whether in guild or comprehensive union situations, the relationship will be marked less by cooperation than by competition.

The competitive model A competitive relationship is one in which competition between senate and union dominates the elements of cooperation. The organizations compete over the right to control negotiations over major issues, and for the loyalty and the support of the faculty. The struggle is for control of the decision-making process and for the right to choose the objectives of the group, to pursue their achievement, and to gain credit for the result. Without compulsory membership or the agency shop the winning of faculty support is a life-or-death matter for the union. Not only must the union almost always win an election campaign to gain representation rights, it must win repeated votes of confidence expressed by the willingness of a major fraction of the unit membership to pay monthly dues.

Even when the constituencies of a faculty senate and a guild union are essentially the same, the activist element in each is self-selected and may be different in composition. The existing senate leadership reflects a certain distribution of political power among subgroups of the faculty, and, if they are convinced of the inadequacy of senate procedures in solving problems, these leaders may take the lead in introducing a union into the equation. Under these conditions not only are the two likely to cooperate, but the union may make strengthening the power of the senate one of its bargaining goals. If, on the other hand, the support for the union comes from those groups outside the political power structure of the senate, then the union will appear to its supporters to be a means of supplanting the current power holders.

Even when the two constituencies are identical and where the existing senate leadership participates in introducing the union, there is no guarantee that the members of the faculty electing to join and pay dues to the union will not generate a new and competitive leadership group.[8] This development is much more likely to occur when a comprehensive union faces a faculty senate, since by definition their constituencies are different and there is often a legacy of resentment between some of the nonteaching professionals and the traditional faculty leadership.

Faced with a choice between two different representatives of the "faculty," administrations are likely to show a clear preference for the senate version, thereby bringing latent competition to the surface. CUNY illustrates this situation in an extreme way. Faculty councils existed in well-developed forms on many of the older campuses, but a university senate was not established until 1968 at CUNY, and it was established at least partly to try to forestall unionization. It was composed largely of regular-rank faculty with limited representation of other members of the "instructional staff," and its assigned jurisdiction overlapped that of a bargaining agent. The regular-rank faculty at CUNY is a minority of the present bargaining unit, and while the senate continues to exist, its role is minimal at the university level and on some (but by no means all) campuses. Both the SUNY and the CUNY unions have challenged administration attempts to deal with the senates in areas in which the unions claim jurisdiction.

The usual prescription for avoiding competition is to define separate spheres of influence for the senate and the union either by law or by administration and union agreement. The customary prognosis for the success of this effort is unfavorable. In the United States it is generally accepted that the effects on conditions of employment of almost any management action create bargainable issues, so that any boundary between bargainable and nonbargainable issues is likely to leak badly. If a division of subject matter could be made effective, the German experience with codetermination suggests that this would result in

[8]When the Academic Senate at the Berkeley campus of the University of California sponsored an independent faculty association, it tried to avoid this possibility by naming an organizing committee and providing that the association would be dissolved unless it achieved about 25 percent membership from the senate by a specified date.

union attempts to capture control of the senate organization itself. What has in the past seemed to be a successful division of responsibility in the British university system, with the Association of University Teachers (AUT) bargaining on economic issues and faculty governance bodies handling academic issues at local levels, appears on examination to be on shaky ground. It has worked because the AUT's local associations do not have the power to bargain in individual universities, and the universities have been able to avoid establishing a national body that could make binding agreements on anything but salary matters.

Where conflict levels are low, union-senate cooperation can work indefinitely and this may be true in a good many situations. The hard fact, however, is that cooperation really amounts to a system of voluntarily shared authority on the part of the union. Just as a governing board in a crisis may revoke the delegation of some of its authority to a senate, so unions may decide to exercise their legal right to bargain on issues traditionally handled by the senate. A decision on the fate of a department or the nonretention of a faculty member that is important to a politically significant segment of the union's membership cannot be left to a final determination by another body without challenge.

If senate-union cooperation is not viable in a conflict situation, the outcome of the resulting competition may not be the elimination of the senate but an integration of the two institutions.

The cooptative model   The simplest description of a cooptative bargaining model is bargained collegiality or collegiality by contract. In the pure version of cooptation the senate, as a formal organization with separate facilities and its own officers, may not even exist on a unionized campus. Conversely, on a campus with a union that is not a formally recognized exclusive bargaining agent, the senate may dominate administration-faculty-union relationships, including the determination of bargaining policy.

Formulating the analysis in this way poses the question of identifying the essence of the problem—the exact nature of the distinction between senates and unions as faculty representatives. Perhaps the heart of the distinction is the role of "collegiality" versus the role of bargaining in decision making. Lawrence De Lucia, the current president of the SUNY union, the United University Professionals (UUP), offers what might be called a union definition of collegiality (1974), when he argues that in personnel matters, peer judgment means "evaluation by peers at the department level . . . if he [the chief administrative officer] rejects peer evaluation, it becomes incumbent upon him to give reasons for his decision. His decision, upsetting peer evaluation, may become the basis for a just cause arbitration."

This description of collegiality can be extended to other academic decisions and is probably representative of the prevailing union opinion. In this view collegiality means decision making by the immediately responsible faculty body with the result binding the administration, unless a reversal is sustained by an appeal from the administrative decision to an independent body.

In the administration's eyes collegiality is a more amorphous and more complicated system. Their version calls for recommendations by faculty committees, often with faculty-administrators participating in the process as part of the peer group and sometimes with the administration influencing the selection of at least some of the faculty members. The decision reached is to be accorded serious consideration and accepted, unless there are overriding reasons for changing it. The authority to override is based on inherent "management rights" and is not subject to review. This type of collegiality implies that decisions by faculty are usually accepted and are changed only after careful consideration for weighty reasons that, except in personnel cases, are reported to the faculty.

Looking at the matter this way suggests that most of the discussion of the effect of bargaining in the senate system really concerns the effect of bargaining on collegiality as a method of making decisions. Unions may have no objections to collegiality in the sense of decision by peers if they participate in the selection of the "peers" who make the decisions, if the process is free of administration domination, and if a favorable decision is binding or, if reversed, subject to objective review.[9] Where the existence of a senate as a separate organization will permit

[9]A provocative statement of the view that collegiality and peer evaluation may leave something to be desired from the standpoint of some faculty members is found in Wollett (1973). Wollett suggests that unions might be better advised to accept administrative initiative in decisions with the right to challenge disputed actions effectively, after the fact.

the administration to make its definition of collegiality prevail, a senate is a threat to the position of the union.

This line of analysis suggests how a cooptative system of faculty representation and participation might work. It may be possible to negotiate a mixture of decision-making procedures. For certain types of decisions (for example, budgetary allocations, academic organization, or administrative appointments) the union may be willing to agree to the acceptance of the administration's definition of collegiality (type I collegiality). For others (for example, personnel decisions) it may insist on the union's definition of collegiality (type II collegiality). Other decisions (for example, salaries) would be the subject of direct bargaining (type III collegiality). Senate-style machinery might be retained for the type I decisions, including independent faculty committees or joint faculty-administration committees with the faculty members selected by and responsible to the union. It would be understood that the recommendations of these committees would be rejected only for weighty reasons. Decisions on type II issues would be made by a system of peer judgment with the right to an independent review of any reversal under certain circumstances. Not only would decisions of the third type be subject to bargaining, but most important, the structure of the overall system, including the allocation of topics, would be subject to the bargaining process as well. The form of representation, the division of subject matter, and the extent of review would themselves be negotiable issues.[10]

The Massachusetts state college system has contracts that resemble this model in that faculty representatives in the governance system are selected by the union. (The romantic attachment to student participation demonstrated in these contracts is another matter.) Other contracts provide for the union to name members to various governance bodies as well. In the next several years it is virtually certain that many unions will achieve some form of compulsory membership or the agency shop, in essence providing them with universal membership. This will give the union more legitimacy as the vehicle of faculty participation and enhance its claim to control the representation system in all of its aspects.

[10]In an early paper Carl Stevens (1972) proposed a similar arrangement in which faculty unions would negotiate "procedural agreements" that would concentrate on setting up mechanisms for deciding substantive issues without making the detailed content of the substantive result the subject of direct bargaining.

The cooptative model differs from the competitive model because the primacy of the union is acknowledged and the distribution of subject matter among the various types of procedural mechanisms is agreed upon by the parties, not legislated. This does not mean that the union will be able to bring all issues into the sphere of bargaining or to require that they be subject to outside review, much less to dominate the outcome of negotiations. The results of collective bargaining to date do not suggest that administrations that know what they want and are competent in bargaining are being overpowered in negotiations.

The arrangement of the sequence of models from cooperation to competition to cooptation does not imply that they are stages in a natural progression from one to the other. Senate-union relations at most organized institutions are in the cooperative phase, some are in the competitive phase, and in a few the two systems show signs of becoming cooptative. Where guild unions exist, the close correspondence between the constituencies of the two organizations make cooptative arrangements a natural development if the proportion of faculty who are union members continues to rise.

In large institutional systems with comprehensive unions competition will be harder to replace with cooperative or cooptative arrangements. In these unions there are conflicts of interest between faculty and other professionals, among faculty in different types of institutions, and even among faculty in different institutions of the same type. An administration or a subgroup of faculty may be tempted to try to work outside the normal union negotiating channels to deal with specific problems important to a minority of the union membership, thereby perpetuating a competitive relationship.[11]

In summary, the predictions that senates would be displaced from the decision-making process by unions have proved to be exaggerated or at least premature. The variety of possible relationships between senates and unions has been underestimated, and extended periods of cooperative relations appear to

---

[11]At SUNY the faculty in the health science centers has maintained a separate identity within the union and has been able to get separate procedures to handle their problems. The faculty at the university centers has tried to develop a unified stand on some issues within the union, and the NTPs have retained their own internal organizational structure. The administration has tried to maintain the faculty senate as a forum for the consideration of academic issues.

be possible, particularly with guild unions. An integration of union and senate functions is at least one possible outcome, with the unions as dominant partners but with senate-style collegiality surviving in important areas of academic decision making. If something like this last system is to develop, however, it will have to be at administrative initiative. Unions are unlikely to make the self-denying distinction between issues on their own, and senates are not usually in a position to bargain for this division. The initial development of the pattern and the policing of its retention will be the administration's responsibility.

When academicians gather to discuss faculty unionism, the air is filled with calls for the development of a genteel alternative to the "industrial union model." Alternatives to the industrial model of academic unionism already exist in the various forms of faculty representation currently operating in the 90 percent of the four-year colleges that are still unorganized. The choice of a faculty union as a bargaining representative with legal status may well mean a replacement of the existing organizational structure, but an administration that really believes in the old-time collegial religion may be able to retain its procedures over substantial areas of academic decision making.

UNIONS AND UNIVERSITY MANAGEMENT Turning from union-senate to union-administration relations, it appears that the predictions of increased tensions and a higher level of conflict under unionized conditions are accurate. Even Rutgers' President Blaustein, whose generally favorable assessment of that relationship has attracted considerable attention, agrees that collective bargaining has "thrust administrators into a management role," but he argues that this change is desirable and long overdue. The most serious new problem he identifies is "creeping legalism," but he believes this is an independent development and not introduced by trade unionism (1973, p. 6).

The principal merit of Blaustein's analysis is that he identifies the changes taking place in the internal relations of colleges and universities[12] and emphasizes that many of them exist inde-

---

[12]Blaustein's "chamber of horrors," often attributed to unionism, is (1) a more explicit system of governance, (2) the deterioration of faculty quality, (3) the deterioration of department and school autonomy, (4) the polarization of the campus, (5) the decline of the senate, and (6) the replacement of consensus by bargaining in decision making.

pendently of unionism and that unionism is as much an effect as a cause.

The AAUP officers at Rutgers may not agree with all the details of Blaustein's portrayal; in general it appears to be a reasonably accurate one. But Rutgers's situation is highly atypical. The impetus for organization was at least partly a shared concern by the administration and a large, active AAUP chapter that the new public-employee bargaining law and a reorganized, and presumably more centralized, system of higher education might combine to threaten Rutgers' preferred position in that system. The AAUP was able to demonstrate support from 80 percent of the faculty, to agree with the administration on a definition of the bargaining unit, and to be recognized as the exclusive bargaining agent without going through the trauma of a representation election. Rutgers had previously experimented with a mixed academic senate with quite modest success from the faculty's point of view, and the AAUP supported the development of a faculty senate to participate in governance. (One unfortunate aspect of unionism that Blaustein detects is the effort by the AAUP to dominate the senate.)

Creeping legalism is a disease that affects unionized and nonunion universities alike (and virtually all other American institutions), but the union is a carrier that introduces legalism in a virulent form to the campus as a whole in a remarkably effective way. It is one of the great accomplishments of American unions that the grievance procedure has introduced due process and the academic version of what Sumner Slichter called "industrial jurisprudence" to employer-employee relationships. In the absence of unions legalism might have made due process available to prominent and controversial figures, but unions help to make it available to obscure assistant professors in departments of library science. Colleges and universities have long been vulnerable to charges of casual and erratic protection of the employment rights of nontenured faculty. With the loss of protection provided by a buoyant academic labor market and a serious oversupply of qualified new entrants to the profession, faculty members need and would in some way have secured more formal methods of job protection.

Nevertheless, the necessity for meeting the standards of what the typical union regards as due process may be incompatible with the subjective process of evaluating faculty performance in the institutions where such evaluations are taken seriously in retention and promotion decisions. Effective peer evaluation may not survive open personnel files, the right to reply, and, possibly, appeals to other forums. Administrators understandably appear to find amusement in the not infrequent instances in which a union pursues a grievance against a personnel decision made by their faculty colleagues (and sometimes fellow union members) sitting in peer judgment. Perhaps they should be wondering how the system will work if the faculty participants come to agree with Wollett's observation that "self-governance that thrusts the faculty into the performance of managerial functions serves primarily the interests of the administration" (1973, p. 36). Many faculty members have accommodated to the pressures for less rigorous standards of performance for students; they may be amenable to doing the same for their colleagues.

No other organized institution has had as high a level of conflict for as long a period as CUNY. Virtually all social relations in New York City seem to be more problem-prone than anywhere else, and faculty unionism is no exception. CUNY is a gargantuan complex of institutions of great heterogeneity exposed to the problems of higher education in their most extreme form—for example, open admissions. Nevertheless, the level of sustained hostility in the union-administration relationship is unusual, particularly in view of the changes in the leadership on both sides that have occurred since the bargaining relationship was established, a factor that sometimes lessens the tensions created by the shock of adjusting to the introduction of collective bargaining.[13] During 1974 a new board of higher education was appointed, and this may lead to a change in the character of the relationships.

During the first three years of the CUNY agreement, 1969–1972, 629 formal written grievances went through the first step (the campus president) of the grievance procedure. Another 30

[13]Since the bargaining election three of the four principals have changed: Albert Bowker and Bernard Mintz have been replaced by Robert Kibbee and David Newton as, respectively, chancellor and vice-chancellor with responsibility for administration-union relations. Belle Zeller, long-time head of the Legislative Conference, remains as head of the merged union, but Israel Kugler, former head of the AFT-controlled lecturers' unit and an officer in the merged organization, no longer plays a major role in the union. There appears to have been less turnover in the legal representatives.

class grievances were initiated at the second step (the chancellor) (Benewitz and Mannix, 1974). This record means that each year about 15 grievances per 1,000 unit members got to this stage. Unfortunately comparable data do not exist for other institutions, but our own guess is that the 659 total may be two or three times the total grievances in all other organized institutions.[14]

Compared to the private industrial sector, an unusually high proportion of these grievances was taken to one of the nation's more expensive labor arbitration forums. Newton (1973) reports that during approximately the same three-year period more than 200 cases were filed for arbitration (some of them undoubtedly later withdrawn), but only 61 cases were actually decided by August 1972.

If Newton's figures are combined with those from Benewitz and Mannix, we can conclude that about one-third of the 623 individual grievances filed at step 1 eventually were filed for arbitration and that at least 10 percent and perhaps as high as 15 percent actually were carried through to final decision. Looked at another way, of the approximately 250 grievances denied at step 2, about 80 percent were filed for arbitration, and somewhere between one-fourth and one-third actually were arbitrated.

There is no question that the situation at CUNY is a difficult one, but in our opinion the best explanation of the conflict is the heterogeneity of the bargaining unit.[15] The administration seems to believe that the union (the Legislative Conference before the merger) does not represent the true interests of the full-time career faculty and that many of its demands are in response to the pressures from a diverse set of militant membership caucuses. During the difficult and prolonged negotiations for a second three-year contract, the administration declined to

---

[14]According to the Benewitz and Mannix study, the grievant won one-sixth of the cases at step 1; about 55 percent of the denials were taken to step 2, where the grievant won in one-eighth of the cases.

[15]The New York Public Employment Relations Board has faced the most difficult bargaining unit determination problems in the country in the several SUNY and CUNY cases. In no other instances have the bargaining unit decisions been so important in determining the character of the relationships, and, in our opinion, they have consistently been unfortunate in their consequences.

put the annual salary increments into effect on the defensible ground that it would be making a major concession in advance of an agreement. In the context of a deadlocked negotiation this move probably did more to nearly double membership in the Professional Staff Congress (PSC) than any other single factor. The membership proportion was at an all-time high of about 40 percent in 1974. If membership continues to rise, the union will gain in credibility as the representative of the group and the administration's position may change. The new New York Board of Higher Education also may bring some change to the situation.

CUNY Vice-Chancellor David Newton has provided a sketch of the escalated bureaucratization that has occurred at CUNY (Newton, 1973). It involves additional internal staff, more outside professional help, a great deal of staff time diverted to contract administration, and greatly increased expenditures on promulgating and administering procedures. His "conservative" estimate of the cost of financing the administrative side of the CUNY system is $2 million in 1973 for a bargaining unit of some 17,000 members. In addition to these costs Kibbee (1973) stresses the effect of the rhetoric of the "negotiating struggle" in shaping the "generalized view of the administration by the faculty" and the consequences of this for day-to-day educational relationships. One of the happier aspects of the CUNY situation is that the relationships on many of the local campuses seem to be less conflict-ridden than at the higher levels.

In most organized institutions the administration-union relationship is more like that at Rutgers than at CUNY. The escalation of bureaucracy is widespread in the form of more staff, more explicit and more detailed procedures, and more records, meetings, and reviews. Blaustein is right in emphasizing that all these trends were set in motion independently of unionism, but the unions are a remarkably effective device for hastening and elaborating the process. The recognition that the new procedures may increase the probability that justice is done in individual cases does not change the fact that there are substantial costs involved.

One man's loss of flexibility and discrimination in decision making is another man's limitation of arbitrary authority. In the short run the impact of bargaining may change the atmosphere of informal administration that many faculty and administrators feel existed previously to one of restricted authority through formalization and rationalization. In the long run, however, administrations may gain more freedom on more important issues by adopting a more aggressive adversary stance than appeared appropriate to a consensus system of decision making.

Collegiality guaranteed by contract may be given less scope to operate than delegated collegiality had. The contribution of lawyers to drafting contracts is a facility with the language of the law and a training to anticipate and provide for dealing with the worst possible occurrence in his client's interest. A governing board that feels that in a crisis it can withdraw delegated authority without challenge will be willing to delegate authority over a wider range of decisions than it will grant irrevocably in a legally binding contract. The union's answer to this argument is that its specialty is forcing the board to grant contractually more authority than it would ever grant voluntarily. The net result depends on relative bargaining power, and in higher education, at least in the four-year sector, this has not been seriously tested.

Finally, collective bargaining legitimates adversarial behavior on both sides of the table, and this may give management an advantage. Bargaining strategy accepts the advancement of extreme demands as a normal tactic, and this encourages not only thinking about the unthinkable but actually publicly proposing "unthinkable" changes. Bargaining means "packaging" gains and concessions so that an explicit tradeoff becomes possible. The resulting decisions need be acceptable to only a majority of those voting on the ratification of the contract. Forms of productivity bargaining are more likely to be achievable since a faculty concession on work load, for example, can be linked to higher pay or other benefits. Faculties enjoy the protections of many well-established "work rules" that might be difficult to challenge directly through traditional procedures but that might be changed as part of a bargaining package. Sophisticated administrations may in the next decade be able to take advantage of these characteristics of bargaining to make more changes more easily than they could through traditional structures.

UNIONS AND STATUS EQUALIZATION Status equalization is the reduction of differentials in pay and privilege that have existed between groups of academic staff and between different types of academic institutions.[16] A century ago the British socialists Sidney and Beatrice Webb identified the establishment of "the common rule" as a major goal of trade unionism. Much public discussion of faculty unions presumes a devotion to uniformity and equality that is exaggerated, but there is no question that employee organizations typically require a justification of differences in treatment in more explicit and objective terms than managements are likely to introduce on their own. The two areas of potential equalization that will be discussed in this section are tenure and pay.

Unions and Tenure A credible threat to the traditional practices of academic tenure may be the most important single cause of unionization in a college or university.

Tenure is the academic version of job security, and its classic defense is its function in protecting faculty members in their intellectual independence in teaching and research from popular or political reprisal.[17] In addition to providing a bulwark of academic freedom in this sense, tenure should be considered as part of a system of personnel and salary administration. In this connection some of its important aspects are:

1 As a desirable condition of employment, it is one of the benefits that attract quality recruits to the profession.

2 The expensive and virtually permanent commitment it implies exerts great pressure to ensure quality of performance before tenure is awarded. The up-or-out decision after the expiration of the probationary period embodied in most tenure systems discourages taking the easy way out by making repeated short-term appointments of persons judged not to merit a long-term commitment.

3 Tenure plays a central role in the whole apparatus of collegiality and peer evaluation if this apparatus is to function effectively. Innumerable academic decisions made by faculty members are more objective than

---

[16]The awkward but neutral term *status equalization* is used to avoid the depreciatory overtones of *leveling* or *homogenization* on the one hand and the laudable connotations of *correcting inequities* on the other.

[17]Walter P. Metzger (1973) has contributed a historical review of the development of tenure for the Commission on Academic Tenure in Higher Education.

they would be if tenure did not protect those involved in the decisions and those affected by them from reprisals from their colleagues, from students, and from administrators.

4 In spite of administrators' impatience with the limits tenure places on their authority, they nevertheless are prime beneficiaries of faculty tenure. It protects them from constant pressures from students, other faculty, alumni, political factions on and off the campus, legislators, and a host of other groups to get rid of one or another faculty member for one or another reason.

5 It is an integral part of the system of salary administration. The operation of tenure means that a system of progressive advances in pay starting from a remarkably low level can be used to motivate performance. Surely the prospect of achieving a tenured career is one of the reasons that institutions of higher education are able routinely to recruit highly trained men and women in their late twenties with a lifetime record of top academic achievement for annual salaries of about $13,000 in 1973.

Tenure has its seamy side as well. The argument against it today is discussed in terms of "tenuring in," the situation that arises as the proportion of an institution's staff with tenure increases. Percentages of tenured staff of 70 or 80 percent are common in mature institutions, although the proportion overall is about 50 percent (Metzger, 1973, p. 233).

Introducing new faculty members into a system that has reached a "steady state" depends on the rate of retirement, death, or resignation at one end and the level of recruitment and the rate of promotion to tenure at the other. It is not generally recognized that the "tenuring in" problem not only affects the rate of new recruitment and the proportion of probationary faculty awarded tenure but also leads to attempts to minimize the number of entry "ladder" appointments that might lead to tenure, to reducing the rate of promotion of faculty already tenured, and to drastically reducing the chances of lateral movement from one institution to another for all faculty with salaries much above entry levels. Unions thus are concerned not only with attempts to limit or abolish tenure but with the pressure that "tenuring in" produces for hiring part-time faculty, adjuncts, or lecturers, for holding down the proportion of eligibles given tenure, and for quotas in rank distributions.

The lengthy progression in salary and rank found in most public institutions does not denote changes in job content—professors and assistant professors do similar work—but is part of an incentive system to motivate behavior. As a faculty ages, it is likely to get increasingly expensive in salary terms. It is not surprising that some faculty members, both inside and outside of unions, suspect that much of the expressed concern with flexibility and obsolescence is really a concern with salary costs and the intriguing prospect of replacing expensive senior staff with inexpensive junior staff.

The other major argument against tenure is that it permits faculty to be unresponsive and irresponsible in meeting the needs of the institution and of their students. Discharge of a tenured faculty member is rare, and a system of discipline short of discharge is only now being developed. This again is a highly principled stance that has more pragmatic personnel overtones. A great deal of what is called governance by consensus or collegiality is really forced by the difficulty in getting faculty protected by academic freedom and tenure to do anything they really do not want to do or at least to get them to do it well. It is very difficult to elicit quality performance of an intangible professional service by discipline or compulsion. The client's replacement of one professional by another is one remedy, but at present, tenure stands as a barrier to this solution in higher education.

Again it is not surprising that faculty members and union officers suspect that the weakening of tenure is designed not only to enhance flexibility, intellectual dynamism, and responsiveness to societal needs but also to lower costs, to raise work loads, and to make faculty more subject to administrative direction and control in a wide range of day-to-day operating conditions.

In fact, administrators down through department chairmen have much more control over their faculties than is implied in tenure discussions. Promotions or pay increases can be manipulated to reward or punish individuals. Access to support services, research support opportunities for additional income, the assignment of offices, reduced teaching schedules, scheduling of classes, committee assignments, and travel opportunities—all can be used to influence behavior. The inclusion of rules governing many of these items in the collective bargaining agreements of faculty unions attests to their use and importance. Discharges of tenured faculty may be rare, but a substantial number are undoubtedly encouraged or harassed into leaving their jobs, and managerial control over a larger number is enhanced by the use of other aspects of the "reward system," of which tenure is one part.

Tenure and security of employment   Most collective bargaining contracts leave tenure arrangements unchanged, either by explicit language that maintains existing policies or by omitting any reference to the subject. Others, like the St. John's agreement, may have strengthened tenure arrangements by including language that expands previous rights.

The most significant fact about collective bargaining on tenure is that, in spite of all the discussion of weakening tenure, on balance the group enjoying some form of security of employment has been expanded and "nonreappointing" probationary faculty members has been made more difficult. In general, where some members of the bargaining units have not had tenure or security of employment prior to unionization, there has been movement toward an expansion of coverage.

At CUNY the official basis for setting up two distinct bargaining units initially was that the members of the faculty group were tenured or eligible for tenure, while the lecturers' unit membership was not. Unfortunately for this distinction the first contract negotiated by the AFT on behalf of the lecturers provided that lecturers given a sixth full-time appointment would be granted a "certificate of continuous appointment." This meant a "guarantee of full time reappointment subject to continued satisfactory performance, stability in academic program, sufficiency of registration and financial ability."

The 1973 CUNY contract for the now-merged units calls for multiple-year appointments for certain administrative positions. After a probationary year, two- or three-year appointments will be the norm, thus increasing security of employment short of tenure for this group.

The SUNY agreements and associated board policies are noteworthy for including a remarkably elaborate set of personnel policies for nonteaching professionals (NTPs) that dramatically improved their position. The change in the status of the NTPs reflects the balance of power within the Senate Professional Association (SPA) during the first three-year contract, when the SPA was led by Robert Granger, an NTP, and the proportion of NTP membership in the SPA was about 40 percent. In 1973 an internal upheaval took place, which resulted in Granger's being replaced by Lawrence De Lucia as president of the SPA (now the United University Professionals, UUP). De Lucia is a faculty member at one of the four-year colleges. Enough NTPs were unhappy with the new situation so that an effort was made, in alliance with the Civil Service Employees Association, to secede from the UUP by petitioning for the formation of a separate bargaining unit. The New York PERB refused to approve the severance.

As of 1974 the NTP proportion of UUP membership is about 22 percent, in line with their proportion in the whole bargaining unit. The change in proportion is primarily due to increased faculty membership. Now that the NTPs' job conditions are greatly improved, the next objective of the UUP is likely to be parity of treatment for the faculty at the two- and four-year colleges with those at the university centers.

The revolution in NTP status began during the first contract period (1970–1973) with provision for a system of promotion for NTPs and a system of peer evaluation in memoranda of understanding. It was continued at the negotiation of the second contract in 1973.[18]

The first memorandum established four professional ranks designated I to IV, with each NTP position placed in one of these classifications. Criteria for promotion were established, and a promotion review panel was set up on each campus, composed of NTPs elected by the NTP chapter. Appeals of position classifications and requests for promotion are reviewed by this panel before going to a university review board for final decision.

The other memorandum of understanding deals with the evaluation of performance. An elaborate procedure for evaluation by supervisors is called for with appeals from unsatisfac-

[18]These provisions have not been made part of the body of the agreement. During the first contract period, negotiations resulted in two separate memoranda of understanding on promotion and peer evaluation. The second contract negotiation produced an agreement and a separate document, *Revision of the Board of Trustees' Policies,* in the form of a new Article XI of the policies dealing with the appointment of professional staff. The memoranda were not covered by the grievance procedure.

tory ratings going to a campus committee on professional evaluation, three of whose five members are elected at large by the NTPs. Further appeals are available, first to the campus president and then, under certain circumstances, to the chancellor of the university.

These arrangements are something of a work of art, exceeding in complexity any system of personnel evaluation of which I am aware. Their most significant features are the peer reviews by elected members of the professional staff and the multiplicity of appeals procedures. Even without formal tenure they must present formidable obstacles to termination.

The 1973 *Revision of the Board of Trustees' Policies* rounds off the system. One portion deals with the appointment of persons to the professorial or librarian ranks and provides for term appointments for a maximum of three years at the rank of instructor or above and for "continuing appointments" (the euphemism for tenure) after that time if the person is reappointed.

The major part of the revision deals with the establishment of a system of permanent appointments for all professional employees. A professional employee who has served two years on a campus, who has a professional title, and who has a total of seven years' service anywhere in the university as a professional employee must be given a permanent appointment if reappointed for a third year.

The achievements of the professional employees of SUNY in their four years of academic bargaining are extraordinary. In that time the almost 4,000 SUNY professionals have come close to reproducing a system of personnel administration paralleling that of the professorial staff. The two sizable groups that have benefited most from faculty unionism are the almost 4,000 professional employees at SUNY and the 3,600 CUNY community college teaching faculty.[19]

The CUNY and SUNY agreements are outstanding examples of the extension of security of employment to substantial numbers of new groups of academic staff, but there is also a general

---

[19]The CUNY community college faculties were brought to parity in salaries by rank with the senior colleges, resulting in increases of 43 percent in the first two years of the contract. The next largest gains are probably those won by the St. John's University faculty in economic and noneconomic matters and those of the Pennsylvania State College faculty.

tendency to extend faculty privileges to the other titles included in the bargaining units.

Unions and instant tenure "Instant tenure" is one of the colorful phrases that appeared early in faculty bargaining. It is a misleading phrase in that no union has demanded, much less achieved, instant tenure for its faculty clientele. But as unions have pressed for "due process" for probationary faculty, the wide gap between the different procedures applied to the termination of tenured and nontenured faculty has been narrowed a good deal as more stringent procedures are required for nonreappointment. Instant tenure is an exaggerated description of the result, but the phenomena it represents are real.

Once again, the unions are reacting to a change in the institutional environment, not initiating one. Demands for due process are ubiquitous in American society, and the traditional processes of nonreappointment in higher education are unusual in the degree of secrecy and lack of review that have been maintained. In the not-too-distant past new recruits to the profession entered the pyramid of institutions of higher education at the highest prestige level available to them and, if unsuccessful at that level, found it easy to move laterally or to a lower stratum, possibly even at an increase in pay. With a reduced demand and an increased supply of job candidates, institutions at all levels find themselves able to raise their standards of recruitment and their standards of performance. It is both easier than it was to fail at a position at one level and harder to make a successful transition to another position. Institutions that 10 years ago were glad to hire a holder of a Ph.D. degree and that granted tenure to virtually all eligibles are reviewing sheaves of applications, lengthening probationary periods, requiring records of research and publications, and reducing the proportion of probationary faculty awarded tenure.

Litigation has been used to press for due process, but most of the pressure for new procedures has come from the unions. The demands have taken several forms:

1 *Specification of procedures of evaluation.* Bargaining agreements commonly specify the character of reviews, a calendar of notifications, and reports of results. When department chairmen are required to observe these procedural niceties, the results are often less than ideal. Flaws of procedure can be challenged in a grievance hearing, and a large fraction of CUNY's hectic grievance record has resulted from complaints that procedure was not followed. CUNY has tried to reduce procedural complaints by negotiating a requirement that a faculty take positive steps to initiate the required action before a claim of omission can be made.

Complex procedures that create unpleasant duties for collegial supervisors or evaluators obviously reduce the likelihood that adverse actions will be taken. If an adverse evaluation must be based on frequent formal observation, if conferences are required at which evaluation reports must be defended against the faculty member and, perhaps, the union representative, and if decisions must be defended before an appeals panel, the administrative stamina needed for effective action may be lacking. Identifying specific contracts would mean imputing motives without information, but on a reading of some procedures it is hard to avoid the suspicion that they have been devised with strategic intent to discourage administrative authorities as well as to provide substantive protections.

2   *Open files.* Peer evaluation has often been done anonymously in committee on the basis of confidential reports secured from persons inside and outside the campus who are familiar with a candidate's work and area of interest. In other cases the membership of evaluation committees is known, but their deliberations are secret. A large number of negotiators have struggled with the obvious problems of equity created by these arrangements. The candidate would like to be sure that all information was considered, that the information was accurate, that extenuating circumstances were recorded, that the persons expressing opinions were qualified to do so, and, finally, that the decision reached was consonant with the evidence. On the other hand, candid expressions of opinion may be difficult to collect if the evaluators are asked to render sensitive judgments solely out of a sense of professional obligation at the risk of personal unpleasantness and possible reprisal.

The trend in contracts is to try to deal with this problem by keeping two sets of files. At a minimum, evaluations made at the time of appointment are kept confidential. Most contracts also try to protect the anonymity of outside evaluators at all times. Official correspondence and all formal evaluations by chairmen, deans, or committees of observers are usually available to the faculty members, and responses can be entered in the record.

Because all the documents are not available and the deliberations of the review committee itself are closed, the question arises as to how full an explanation of the action taken will be provided—that is, will reasons for adverse actions be given?

3   *Reasons for denial.* The key argument against giving reasons for an adverse action is that it implies that the reasons must meet some standard of adequacy if the action is to be regarded as justified. In some instances giving reasons would compromise confidentiality, but the real danger is that the published reasons may then have to be defended and that over a succession of cases a kind of public common law would develop with the citing of precedents and a need to prove distinctions among apparently similar cases.

These same considerations are cited as grounds for requiring that the justification of decisions be made available to the faculty member. Unless the bases for the decisions are revealed, how can arbitrary or discriminatory actions be challenged?

The 1974 SUNY agreement illustrates one method of handling grievances involved in the denial of tenure. If the first-level peer review committee recommends against the faculty member, no reasons need be given. If there is a second-level academic review committee in the institution and it makes a negative recommendation, the campus president gives the candidate the reasons for the action, but no appeal is possible. If the campus president reverses a favorable recommendation of an academic review committee, he must give reasons, and the staff member has the right to some form of a review.[20]

On the other hand, the AFT union at Southeastern Massachusetts University has negotiated a special grievance procedure for reappointment, pay increases, tenure, and promotion, which calls for "access to all written evaluation materials" used and a statement of the "grounds for the decision" to go to the faculty member (SMU Agreement, 1973, p. 25).

4   *Appeals in academic cases.* In unionized four-year colleges appeals from academic decisions to outside bodies have been strongly resisted. The collective bargaining contracts tend to distinguish carefully between a grievance procedure to appeal from disciplinary actions and a procedure for grieving the interpretations of the provisions of the contract, including the procedures for academic review.

Where they exist, as at SUNY and CUNY, the disciplinary grievance procedures could eventually turn out to be an underrated innovation. Discipline against faculty members has been rare in the past, and spelling out procedures for discipline could be interpreted as implying that they might be less rare in the future. (So far these procedures seem to have been little used.)

The CUNY provision (Article 21, CUNY Agreement, 1973) states that

[20]In the two SUNY collective bargaining agreements, the various memoranda of understanding, and the *Revision of the Board of Trustees' Policies* the word *tenure* does not appear.

discipline can be imposed for "(a) incompetent or inefficient service; (b) neglect of duty; (c) physical or mental incapacity; (c) conduct unbecoming a member of the staff. This provision shall not be interpreted as to constitute interference with academic freedom."

Proceedings are to be held before a three-member committee made up of one nominee from the personnel committee of the college concerned, one named by the university faculty senate, and a chairman chosen from outside the college by the first two members. Appeals may be made to the New York Board of Higher Education.

CUNY pioneered the outside arbitration of academic grievance cases with the arbitrator barred by the famous "Nota Bene" clause from reviewing the exercise of academic judgment. The Nota Bene clause, as such, does not appear in the 1973 agreement, but the substance remains. Appeals from decisions of nonreappointment have been the most common type of grievance and arbitration cases at CUNY in spite of this limitation. According to Benewitz and Mannix (1974), about 80 percent of all grievances involved reappointment or promotion.[21]

The CUNY method of handling this problem set a pattern of protecting academic judgment from outside review that has been followed closely by other bargainers. As a result, the decision of whether to award tenure has been retained as a judgment made by the faculty and the administration up to this time, with limited outside review.

The CUNY 1973 Agreement breaks some new ground. Under a new procedure the arbitrator may decide in favor of the grievant in an academic case, and if he then concludes "that there is a likelihood that a fair academic judgment may not be made on remand if normal academic procedures are followed, the Arbitrator shall remand the matter . . . to a select faculty committee of three tenured full or associate professors of the City University of New York" (p. 23). The committee is to function essentially as a faculty review committee on the merits of the case. Note, however, that the select committee is available only in a restricted set of cases, that it is made up of internal faculty, and that its decision is apparently not binding on the administration.

The introduction of these four elements into the tenure review process by faculty unions represents a major change in the way the system has operated, particularly in the colleges

---

[21]According to a study of step 1 grievances at SUNY by Herman Doh and Stanley Johnson, 85 of 180 cases filed in 1971–72 involved appointment, reapppointment, tenure, or promotion issues. Even though their classification is different and possibly more inclusive than that of the CUNY study, the proportion is much lower (National Center, *Newsletter*, May/June 1974).

and universities that have taken tenure most seriously. In community and state colleges covered by tenure laws some elements of due process have been available in the past, but even here it appears likely that the new systems are more procedurally elaborate. In spite of the development of these procedures, the tenure review process is an example of a bargaining issue on which administrations have resisted any really significant inroads on the academic content of internal decisions.

Nontenured faculty, as the least favored of the professoriate, have been formally guaranteed procedural justice in unionized institutions, whereas previously they had to take the provision of justice on faith. Undoubtedly more justice is probably now being done, and certainly more justice is being *seen* to be done, which is important in itself. This does not mean that nontenured faculty are more likely to be promoted as a result. At CUNY, for example, it is probably true that, in spite of the new procedures and the vigorous and expensive prosecution of nonreappointment cases by the union, the proportion of eligible faculty being awarded tenure each year is smaller than was the case before unionization.

Junior faculty may be in the same position as senior faculty who have made relatively few positive gains from unionism but who may have benefited from a mitigation of possible negative developments in an unfriendly environment. Because the position of all nontenured faculty is much more unfavorable than it was formerly, it is important that negative decisions be seen to be procedurally fair. On balance, the procedural complexities and greater openness that bargaining has introduced do not seem to have been serious barriers to the continued exercise of academic judgment. The price in administrative expense and complexity has bought benefits by protecting a system that can still be meritocratic if the administration and the tenured faculty really want it that way.

There is a danger that over a period of time union pressure will eliminate the distinction between outside review on procedure and the review of academic judgment. If this happens in those institutions where a system of peer evaluation has operated effectively in selecting and providing persons of scholarly promise, the adversary nature of the arbitration process and the emphasis on the formal record could pose a threat to the maintenance of academic "quality." This could be particularly true if arbitrators were drawn from outside the institution. This possibility is mitigated by a number of factors. Institutions that take tenure seriously appear to be in the minority,[22] although they are a large and an inordinately important minority, and few of them have unionized to date. Even where the screening is taken seriously, it is not necessarily true that outside review by carefully selected academic persons would be less effective than internal selection; in fact, it might be more effective in protecting faculty quality.

In summary, unionization has had a substantial effect in extending security of employment similar to faculty tenure to other members of the academic staff. This may have significant financial and administrative costs but is unlikely to affect academic affairs directly. Unions have introduced lengthy and tedious procedures of selection, evaluation, and review of appointments, nonreappointments, and promotions. These are expensive and bureaucratic in operation, but until there is more evidence than exists to date that the academic content of decisions has changed for the worse, no final judgment can be made.

Is tenure negotiable?   So far, the discussion of status equalization has assumed that the faculty unions are the aggressors in trying to expand the areas of academic privilege. In the long run, in some institutions it may be the administration that takes the offensive—at least as far as tenure is concerned.

The abortive contract negotiated by the AFT at the University of Hawaii but overwhelmingly rejected by the faculty attracted a great deal of attention because it contained a provision that weakened the tenure system. Part of the proposal was the modification of the up-or-out system by the concept of an "extended" appointment. Persons completing the probationary period and not going "up" to tenure need not have gone "out" but could have been awarded five-year term appointments and retained on the staff. Faculty with tenure would presumably have retained it, and new tenure appointments could have been made, but under the new system a new category of possibly

[22]The Commission on Tenure found that in all institutions combined, 42 percent awarded tenure to all candidates considered in Spring 1971. Only 25 percent denied tenure to as many as 30 percent of the candidates (Commission, 1973, Table 4).

long-term nontenured faculty would have been established. The possibility of an indefinite succession of term appointments was regarded as the thin edge of the wedge of an attack on tenure overall.

The administration initiated the proposal in bargaining, and the union could have rejected it outright and struck, negotiated its withdrawal by granting other concessions, or accepted it with or without securing compensating administration concessions. The AFT took the last alternative. If the AAUP wins bargaining rights and the same demand is pressed, they will face the same set of choices. Whatever their decision, tenure will be established as a negotiable item.[23]

If a frontal assault on the academic version of tenure is launched and succeeds, it will probably be replaced with its civil service equivalent in public institutions. A wave of organization would be stimulated. Under these conditions it is possible that management might gain more initiative and control than the present system permits, but experience with the operation of unionized civil service systems indicates that it is not obvious that the difference in practice actually realized would be significant.

Salaries and Salary Administration   Measuring the impact of unions on the level of salaries will attract increasing attention as collective bargaining spreads and more experience is accumulated. At this moment the data are too sparse to permit econometric analysis of any sophistication to be undertaken for the four-year institutions. The heterogeneity of institutions by size and type requires their separation into categories (the AAUP salary survey uses five categories), and there are only 60 to 70 separate four-year contracts to analyze. The data source most often used for the simpler analyses of salaries in higher education is the AAUP survey, published annually in the summer issue of the *AAUP Bulletin*.

Salary practices in institutions of higher education make it difficult to collect and analyze data to test the effect of unioniza-

---

[23]William Van Alstyne, the AAUP president, advances the suggestion that tenure might be considered a nonnegotiable subject that would be the faculty equivalent of an inherent management right. In Hawaii the law contains a strong management-rights clause that alone might rule out this interpretation, and, in general, tenure seems almost a classic "condition of employment" and therefore bargainable under virtually all laws and court decisions.

tion. Changes in salary by rank of individual faculty reflect general salary increases, the granting of pay increases to individuals within a rank, and promotions to a higher rank. Averages computed for a single institution are affected by all these, plus changes in the number employed at the different pay levels. Changes in averages for groups of institutions are the result of all the foregoing, plus changes in the set of institutions reporting over the years and changes in the distribution of employment among the institutions. Isolating the effect of unionization is a difficult task.

One method of coping with these problems is to use pairs of union-nonunion comparison institutions chosen to resemble one another in all other pay-determining variables. Robert Birnbaum (1974) did such a study for 88 pairs of institutions. He concluded that the average unionized institution had increased a pay advantage of $47 in 1968–69 to $824 in 1972–73. Birnbaum divided the institutional pairs into four categories[24] and found that in all categories unionized institutions increased their advantage over their unorganized counterparts, although the results for two groups were not statistically significant.

Not only is it hard to isolate the differential effect of unionism on salaries, but it is even difficult in many cases to calculate the correct percentage rate of increase from the collective bargaining agreements. Both the Rutgers and CUNY agreements, for example, do not contain a percentage increase figure; instead they reproduce salary scales and describe movements on the scale. Without other information an average percentage increase cannot be calculated, which may not be an accidental result. In other contracts—for example, Wayne State University—an across-the-board increase is specified, but then other adjustments are described in a way that presumably is clear to the administration and the union but is hardly clear to the outside analyst.

Under the circumstances we will fall back on advancing two propositions as to the behavior of average salaries under collective bargaining, based on an unsystematic mix of interviews, case studies, contract analysis, and intuition.

[24]Public universities, public four-year colleges, public two-year colleges, and independent colleges and universities. The differentials in public two-year colleges and independent colleges and universities did not meet statistical tests of significance.

1 In the general case faculty salaries in public institutions of higher education have moved upward more or less in line with the salaries of the state civil service as a whole. This means a range within one percentage point plus or minus of the state employees' increase for the year. Examples of this pattern appear to be SUNY, Wayne State, and the New Jersey institutions, including Rutgers.

2 In a number of special situations unions won increases substantially greater than civil service increases or the "going rate" in academia generally in the early years of negotiations, but the rate then declined to the equivalent of the civil service rate. St. John's, for example, started at 12 percent in the first year, dropped to 9 percent in the second, and then to 5.8 percent for each of the next two years. The Pennsylvania state colleges are unlikely to maintain the rate of 5 percent every six months in their first three-year contract plus annual increments and fringe improvements. Central Michigan University and Oakland started off with increases of between 7 and 8 percent, and Oakland at least has tapered off to a 5.9 percent rate in its 1973 settlement. The first St. John's contract followed several years of institutional upheaval and reflects the resolution of a difficult internal situation. The other examples seem to represent "emerging institutions" whose faculties, possibly with tacit administration support, were trying to move up a notch or two in what the British would call the academic league standings in faculty salaries and perhaps also in institutional quality. Unionism has been the method used by faculty and administrations to gain ground on the "elite" universities in their states.

In the current climate the limits to this kind of academic boot-strapping are narrow, and the civil service pattern, modified somewhat by differences in pay practices, is most likely to prevail in the long run.

Salary Structure The status equalization theme raises more questions of salary administration and salary structure than of general salary changes. Are there any discernible tendencies for unions to negotiate systematic changes in internal salary relationships?

There are several different dimensions of this question that can be studied, and there is enough evidence available for three of them to report in some detail:

1 *Changes in differentials among ranks.* The AAUP surveys show that over five years, 1968–69 through 1972–73, the three major ranks—assistant, associate, and full professor—each reached annual increases in pay

totaling 30, 30, and 29 percent, respectively, although the pattern of change was slightly different from year to year. These data show a stability of rank differentials for the system as a whole. Some of the unions have been negotiating across-the-board percentage wage increases that would have the same effect. Others provide for a wide variety of adjustments that tend to favor lower-paid faculty members to some extent.

Examples of the latter are the first St. John's University contract, which called for generous percentage increases or an absolute dollar-minimum increase, whichever was greater. Central Michigan University has used the device of across-the-board percentage increases plus a uniform dollar amount. Both of these approaches result in somewhat larger percentage increases for lower-paid faculty.

Perhaps the most egalitarian four-year contracts in existence are the two CUNY agreements. In the first contract the major move in that direction was the equalization of salary scales by rank for the senior and the community colleges. At the same time Table 14 shows a reduction in percentage differentials by rank from the differential existing in the year prior to the first contract and those prevailing in the final year of each of the two agreements. The trend toward a reduction of differentials is uniform through the table, with the rate of reduction increasing during the second three-year contract period. Because CUNY publishes salary schedules in their contracts instead of announcing an average percentage salary increase, little attention has been paid to the low rates of general pay increases built into the scales in the second contract. Salary schedules were raised a flat $600 for the first year, $750 for the second, and $850 for the third. These amounts for the first year produce percentage increases for those persons already at the top of the scale for professor, associate professor, and assistant professor of 1.9, 2.4, and 2.9 percent, respectively. The total increases over the entire three-year contract at the top of each rank will be 7.0, 8.6, and 10.6 percent. This compares with the three-year totals of over 20 percent for the same ranks in the first contract.

Those professors not at the top of the salary range for their rank

TABLE 14 Salary ratios by rank, CUNY	Prof./asst.	Assoc./asst.	Asst. prof.
1968–69	152.9	123.5	100
1971–72	150.1	122.4	100
1974–75	145.4	120.3	100

SOURCE: Calculated from the CUNY agreements. Salaries are for the top step of each rank in each year.

receive annual increments in pay of $1,250 each year; assistant and associate professors each receive increments of $1,000 each year. If we choose a member of the faculty who receives an increment in each year plus the three general increases in the schedule, the combined increases in salary would be much more substantial: 21.6, 23.1, and 29.2 percent[25] over three years for professors, associate professors, and assistant professors, respectively.

The degree of emphasis on flat, relatively uniform dollar amounts of pay increases in the CUNY contracts is unusual. It operates to reduce percentage differences between salaries by rank as portrayed in Table 14. The emphasis on annual automatic increments in pay rather than general increases in the salary schedule explains why the promotion problem and the limits in the proportions in the several ranks are so important to the CUNY union. A person at the top of the salary range for his rank receives only the relatively low general wage increase unless he can move to the next higher rank. An associate professor at the top of his salary range at the end of the first contract received an annual salary of $25,500. If he were promoted to professor at that point, he would be paid $30,975 by the end of the next three-year contract; if he remained an associate, he would be getting $27,700. The promotion means the difference between a pay increase of 22 percent and 9 percent over three years.

It would be a mistake to assume that the union has initiated the policy of reducing differentials. CUNY salaries were tied to lower-school salaries prior to unionization, and schedules were rising as unions in the lower schools won increases. It is reported that there was some administrative concern with the political effect of the rising levels of the top of the professors' scale, and holding this ceiling down has resulted in the compression of differentials. Even so, two CUNY units had the highest-paid faculties in the nation, according to the 1974 AAUP survey report.

Although the AAUP data suggest that rank differentials have been maintained over the whole system, increases in pay that are "tapered" to favor lower-paid faculty have occurred in nonunion situations. The unions have reinforced this tendency and made it more general, but the overall trend seems to be little influenced by these efforts.

2 *Compensation differentials in two- and four-year institutions.* Baseball pitcher Satchel Paige's famous saying, "Don't look back, something may be gaining on you," might well have been directed at the faculty

---

[25]The corresponding figures for the first three-year contract were 40.5, 41.7, and 48.8 percent. Note that since the increments are in absolute dollar amounts the percentage increases would be even larger if we measured the gains at the low end of the salary range rather than at the top end.

of four-year colleges. In terms of average compensation community college faculty have been closing in on their four-year college brethren for many years, with and without unionism.

The AAUP surveys for the academic years 1966–67 and 1972–73 illustrate the position of the faculty in two-year public institutions relative to four-year public institutions. Although the institutional categories used to report the data are different in the two years, the main outlines of the relationship are clear from Table 15. In 1966–67 the compensation for every rank in all four-year public institutions (except for associate and assistant professors in teachers colleges) equaled or exceeded that of the corresponding ranks in the two-year colleges. In the different classification of 1972–73, of all the nine rank categories in four-year institutions, only the compensation of the full professors in public doctoral universities exceeded that of their counterparts in two-year institutions and then only by 6 percent.

Another indication of the changing relationship between two- and four-year colleges that reflects the effect of unionism is the fact that none of the 70 institutions with the highest average compensation in 1966–67 was a two-year college, but by 1973–74 11 of the top 70 institutions were two-year colleges and all 11 were unionized.[26] Seven of the 11 were CUNY community colleges, 3 others were located in metropolitan New York, and the other entry was the Chicago city colleges.

This record emphasizes the role of the comprehensive union at CUNY in raising the compensation of the CUNY community college faculty by negotiating salary parity in 1970. It may be that a separate community college bargaining unit would have raised the salaries of their group relative to those of the four-year faculty, but we doubt if the differential could have been eliminated in three years with separate bargaining. Achieving parity in salary scales in the first three-year contract at CUNY required that the two-year faculty by rank receive annual percentage increases more than double those of the four-year faculty.

In the SUNY system there are pressures for parity between the four-year colleges and the university centers and between NTPs and teaching faculty, but there is relatively little public evidence of pressure for parity for the two-year campuses. This may be because of their relatively small size and because they are not community colleges but agricultural and vocational schools. One suspects that the pressure is only delayed.

[26]As were 19 of the four-year institutions. Note that some institutions on the 1973–74 list may not have existed in 1966–67 or may not have participated in the survey. The 1973–74 data are from the *Chronicle of Higher Education,* May 6, 1974, p. 6.

TABLE 15		Two-year colleges	Teachers colleges	Liberal arts	Universities
Compensation ratios by rank and type of public institution					
1966–67					
	Professor	100	105	106	122
	Associate	100	92	100	106
	Assistant	100	94	101	105
1972–73		*Category III*	*Category IIB*	*Category IIA*	*Category I*
	Professor	100	89	97	106
	Associate	100	90	96	98
	Assistant	100	88	94	95

KEY: Category I—universities granting 15 or more earned doctorates in the past three years in at least three unrelated disciplines. Category IIA—institutions awarding degrees above the baccalaureate not in I. Category IIB—institutions awarding only the baccalaureate or equivalent. Category III—two-year institutions with academic ranks.

SOURCE: *AAUP Bulletin*, Summer 1967, p. 150, and June 1973, p. 194.

Once again we have a situation in which the changing environment of one sector of higher education is leading to a change in traditional relationships. The community colleges are expanding in size and function, they are the legislators' favorite sector of higher education, and their close links to the lower schools have helped them benefit from the militant union campaigns in this sector. All of these factors are basic to an explanation of their relative gains.

Unionization also has been an independent factor in the community colleges' improved position. More than a third of all community college faculty are unionized. In California nearly all of the nation's largest system (96 institutions, 24,000 teaching faculty) engage in collective negotiations under a "meet and confer" bargaining law, but these situations do not meet the test of unionization used in this study. If they are regarded as bargaining, almost half of all community college faculty is engaged in bargaining. Some part of the advances of this group results directly from this bargaining activity. The community colleges of CUNY are the most visible example of gains from unionization in the context of a comprehensive bargaining unit. Organization has given independent community colleges less obvious but nonetheless real benefits and has improved their relative position.

3 *Retrenchment and merit pay policies.* As more institutions find themselves forced to reduce staff, the importance of policies on "retrenchment" rises and provisions dealing with these procedures are appearing in agreements. Some agreements are silent on the problem; examples are Central Michigan, Oakland, and CUNY. St. John's and Rutgers provide for joint consideration of the problem by the union and the administration, with the St. John's agreement explicitly giving weight to the faculty's "worth" to the institution. But most agreements that mention retrenchment provide for reductions in staff to be made in inverse order of seniority, with some qualifications about the scope of the seniority districts and the ability of those remaining to carry out the educational program. Examples of agreements of this type are those at SUNY, Wayne State, Rhode Island, Southeastern Massachusetts, and the Pennsylvania state colleges. With the best intentions one wonders whether significant departures from seniority will occur when institutions such as Rutgers and St. John's actually face a retrenchment problem.

Discussions of faculty unionism sometimes are carried on under the assumption that unions are invariably hostile to differential pay for "merit." In rebuttal union sympathizers often point out that unions of entertainers, musicians, professional athletes, newspaper and television reporters, and columnists operate by negotiating basic pay scales while leaving individuals limitless scope for individual bargaining. Union officials have, on occasion, spoken out against the "star system" in academia, but there appears to be no evidence that any union in a four-year college institution has tried to limit the payment of special salaries or accelerated movement up a salary scale.

Where contracts contain salary scales, there is typically no mention of whether an overscale salary may be paid. CUNY's agreement calls for $250,000 to be provided to create 50 distinguished-professor chairs that are not necessarily permanently assigned to individuals or equal in value. In the first year of its agreement the SUNY union negotiated money for a general increase and for payment of annual increments but did not include funds for merit increases. In the second year's pay negotiations merit increases were provided, but increments were eliminated.[27] The current CUNY contract makes no provision for increments but provides funds for "discretionary" increases, which can be used to reward "merit" or "correct inequities" as the local group decides.

It is probable that a substantial part of the total salary budget of a symphony orchestra is devoted to payments above salary scales to individual performers. If a unionized institution were to use a substantial part of its salary budget to pay above-scale salaries to a

---

[27]The agreement required that merit increases be limited to no more than 30 percent of faculty and 25 percent of NTPs to try to preserve the merit principle. This limitation is not included in the new contract.

significant number of faculty, one wonders if the method of distribution would be a matter of indifference to their colleagues and the faculty union. Agreements often provide funds specifically for merit pay and sometimes specify a method of deciding on their distribution. It may be that the ability of administrations or peer committees to make differential pay adjustments will be eroded by the democratization of pay systems, but experience to date has not produced any evidence that this has happened.

In summary, the individual institutions of higher education have been stratified internally into occupational groups with substantial differences in job security, working conditions, and pay. The various types and levels of institutions have also been part of a stratified system of higher education, with significant differences among the sectors in the same characteristics. As higher education evolves toward a system of mass higher education, many of these relationships are changing. Faculty unions appeal to some of the affected groups as a way to take advantage of the new situation to improve their position. Among these groups the most prominent are the nontenured regular-rank faculty; the irregular teaching ranks, and the nonteaching professionals at university-level institutions; and the staffs of the lower-level institutions as a whole. The faculty unions also gain support from some of the more privileged groups as a method of protecting their existing position from erosion in a new environment. The less privileged groups and institutions have so far been more active in their concerns, and their aspirations are more in tune with the temper of society as a whole. As a result faculty unionism has been part of a holding action for the established faculty and the university sector, with most of the gains accruing to the other sectors of the academic and professional staff and to the "emerging" four-year institutions and the community colleges.

6. Community Colleges Without Community

by Bill Aussieker

While four-year institutions have dominated the discussion on faculty unionism, more two-year than four-year institutions have chosen bargaining agents, and two-year institutions have been bargaining for a longer period of time and have more experience with its effects.[1] Community colleges account for 80 percent of the faculty bargaining agents in higher education, 60 percent of the unionized institutions, and approximately one-third of the unionized full-time faculty.[2] As of June 1974, more than 100 two-year college bargaining relationships were operating under a third contract, while only two four-year college bargaining relationships were doing so.

For most students of faculty unionism the extensive experience of community colleges with bargaining and faculty unions has been of less interest than the similarities and differences between four- and two-year college bargaining experiences. The general belief is that two-year and four-year experiences are not comparable. According to this argument, two-year institutions and faculty have a history more closely linked to the

[1]Two-year institutions were defined as institutions with a program offering at least two but less than four years beyond the twelfth grade of college-level studies that either lead to an associate degree or are wholly or mostly creditable toward a baccalaureate degree: junior colleges, community colleges, technical institutions, and normal schools.

[2]Community colleges are comprehensive public two-year colleges that offer academic, general, occupational, remedial, and continuing adult education. Information for this chapter was obtained from interviews in September 1972 with selected faculty union members and district administrators in seven unionized Illinois and Michigan community college districts and from the files of the Faculty Unionism Project. I thank the 70 people who generously took time from their busy schedules to provide information. All results and conclusions herein are my responsibility.

lower public schools than to higher education, have strictly teaching rather than research and teaching functions, and have less faculty participation in institutional governance. Two-year institutions do possess some characteristics in common with four-year institutions—for example, curriculum, degree requirements, departmentalization, student freedom and initiation, and organizational climate related to faculty service (Angell, 1973, pp. 88–89)—but the differences are thought to outweigh the similarities.

INSTITUTIONAL SIMILARITIES Less widely recognized, and more relevant, is that unionized and unionizable two-year and four-year institutions are not dissimilar. First, unionized two-year and four-year institutions are predominantly public single-campus institutions with an enrollment of 2,000 to 5,000 students and are governed as part of a system of higher education. Second, unionized two-year institutions offer the first two years of higher education and terminal occupational programs; unionized four-year institutions offer the first four years of higher education (including the baccalaureate degree) and terminal occupational programs (including programs that require five years to complete). Third, unionized two-year and four-year colleges fall closest together on a single "quality of institution" continuum of higher education. Fourth, as to institutional mission and organizational development, most unionized institutions qualify as emerging institutions of higher education. Community colleges, approximately 85 percent of the organized two-year institutions, are "emerging" from a history of lower-school association and administrative dominance to autonomy; from the junior college concept of strictly transfer program curricula to more community-oriented, occupational programs; and from the functions of being feeders and temporary retainers of students for state colleges and public universities to independent, distinct functions within higher education. Most of the unionized four-year institutions are also "emerging" from the dominance of state departments of education; from teacher training functions to more comprehensive programs in higher education; and from competition with other segments of higher education to functional differentiation and coordination with other segments of higher education.

In addition to organizational and institutional similarities the faculties of unionized two- and four-year institutions may have quite similar characteristics. According to the 1969 Carnegie Commission *National Survey of Faculty and Student Opinion*, the differences in responses on most faculty items are much less between two-year college faculty and public comprehensive four-year college faculty than between two-year college faculty and faculty of other types of institutions (Bayer, 1970). Not unexpectedly, in regard to faculty attitudes toward collective bargaining (see Table 16), the two-year faculty and public comprehensive four-year college faculty attitudes and characteristics are the most similar. Both groups are also more organized, as measured by membership in the AAUP, the AFT, the NEA, and other faculty "unions" (see Table 17). The more favorable collective bargaining attitudes of two-year comprehensive college faculty are probably attributable to a greater familiarity with unions and collective bargaining than to more liberal political and social beliefs. Twenty of these institutions in the

TABLE 16 **Collective bargaining attitudes of faculty by type of institution**	*"Collective bargaining by faculty members has no place in a college or university."* Percentage strongly disagreeing or disagreeing
All institutions	59
Doctoral-granting institutions	
Research and doctoral I	53
Research and doctoral II	53
Doctoral I	58
Doctoral II	56
Comprehensive colleges and universities	
I	63
II	66
Liberal arts colleges	
I	57
II	61
Two-year colleges	68

SOURCE: Carnegie Commission on Higher Education (1973*a*, p. 93).

TABLE 17 *Percentage of organization membership by SRC quality*

SRC Quality	AAUP	AFT	NEA	Local/ state	State, county, and city	Other	No org.*
University							
High	25.2	.5	5.6	2.5	5.1	3.5	57.6
Medium	28.7	1.2	8.7	4.2	5.6	4.5	47.1
Low	27.3	1.1	13.5	8.4	8.1	4.8	36.8
College							
High	30.4	2.1	10.5	9.0	6.9	7.4	33.7
Medium	22.3	.5	18.5	18.0	10.5	9.6	20.6
Low	25.0	1.2	22.4	14.5	11.8	9.7	15.4
Two-year	12.6	3.5	19.9	24.5	13.4	19.2	6.8

SOURCE: Carnegie Commission Survey of Student and Faculty Opinion, 1969.
*Includes "No answers" and "Don't knows."

Carnegie survey sample were unionized at the time of the survey (Trow, forthcoming).

A final comparison between two-year and four-year college experiences can be made in the area of faculty-administration relationships. In both public two-year and four-year institutions faculty members have generally worked under relatively authoritarian management, received increases and improvements in working conditions through changes initiated by civil service commissions, government personnel boards, or school boards at the prodding of faculty or other employee associations, and defined advancement narrowly to *this* job at *this* institution and not mobility from the job or the institution.

This discussion of the similarities between unionized two-year and four-year institutions and faculty illustrates that analysis of the rich community-college bargaining experience is at least as instructive as an analysis of the relatively fewer examples of faculty unionism in the four-year institutions. Whether generalizations from the community college experience can be transferred completely to the four-year colleges will be determined by the course of bargaining, but the issues are identical. The causes and effects of faculty unionism are of major importance in the two-year and four-year segments of higher education.

Explanations for the spread of faculty unionism usually include public-employee collective bargaining laws; the financial crunch, student unrest, political reprisal, and other environmental adversities; and the problems of faculty and administrators caused by various structural and functional changes (growth, diversification, and new organizational and administrative forms).

THE EFFECTS OF BARGAINING LAWS About three-fourths of all unionized faculty and almost two-thirds of the unionized two-year faculty are in states with comprehensive public-employee bargaining laws. The effect of these laws on faculty unionism in the community colleges cannot be understated, but it has been slightly different than the four-year experience. First, the liberalization of public-employee bargaining laws generally followed militant teacher, police, sanitation, transit, welfare, and health-care employee unionism in New York City, Chicago, Detroit, Boston, Philadelphia, and Trenton. Two-year institutions administered as part of a K–14 district and staffed with faculty experienced in public-school teacher–union–school board relationships were sensitive to the union activity in the public schools and other local public agencies. For example, more than half of the community college faculty in seven Illinois-Michigan districts were former members of local lower-school teacher unions before becoming college faculty members, and prior union membership was regarded as one reason for the rapid organization of the college districts once they were administratively separate from the lower-school districts. The intervention of local political figures and AFL-CIO officers into the community college bargaining process in these districts was also regarded as part of the "multilateralism" endemic to the larger public-employee unionism phenomenon.

A second difference between two-year and four-year union activity related to law is that a sizable portion of the earliest incidents of faculty unionism in community colleges occurred in states without enabling collective bargaining legislation, for example, in Colorado, Washington, Illinois, and Maryland. Without benefit of the orderly recognition procedure specified in various strong bargaining laws, recognition usually followed a protracted guerrilla organizing campaign, which generally culminated in a representation election sponsored by the local community college board of trustees. For example, the Chicago City Colleges (CCC) were organized by the Cook County College Teachers Union (CCCTU), AFT Local 1600, in a 1966 board-conducted faculty preference election in which the CCCTU was preferred over the Chicago affiliate of the Illinois Education Association. In subsequent negotiations the CCCTU negotiated the exact scope of union recognition and security rights with the CCC board of trustees. The bargaining relationships, including the CCC-CCCTU, which began in a "no-law" environment, have functioned continuously over as many as four different two-year contracts. The CCC-CCCTU and other "no-law" bargaining relationships differ from permissive-law relationships in that they have had greater strike activity, accounting for over half of the faculty-days lost to strikes in two-year institutions from 1963 to 1973, and they have relied upon the courts for mediation, fact finding, and arbitration.

A third legal difference is that some organization has occurred in states that forbid public-employee organization or even exclusive recognition of a faculty bargaining agent. Successful organization is dependent on the strength of the faculty organization and public support for unionism. Attempts have been made to organize the faculty of Arapahoe College, Colorado; Frederick and Baltimore community colleges, Maryland; Brevard, Broward, and Indian River community colleges, Florida; Delgado College, Louisiana; and the North Carolina and Virginia community college systems. The only ones successfully unionized were Baltimore Community College and, after a faculty strike, Frederick Community College. The Delgado College AFT local struck the college and filed suit to obtain benefits guaranteed by state law but has never concluded an agreement or obtained exclusive recognition. The Arapahoe NEA-affiliated faculty association was able to negotiate an agreement with the college, but it was suspended by the state attorney general.

The California Experience

The best example of a state law's preventing unionization—that is, exclusive recognition—and the most disparate state as far as actual and potential faculty unionism in the two-year colleges is concerned is California. California's Winton Act permits negotiations through negotiating councils of all organizations representing certificated employees. Seats on the councils are awarded in proportion to organization membership. The Winton Act, as interpreted by the California courts, does not permit exclusive recognition of a faculty organization even if no other organization has the minimum membership needed to secure a seat on the council. Binding agreements between community college districts and faculty representatives have also been prohibited by court interpretations of the Winton Act. As a result California has no exclusive faculty bargaining agents, although the state has more than twice as many two-year institutions and four times as many two-year students on a full-time equivalency basis as New York.

The faculty of the California community colleges is not unorganized.[3] More than 90 community college faculties have established negotiating councils composed of faculty external and internal (senate) representatives who meet and confer with representatives of the community college or college district administration. In many districts the organizations represented on the councils are affiliated with the AAUP, the NEA, the AFT, or local or statewide faculty organizations,[4] and the faculty organization-administration relationships in the districts are clearly a form of bargaining. Although without formal recognition or binding contracts, California bargaining is similar to the independent faculty senate or association bargaining agents found in Michigan and New York community colleges.[5] The latter districts have had strikes, binding arbitration, fact finding, and mediation that are uncommon to internal faculty rep-

[3]For a more detailed description of bargaining in the California community colleges, see Aussieker (1974, pp. 40–49).

[4]Faculty organizations include the California Higher Education Association-Community College Association (California Teachers' Association-NEA); California Federation of Teachers-Community College Council (AFT); Faculty Association of California Community Colleges (independent); Academic Senate of California Community Colleges (institutional membership—independent); and the California Junior College Association (institutional membership of administrators, trustees, students, and faculty—independent).

[5]For example, in Michigan: Macomb County Community College, Grand Rapids Junior College, and Kirtland Community College; in New York: Fulton-Montgomery Community College, Schenectady County Community College, and Ulster County Community College. All of these independent faculty bargaining units obtained exclusive recognition after an extensive period of moderately successful use of faculty senate representation.

resentation procedures, but much of their bargaining process is interwoven with the traditional faculty senate–district administration governance process.

The California experience is also instructive about the nonlegal factors working against bargaining agent representation. These factors are extensive faculty organization input on state legislation affecting community colleges and on the actions of the California community colleges chancellor and board of governors (the state public two-year institution governing board and administrative unit); the "most-favored" segment of higher education treatment by the California state legislature and governor; widespread, historical reliance on effective internal faculty representation and bargaining schemes in local governance; and a mature and relatively stable community college system overall (Aussieker, 1974).

FINANCIAL DIFFICULTY AND EDUCATIONAL REFORM
While financial difficulty and educational reform measures initiated by elected or appointed public agencies may have some relationship to the future organization of community college or four-year faculty, both factors had little relationship to almost 85 percent of faculty unionization in the two-year colleges.[6] Most of the two-year faculty organization occurred during times of rapid growth and financial benevolence. Between 1965 and 1969 enrollment in public two-year institutions increased approximately 60 percent. Total current fund revenues for these institutions increased over 110 percent, and government support revenue increased almost 90 percent. This was a period of extensive organization of two-year public college faculty (U.S. Office of Education, *Digest,* 1972, Table 100, p. 75, and Table 113, p. 78; 1967, Table 2, p. 11; and 1970, Table 2, p. 3). Over the same period, the rate of growth of public four-year colleges and universities and their revenues was less than half of the two-year college rates.

In a similar vein state reprisals against higher education

[6]The community colleges in the University of Hawaii system are notable exceptions to this generalization. The university's relationship with the state legislature had deteriorated to the point of budget cutbacks and the passage of a bill to suspend tenure for one year and to institute a tenure review every five years. Like innocent bystanders the six community colleges in the system were hit by this hostility directed toward the universities.

began after the 1965–1969 growth of faculty unionism in the two-year colleges. In contrast to the variety of bills passed by state legislatures to curb the "excesses" of four-year college activities, the same legislatures and other state agencies were almost embarrassing in their endorsement of the community college concept and their munificent support for it during the 1960s and early 1970s. Recent events suggest that state legislatures in several states have, with supplementary appropriations, rescued community districts from the financial impact of falling or leveled enrollment and ceilings on the local property tax rate. For example, a 1973 California law gave $35 million in new state funds annually to the community colleges and set 40 percent as the minimum level of state support of community college financing.

The Michigan Experience For community colleges the cause-and-effect relationship between political repression and unionism may be reversed; that is, political attacks followed rather than preceded unionization. For example, public education in general has attracted the ire of the Michigan state legislature since 1970. Two bills were passed: one to remove the tenure provisions of bargaining agreements and the other to terminate state retirement coverage of faculty in community colleges and other public institutions of higher education. A third bill required a minimum amount of classroom instruction for each faculty member in all public institutions but was directed at four-year faculty, because the community college faculty work load already exceeded the law's specified level of student contact and class hours. None of the three bills has been implemented because of court action brought by the Michigan Educational Association (MEA) and other faculty groups.

In addition to the hostile actions of the Michigan legislature, local politicians have used tactics to defeat their opponents that have produced unfortunate backlash effects on community college district tax override measures. (Override measures may have been necessary to cope with budget increases caused by aggressive faculty union bargaining.) These politicians publicized community college faculty salaries and work loads—for example $16,000 or more for a 30-hour work week over a nine-month period—and announced that their opponents were supported by local faculty associations or the statewide educational association. This type of political strategy has been most effective in the rural and economically depressed areas of the state.

To combat the increasingly hostile political and legislative atmosphere, the Michigan Educational Association assessed members $5.00 each to set up the MEA Political Affairs Council. Early efforts of the council included financing mass media "spots" for selected state assembly candidates in rural districts and expending large sums of money on "hopeless" candidates.

The MEA considered the council's efforts to be a warm-up for the 1972 elections that ended in the defeat of the MEA's property tax proposal, which received fewer votes than the probusing option of an antibusing initiative; that saw the election of several unfriendly state legislators; and that brought no significant change in the statewide-elected board of education. Future MEA efforts seem doomed in the "Auto State" by a pervasive Michigan voter attitude that links VWs, automobile pollution standards, and busing with education.

The political efforts of the MEA, increased state funding and regulation of community colleges, legislative intervention in local bargaining disputes, political organization of students, and the increased industrial relations sophistication of district managements were part of a larger scenario leading toward more centralized statewide or areawide bargaining among the Michigan community colleges. In preparation Detroit area MEA and MFT faculty bargaining agents sought common contract expiration dates, and the district boards sought mutual aid pacts. However, by Spring 1974, although no faculty agents or districts were involved in multidistrict bargaining, some Detroit suburban lower-school districts were negotiating on a multidistrict basis.

Political developments similar to those in Michigan have occurred in Illinois, New Jersey, New York, and Pennsylvania. Only in Pennsylvania could legislative and public demands for greater accountability, heavier work loads, and increased performance by higher education faculty with less job security and lower economic rewards be construed as exacerbating faculty organization among community colleges. Less certain than the relationship between financial-political difficulties and faculty organization is the degree to which faculty anticipation of these difficulties (or student unrest in particular) led to organization.

Although we can only speculate from past events on this issue, so far the pessimistic financial projections for community colleges have proved inaccurate, and organization in anticipation of legislative hostility may be a self-fulfilling prophecy.

ORGANIZA-
TIONAL CHANGE
AND RAPID
GROWTH
An earlier chapter in this book advances the notion that faculty unionism is best understood in terms of rapid organizational change.

Organizational change in community colleges over the past decade has been induced, in part or in whole, by the rapid, absolute, and relative growth of the public two-year segment of higher education. From 1960 to 1970 the number of public two-year institutions increased from 310 to 654, and enrollment increased from 355,967 to 2,089,723. Enrollment in public two-year institutions almost tripled, and the average enrollment increased from less than 2,000 students to 3,200. Even at a time of universal growth in higher education the growth rate for public two-year institutions was four times greater than the rate for all institutions of higher education (U.S. Office of Education, *Digest*, 1972, Tables 89, 92, 113).

The growth rate of public two-year institutions has varied from state to state. Among the fastest growing systems were those in Illinois, Florida, Michigan, New York, Pennsylvania, New Jersey, Minnesota, and Washington. The Texas, California, Iowa, Georgia, Mississippi, and Kansas systems were highly developed by the beginning of the 1960s.[7] With the exception of Kansas and Florida, states with recently or rapidly growing community college systems are highly organized.

Caution should be exercised in interpreting the relationship between rapid growth and organization because states with new and/or rapidly growing community college systems also have strong public-employee bargaining laws (for example, Michigan and New York), but faculty unionism is a clear-cut response to the problems of growth in some districts. Some of

[7]Rates of growth for state two-year colleges were calculated from the rates of increase in number of institutions and enrollees in excess of the national rate. The degree of development of a state's two-year college system was determined from descriptions in Medsker (1960, pp. 208–296). States not classified were those with limited two-year college systems (Oregon, South Dakota) or with a two-year branch university as the state's dominant type of two-year institution (Ohio, Indiana, and Wisconsin).

the frustrations directly related to growth and its disorganizing effects on the academic community were larger classes; sudden changes in teaching assignments and loads; less personal and more formal relations with students, peers, and superiors; a deterioration in informal organization and formal communication and coordination procedures, which broke down frequently under information and decision overload; and the suspicion by all that no one really knew what to do then or in the future. The unionism-growth nexus was evidenced by domination of union leadership by the more senior faculty; contract provisions on maximum class size and teaching load; seniority and faculty preference in teaching assignment and class scheduling; seniority in the assignment of overload and summer classes; guarantees on faculty office space, clerical assistance, supplies, and parking space; and, in some districts, guarantees of faculty participation in the hiring of new faculty. In comparison to the issues of academic freedom, tenure, and due process, the provision of clerical help, office supplies, and parking seems picayune, but to faculty members who have no desk or share a converted closet office with seven other persons, who have to type and mimeograph their exams, and who have to carry their chalk in a locked case, these contract provisions solved irksome problems.

Structural Change

Five different patterns of structural change in response to rapid growth have been identified among community colleges: (1) the expansion of existing institutions by an increase in the size of existing campuses or campus; (2) the creation of new institutions in new community college districts; (3) the expansion of existing institutions within the same district by an increase in the number of campuses or branches of the institution; (4) the expansion of existing districts by the creation of new institutions within the district; and (5) the creation of new community colleges and districts as part of a comprehensive statewide higher education system. For some community colleges all five structural changes occurred within 5 to 10 years. For example, the Hawaii community colleges were formed as part of the University of Hawaii system, the campuses grew in size, new branches were established, new campuses were constructed, and new institutions were formed from the campuses and branches.

We previously emphasized the relationship between the first and second growth-related organizational changes and unionism among public two-year institutions. Table 18 indicates a somewhat weak relationship between size and organization. The relationship would be greater if the California institutions, which comprise about three-fourths of the unorganized institutions in the two largest size categories, were omitted from the population. Table 19 shows that organized public two-year institutions were more likely to be established in the mid-1960s than before 1960 or after 1967.

The third, fourth, and fifth structural responses to growth correspond to six possible organizational structures of public two-year institutions:

1 Single-campus institution—an institution of higher education with only one location, for example, Lansing Community College, Michigan.

2 Main-branch institution—a public two-year institution with programs of instruction being offered at two or more locations, where one location serves as administration for the entire institution, for example, Black Hawk Community College, Illinois.

3 Multicampus institution—a public two-year institution with more than one campus. Each campus is administratively equal to the other campuses, and all campuses are under the control of a central administration, for example, Chicago city colleges.

4 Two-year institutional system—a grouping of several two-year insti-

TABLE 18 Unionized public two-year institutions as a percentage of all public two-year institutions by size and legal environment						
Institution enrollment	Comprehensive		Other		Total	
	%	N	%	N	%	N
Under 200	0	—	0	—	0	—
200–499	60	3	20	9	24	12
500–999	79	19	10	10	22	29
1,000–2,499	80	33	14	26	27	59
2,500–4,999	91	30	22	20	41	50
5,000–9,999	81	21	8	4	34	25
10,000 or more	100	14	21	4	37	18

SOURCE: Opening Fall 1970 degree-creditable enrollment from U.S. Office of Education, *Opening Fall Enrollment* (1972, table 113, p. 85) and U.S. Office of Education *Directory* (1971–1972).

TABLE 19
Unionized public two-year institutions as a percentage of all public two-year institutions by year of founding

Year of founding*	Number unionized	Percentage unionized
Before 1960	71	23
1960–1967	76	42
1968 or later	19	12

*Year institution first listed in *Directory of Higher Education*, or date institution founded or first classes offered according to *World Almanac, 1973* (pp. 318–26). Data unavailable on 27 unionized institutions.

tutions, institutionally autonomous, under the framework or control of a single central administration and governing board, for example, Los Angeles city colleges.

5 Comprehensive institutional system—a grouping of public two-year and four-year institutions, institutionally autonomous, under the framework or control of a single central administration and governing board.[8]

Table 20 presents the degree of organization of public two-year institutions by type of organizational structure. According to the table, organizational complexity has a stronger relationship to the degree of organization than size. Public two-year institutions in comprehensive institutional systems are highly unionized, and multicampus institutions and two-year institutional systems are more unionized than single-campus institutions. Again, the relationship may be spurious, as the community colleges in New York, Washington, Michigan, Massachusetts, New Jersey, Pennsylvania, and Minnesota are heavily unionized, possess the organization characteristics attributed to organizational change, and are covered by strong public-employee bargaining laws.

Although the single-campus community college bargaining relationships numerically dominate the community college unionism scene, the multicampus community college bargaining relationships provide more interesting incidents of faculty unionism. The six Hawaii community colleges in the University of Hawaii system were responsible for the AFT victory in the first bargaining agent election for faculty of the entire

[8]Organizational structure typed according to criteria of the U.S. Office of Education, *Directory, 1972–73* (pp. xii–xiii), and Lee and Bowen (1971, pp. 4–6).

TABLE 20 *Unionized public two-year institutions as a percentage of all public two-year institutions by type of organizational structure**

	Number unionized	Percentage unionized
Comprehensive institutional system	44	80
Two-year institutional system	24	27
Multicampus institution	5	25
Main-branch institution	—	0
Single-campus institution	116	23

*For definitions of types of structure, see text.

system. In the recent decertification election the community college faculty continued to support the HFCT by a 2 to 1 margin over the AAUP-NEA coalition. The gain of the community college faculty in the CUNY full-time faculty bargaining unit in the first contract negotiations is one of the few genuine instances of the much-anticipated leveling and homogenizing impact of unionism. Little is known about how the faculty of the six two-year agricultural and vocational colleges in the NTP-dominated SUNY unit fared in the contract negotiations.[9] The other 25 nominally related SUNY unionized community colleges have been engaged in productive local district-faculty organization negotiations for as long as six years in some districts. The absence of the statewide SUNY chancellor's office involvement in the community college bargaining relationships has preserved the autonomy of the local community colleges, but the tendency of local boards of trustees to defer to county officials in exercising their bargaining responsibilities has weakened the role of the boards and the presidents in institutional governance of some districts (Angell, 1973, p. 102). Twelve unionized community college faculty associations have formed a statewide independent Association of Community College Faculty in order to avoid inclusion in the merged NEA-AFT New York State United Teachers' Union.

Since 1969 the faculty in the 18-college Minnesota junior college system has been represented in wage negotiations with the state junior college board by the Minnesota Junior College

[9]Two-year institutions are virtually ignored in the one published study of unionism at SUNY by Fisk and Puffer (1973, pp. 130–155).

Faculty Association (MJCFA), which is affiliated with the NEA and the Minnesota Education Association. After formal recognition of the MJCFA in 1972 the state board and the MJCFA reached agreement within 18 months. The first contract replaced tenure provisions with academic freedom and job security clauses that specified just cause for termination and provided for binding arbitration of dismissal grievances.

The moderate interest in unionism of the Massachusetts community college faculty (3 unionized of 16 colleges) is explained by college rather than statewide appropriate faculty unions and the legal exclusion of wages from the scope of bargaining.

The five multicampus unionized community colleges are Community College of Allegheny (Pennsylvania), Macomb and Oakland community colleges (Michigan), the Chicago City Colleges, and Seattle Community College. Each district has experienced at least one faculty strike, and the Allegheny faculty strike and one of the CCC faculty strikes were ended by student-initiated court injunction activity. The Seattle and Chicago bargaining relationships emerged in a "no-law" legal environment, one indication of the intensity of faculty grievances in the two metropolitan multicampus districts. The success of the CCCTU in contract negotiations with the CCC has been unmatched by any four-year or two-year faculty union. Among the major gains for faculty in the eight-year bargaining history are a doubling of average faculty compensation, the separation of salary and rank, a reduction in maximum teaching load from 15 to 12 contact hours a week, equal credit for most lecture and laboratory class contact hours in determining faculty work load, and a past practices contract clause that extended the scope of the grievance procedure to include any administrative action unfavorable to one or more faculty members.

Administrative Change

A second kind of organizational change occurred in the administration of public two-year institutions. One frequent change was the separation of the two-year college from the direct control and administration of the lower or K–12 public school district and the creation of a separate community or junior college district. Separation from K–12 administration often removed the college teachers from the coverage of statutory tenure laws (for example, in Michigan) and also removed them from the protection of K–12 teacher organizations, which had represented them in negotiations with the administration (for example, in Illinois, Michigan, Minnesota, New York, and Washington).

A less direct linkage between separation, community college administration, and unionism involves the effectiveness of the new college administration. The first college administrators in the newly created autonomous districts were mostly recruited from K–12 districts. The conversion to a separate community college administration required a different managerial style from that tied in spirit, training, and experience to a K–12 district. This crisis in college administration was most apparent at the middle levels of administration—deans and associate deans. (The college presidents, mostly recruited from outside the district, were more concerned with the college building program, securing community support, and establishing new programs than with internal administrative affairs.) The widespread absence of regulations on personnel matters—no uniform salary administration, favoritism, and individual bargaining as the prevalent means of personnel decision making, and unilateral decisions on faculty working conditions—was frequently cited as an area of faculty dissatisfaction with the administration. The middle and top levels of community college district administration were characterized by faculty members and administrators in seven Illinois-Michigan unionized districts as poor and concerned mostly with nonfaculty matters.

The college administrations' approach in these districts was described as that of traditional management. Common administrative characteristics of the Illinois-Michigan districts after the creation of a separate community college district were decision making with no faculty participation; faculty recommendations ignored by the administration; open conflict among faculty, administration, and board, resolved only by the use of threats against faculty members; and few or nonfunctioning committees of faculty and administrators.

In the Illinois-Michigan districts faculty unionization was hastened by the college administration's opposing tenure; making unilateral changes in faculty working conditions (sabbaticals, teaching assignments, merit pay, and overload teaching assignments, for example); ignoring faculty policy recommendations until administrative proposals on the same policy matter were adopted by the board of trustees; dismissing tenured and nontenured faculty because of program termination; and openly opposing faculty organizations.

Most ensuing faculty union-board contracts can be interpreted as efforts to resolve these problems with the administration. Contracts provided for faculty organization rights; no discrimination against the faculty for union activity; dues checkoff; rights to meetings with the college president; rights to meetings with the board on matters outside the scope of the contract; leaves of absence for union officers; rights to union meetings; guaranteed information from the district; and the use of college facilities and equipment. Contract personnel provisions were uniform salary schedules and salary administration; uniform determination of teaching loads and assignments, sick leave, and sabbaticals; and faculty procedural rights on dismissal or disciplinary actions; but the provision most effective in curbing administrative unilateralism in personnel actions was the right to grievance procedures with binding arbitration.

The loss of administrative flexibility and managerial autonomy, more formal and efficient management practices, increased rules and regulations, improved information, management development, and centralization on personnel decisions were some of the changes in management precipitated by the grievance procedure and union efforts to "improve" management by negotiated contracts. The input of unionism on management was related to composition of the management team. The addition of full-time professional staff to handle grievances and faculty negotiations was particular to those districts that originally negotiated contracts with internal personnel.[10] Most districts employed external labor relations experts and did not hire professional employees to handle faculty unions. Failure to comprehend the board's limits or the specific community college milieu, conflicts between the goals of contract settlement and those of the college, and overemphasis on the legal aspects of contract negotiations at the expense of the problem-solving aspects shortened the average use of internal and external negotiators to less than one year in the districts studied. The management negotiating team usually

[10]In a 1971 study of the faculty union impact on management in Illinois, Graham reports that no public two-year college had hired an administrator to work in the employee relations area (1972, pp. 241–249).

included an academic policy expert and a financial expert, but these persons were internal administrative personnel whose duties were altered to include negotiations and contract administration. This was the extent of the impact of unions on the duties of deans, vice-presidents, and other administrative personnel. Presidents and members of the boards of trustees occasionally were members of the management negotiating team, but from the available evidence the roles of the presidents and the trustees were unchanged by the presence of a union. Their authority was, however, constrained by the union contract provisions.

Most unionized community colleges were subject to three other administrative changes: (1) the establishment of a statewide community college system administered by a special board; (2) the creation of a public two-year college governing board for all such institutions in the state; and (3) the creation of a statewide board of higher education, which governed and coordinated all public institutions in the state.

The governing board changes are associated with different types of institutional control. First, in states without a statewide board, local control is exercised by local governing boards with direct control over single institutions or units. Second, primarily local control also exists in states with local governing boards plus a statewide board that coordinates policy on all state higher education but does not govern individual institutions. Third, combined state-local control exists in states with local boards plus a statewide board that functions as both a coordinating and a governing board for those institutions that offer programs with common elements. Fourth, primarily state control exists in states with only a statewide governing board for all institutions with common elements, and sometimes for all segments of higher education.[11]

Table 21 indicates the relationship between organization of public two-year institutions and the pattern of state control. Administrative complexity, not centralization, appears related to organization because institutions in the combined state-local control category are the more heavily organized. The importance of administrative complexity as an explanation of the incidence of unionism among public two-year institutions

[11]Control and governing board categories were constructed from Lee and Bowen (1971, p. 2) and Martorana and Hollis (1960, p. 6).

TABLE 21
Organized public
two-year
institutions as a
proportion of all
two-year
institutions by
pattern of state
control

Pattern of state control	Number organized	Percentage of total	Total number
Primarily state	38	17	221
Primarily state and local	113	39	287
Primarily local	42	19	227
TOTAL	193		735

KEY: *Primarily state*—primarily under the control of a state governing-coordinating or governing board, for example, Massachusetts. *Combined state-local*—control shared by both a local governing board and a state governing-coordinating board, for example, New York. *Primarily local*—primarily under the control of a local governing board, although there may be a state coordinating board, for example, California.

SOURCE: U.S. Office of Education, *Directory, 1972–73*, Medsker and Tillery (1971, pp. 106–109); and Medsker (1960, pp. 207–295; 304–305).

must again be interpreted relative to the importance of state laws and public-employee bargaining activity.

The intraorganizational structures of the local and state community college faculty organizations have largely emerged in response to changes in community college administration. The tasks of offsetting the adverse effects of increased centralization of authority in public higher education and community colleges and representing community college faculty as opposed to the numerically greater secondary school teachers and four-year college faculty members are responsible for the unique structures of NEA and AFT community college bargaining agencies. For lobbying the NEA-affiliated local associations have relied upon the National Faculty Association of Community and Junior Colleges, a national organization created to give two-year college faculty members a separate voice in the NEA. For lobbying on a state level there are special higher education segments of the NEA-affiliated state associations—for example, the Michigan Association of Higher Education–Michigan Education Association—and sometimes special community college segments, for example, the Community College Association–California Higher Education Association–California Teachers Association. For the purposes of bargaining only the local faculty association is relevant. No statewide personnel or officers are involved in local bargaining matters unless requested by the local organization to serve as consultants or legal counsel.

The AFT locals depend also on the lobbying assistance of

state and national AFL-CIO and AFT organizations. With the AFT, higher education faculty and community college faculty are represented on national and state AFT community college and higher education councils. The officers of these special higher education organizations are irrelevant to the individual locals' bargaining, except as consultants and legal counsel.

More complex are the AFT locals that represent faculty in more than one district or institution. The multicollege locals were formed by the amalgamation of diverse college faculty locals for mutual aid and protection, that is, the complete organization of all community colleges in a metropolitan area and the ability to support strikes and legal costs. For example, the Cook County College Teachers Union (CCCTU) Local 1600 represents faculty in six different community college districts and private and public four-year institutions in the Chicago area. In the CCCTU and other multicollege locals local officers have not interfered in the affairs of the individual college or district chapters. The chapters formulate their own demands, select a negotiating team, negotiate the contract, and administer the agreement. Individual college chapters often ignore the advice and counsel of the local president. For example, the Prairie State College chapter of the CCCTU ignored President Swenson's advice not to go on strike during the college's summer session but to wait until fall.

Although suburban and city college chapters have avoided conflict, the CCCTU has not been free of internal dissent. Two factions exist within the CCC division of the CCCTU: the Council for Democratic Action (CDA), whose followers vary from new leftists and militant blacks to a Wobbly fringe, and the United Progress Caucus (UPC), which represents the present local leadership and the more conservative elements of the union.[12] The composition of the negotiating team reflects the

[12]The pluralism of the CCCTU is not unique to faculty organization. The national AFT convention of 1973 had two separate caucuses—the Progressive Caucus, whose slate was elected as AFL-CIO convention delegates, and the United Action Caucus, which represented the radical membership of the AFT and pledged guaranteed minority representation in AFT leadership, restoration of the secret ballot in convention voting, and impeachment of President Nixon. The Progressive Caucus pledged continued support for the AFT's organizing program, merger with the NEA, a commitment to integrated education, and increased lobbying efforts. All current members of the AFT's executive council are members of the Progressive Caucus.

balance of power between these two factions, and only one member of the negotiating team in the 1972 contract negotiations could be identified with the CDA. Factionalism within the local became more critical in 1972 because some of the CDA leadership lost their jobs as a result of a court decision that overturned an arbitrator's ruling in favor of granting certain faculty members contract renewals and, as a consequence, tenure. The union membership rejected a CDA proposal for immediate job action by the union against the CCC and supported the UPC's proposal for financial support of the dismissed members pending an appeal of the court ruling. The appeal failed to alter the decision, but as part of the 1973 contract settlement the CCC administration agreed to give priority to the dismissed faculty for new jobs in the eight-campus institutions.

Functional Change The final kind of organizational change in the public two-year institutions was related to function. The first functional change was the transition from the junior college or vocational school to comprehensive community colleges. Most junior colleges offered the first two years of degree-credit programs, and vocational schools almost exclusively offered terminal nondegree occupational programs. Community colleges offer balanced degree and nondegree programs, remedial, continuing, and general education, and a variety of educationally related community services.

The second functional change occurred as a direct result of social change, the urban crisis, and the increased enrollment of blacks and other racial minorities in two-year institutions. New kinds of programs and new kinds of administration were needed for the new two-year students; these included ethnic and upward-bound studies, expanded educational opportunities, remedial education, expanded counseling services, joint programs with four-year colleges, skills centers, special learning laboratories, and college recruitment programs.

Both of these functional changes altered the community college faculty labor force. The most fundamental change in the labor force resulted from the junior to community college transition. The emerging community colleges were increasingly staffed with full-time, vocational/occupational, general, and adult education faculty, as well as other full-time professional staff. Formerly part time in status, these more community-oriented instructors comprised at least one-third of the full-time staff. Their attitudes toward the mission and purpose of the community college as well as the administration were quite different from those of the academic and predominantly liberal arts faculty, who formerly comprised as much as 90 percent of the full-time staff. The impetus for faculty unionization came from the full-time academic liberal arts faculty.

The movement of community colleges into programs directed at the urban crisis altered the community college labor force in a second way. To such traditional community college NTPs as librarians, counselors, and administrative professionals were added financial aid counselors, minority admissions officers, basic education directors, vocational program directors, and special counselors. The new NTPs and the more aggressive librarians and counselors form a second segment of community college professional staff with different interests from those of the full-time academic teaching staff.[13]

Most local community college locals or associations are dominated by the full-time liberal arts faculty. In most districts math, physical and life science, English, and social science faculty are overrepresented on negotiating teams and as organization officers, and the gains of most faculty unions are directed more toward the full-time liberal arts faculty than the NTPs or nontransfer faculty. For example, work load differentials between transfer and nontransfer faculty and the M.A. requirement for advancement on the salary schedule have been maintained in unionized districts.[14] However, counselors, librarians, and the nontransfer faculty have become more active in local faculty organization affairs and should obtain some favorable consideration in future contract negotiations.

Full-time NTPs and nontransfer faculty have not suffered as

---

[13]I would estimate the magnitude of change in professional staff composition of community colleges due to the diversification of institutional programs to be about one-third, that is, the professional staff of community colleges changed from 90 percent full-time transfer course instructional staff to 60 percent full-time transfer course instructional staff. This estimate was obtained from studies cited by Medsker and Tillery (1971, pp. 87–90, 97–101) and Medsker (1960, pp. 171–173, 174–191).

[14]In a study of faculty salary differentials in Michigan community college districts "pre" and "post" union, salary differentials within experience, degree, and departmental or divisional groupings and between high and low salaries were found to be significantly greater after unionization (Gram, 1971).

much as part-time faculty. Contract provisions that require sharing overload teaching assignments among full-time faculty have eliminated almost all part-time teaching faculty in some districts. In districts with full-time and part-time faculty in the same bargaining unit the dues structure on occasion has been applied so as to make membership of part-time faculty financially unfeasible and thus to exclude them from active participation. In other districts with separate units for full-time and part-time teaching faculty, full-time faculty teaching overload courses dominate the part-time faculty organization and negotiate the contract. Differentials between full-time and part-time faculty in the rate per class contact hour vary from 50 percent to over 200 percent. However, part-time faculty in some districts have gained continuity of employment, seniority in layoffs due to reduction in attendance, and health and welfare benefits in contract negotiations. It is apparent from this discussion that the leveling and homogenizing effects of unionism are more dependent on the faculty organization's leadership than on the composition of the bargaining unit.

Change and Disorganization

More important than the effects of administrative, structural, and functional changes in community colleges is that each represented an organizational change for the institution and, considered together, more organizational change than most institutions could accommodate without social disorganization. In Michigan, Minnesota, Massachusetts, Illinois, New Jersey, New York, and Washington these organizational changes all occurred between 1963 and 1968. In other states, for example, Texas and California, organizational changes were more gradual, with many community colleges developed and separated from K–12 administration before or after periods of growth and expansion as well as of diversification.

For the less stable community colleges and systems the rapid organizational change destroyed the sense of "community" that had formerly bound together faculty, administrators, trustees, and, to a lesser extent, students. In these turbulent institutions the larger, more structurally complex and more occupationally diverse academic community was in a state of disorganization, and the faculty seems to have resorted to unionism as a means of controlling or moderating changes in a manner more consistent with its interests.

INSIDIOUS COMPARISONS Despite a larger number of unionized institutions, a longer history of unionism, and the increased number of similar non-unionized institutions in similar environments, union and non-union comparisons in the community colleges are tenuous at best because of the limitations of data and the effects of extraneous factors on the results. In spite of these reservations, some

TABLE 22 *Comparisons of standardized compensation and salary at union and nonunion community colleges*

	Average 1965–66	Compensation 1972–73	Increase	Average 1965–66	Salary 1972–73	Increase
Union	$ 9,287	$12,184	$2,897	$8,896	$10,657	$1,761
Nonunion	9,969	12,588	2,619	9,576	11,574	1,998
Difference	$ (682)	$ (404)	$ 278	$ (680)	$ (917)	$ (237)
			t =.722			t = .86
Union/nonunion	$ 93	$ 97	4	$ 93	$ 92	$ (1)
			t = .95			t = .38

	Average 1968–69	Compensation 1972–73	Increases	Average 1968–69	Salary 1972–73	Increases
CUNY	$11,765	$12,595	$ 830	$10,190	$10,419	$ 229
California	11,251	12,728	1,477	10,603	11,651	1,048
Difference	$ 514	$ (133)	$ (647)	$ (413)	$ (1,232)	$ (819)
CUNY/California	$ 105	$ 99	t = 1.22	$ 96	$ 89	t = 1.49
		t = 1.25			t = 1.50	

	Chicago City Colleges	Los Angeles City Colleges	Peralta Colleges
1964–65	$6,379–$14,823	$5,544–$10,786	$5,931–$11,764
1971–72	$7,993–$17,229	$7,434–$14,641	$6,609–$13,103

NOTE: Parenthetical figures are nonunion differences or net increases. All salaries and compensation have been standardized on the basis of 1967 U.S. Urban Average Cost.

SOURCES: First section from "Further Progress" (1967, pp. 160–195); and "Surviving the Seventies" (1973, pp. 215–258). Second section from "The Threat of Inflationary Erosion" (1969, pp. 219–253); and "Surviving the Seventies" (ibid.). Third section from Chicago, Cook County College Teachers Union, *Agreement* (1969, pp. 47–49); Chicago Public Schools Board of Education (1964, pp. 41–42); California Community Colleges System, Office of the Chancellor, (January 1972, pp. 35, 51); and California State Department of Education, Bureau of Junior College Education (1964, pp. 26, 39).

comparisons on compensation, salaries, and governance are essential.

Compensation and Salaries

Table 22 presents three comparisons of compensation and salaries for unionized and nonunionized community colleges. The salary and compensation figures have been standardized for differences and changes in the cost of living in the areas where the sample colleges are located. The first comparison is of the average faculty salary and average faculty compensation from the annual AAUP surveys of faculty compensation for 1965–66 and 1972–73 at eight matched community colleges.[15] The year 1965–66 was selected because it was the last year before the extensive unionization of community colleges. Unionized and nonunionized community colleges in California, Illinois, Michigan, and New York were matched according to size, as measured by the number of full-time teaching faculty, and changes in size, as measured by the percentage of change in the number of full-time teaching faculty from 1965 to 1972. The latter criterion was selected to reduce the effects on average compensation and salary of the increased number of full-time faculty hired during the comparison period. It was assumed that the changes in the number of full-time faculty uniformly reflected the presence of new faculty hired at the lower levels of the salary schedule. Not included were vocational-technical institutions (for example, SUNY and Wisconsin), CUNY community colleges and other community college faculty included in bargaining units with four-year faculty, and the Washington and Pennsylvania community colleges (not included because bargaining generally did not begin in these institutions until 1971–72).[16]

---

[15]The matched sample and the AAUP survey comparison design were previously used by Birnbaum (1974, pp. 29–33) in a study on the effects of unionism on faculty compensation.

[16]The inclusion in the sample of the three CUNY institutions for which data were available and the matched-pair institutions raises the averages for both unionized and nonunionized institutions but does not alter the degree and direction of change. Inclusion of the six SUNY two-year institutions, the one Wisconsin vocational-technical institute, and the seven matched-pair institutions lowers the averages of the unionized institutions and significantly alters the degree and direction of change. Because the community colleges were matched with vocational institutions, the significant nonunion advantage shown should be interpreted as an indication of the adverse salary conditions in the vocational institutions and not as a pecuniary disadvantage of faculty unionism.

According to the first comparison in Table 22, unionized community colleges had greater increases in standardized average compensation, and nonunionized community colleges had greater increases in standardized average salaries. As the ratio of union and nonunion averages shows, union compensation improved relative to nonunion compensation, and nonunion average salary declined slightly relative to union salary. None of the changes was significant at the .10 level according to two-tailed t-test values. Using figures not standardized for changes in cost of living, unionized community colleges show significant increases and relative gains in compensation, and insignificant increases and relative gains in salary over nonunionized community colleges, as follows:

	Average "money" compensation		Average "money" salary	
	1965–1966	1972–1973	1965–1966	1972–1973
Unionized	$ 9,630	$16,958	$8,863	$14,621
Nonunionized	$10,113	$16,732	$9,705	$15,358

Significant improvements in the union average compensation are not necessarily the result of bargaining. The AAUP average compensation figures include district payments for FICA and workmen's compensation and unemployment compensation, which are mandated by state law and are the function of a state public-employee or teacher retirement plan and not a subject of bargaining. Data on bargainable fringe benefits (health, dental, and life insurance) indicate a similar level for both unionized and nonunionized community colleges in the first comparison sample.[17]

Conversely, significant increases in nonunion average salaries could be due to bargaining pressures not channeled through unions but through other organizations in the colleges—faculty senates, for example, or to the effects of salary increases in neighboring unionized community colleges.

[17]Data from the Michigan Education Association (1972, pp. 1–16) and the California School Board Association.

The second comparison of standardized average compensation and salary data from the AAUP faculty compensation surveys is a matched-pair sample of the six CUNY community colleges for which data were available and six California community colleges. The CUNY and California sample was chosen in order to minimize the effects of unions upon nonunion compensation used in the analysis, but, as noted earlier, the inclusion of the California institutions maximizes the effects of nonunion bargaining upon the results. In addition, the uniqueness of the California system increases the effect of environmental influences. The colleges again were matched by size and changes in size of full-time teaching faculty. This second comparison is for 1968–69 to 1972–73. The year 1968–69 was the last for which CUNY salaries were not determined by collective bargaining. As seen in Table 22, the California standardized average compensation and salaries increased more than the CUNY averages, and the California compensation and salary averages improved relative to the CUNY colleges. The California advantages in salary and compensation increases and relative gains were not statistically significant at the .10 level, according to two-tailed t-test values.

It should be emphasized that CUNY compensation and salaries increased more and gained relative to the California averages when calculated on a nonstandardized money basis. On a nonstandardized money basis the CUNY community colleges show significant increases and relative gains in compensation and insignificant increases and relative gains in salary over the California colleges, as follows:

	Average "money" compensation		Average "money" salary	
	1968–69	*1972–73*	*1968–69*	*1972–73*
CUNY	$14,756	$20,291	$12,759	$16,785
California	$12,788	$17,004	$12,051	$15,548

The significant "money" gains of the CUNY community college faculty were the result of contract negotiations that raised the CUNY two-year salaries to parity with the senior colleges and were not the result of independent union-bargained increases in the CUNY salary levels.

The third comparison in Table 22 is among the Chicago City Colleges, Peralta Colleges (Oakland), and the Los Angeles City Colleges. All three are multicampus community college districts serving metropolitan areas. As described above, the Chicago City Colleges faculty has been represented since 1966 by the militant Cook County College Teachers Union, Local 1600, AFT-AFL-CIO. The Los Angeles City Colleges faculty has been represented by a negotiating council of AFT, NEA, and independent faculty representatives, and the Peralta faculty has been represented by a tripartite districtwide committee that includes students, administrators, staff, and faculty senate representatives. Table 22 presents the 1964–65 and 1971–72 standardized ranges for the three districts. From 1964–65 to 1971–72, the Peralta Colleges minimum and maximum full-time teaching salaries declined relative to the Chicago salaries, and the Chicago minimum and maximum teaching salaries declined relative to the Los Angeles salary levels. Again, the results are interesting but inconclusive.

The nonstandardized or "money" salary ranges are as follows:

	Chicago City Colleges	Los Angeles	Peralta Colleges
1964–65	$ 6,150–$12,290	$5,500–$10,700	$6,050–$12,000
1971–72	$10,415–$22,450	$9,130–$17,980	$8,777–$17,401

The same results are obtainable from the standardized "money" salary ranges in Table 22, except that the CCC minimum salary is higher than the Los Angeles minimum.

Other comparisons of unmatched samples, or matched samples with different base years, different matching criteria, and cross-sectional analysis, may find a significant union or nonunion salary differential.[18] The insignificant results of all three

[18]See Birnbaum (1974), who found insignificant increases in average compensation of unionized community colleges; see Aussieker (1974, pp. 46–47) for a nonunion differential. Nonunion increases in compensation and salaries and relative gains were also found by a matching of CUNY and California and unionized and nonunionized community colleges only on the basis of the number of full-time teaching faculty for either 1968–69 or 1972–73. These nonunion advantages were not significant at the .01 level according to two-tailed t-test values.

comparisons in Table 22 and the related comments illustrate the importance of broader economic, political, or public-employee phenomena in salaries and compensation and the insidious nature of union and nonunion comparisons using the data available at present.

Governance One common argument against faculty unionism is that it will reduce faculty participation in academic governance. Two research efforts undertaken to determine the impact of unionism on faculty participation in community colleges concluded

TABLE 23
Level of faculty participation in institutional governance on various decisions for unionized and nonunionized community colleges

	Level of faculty participation	
Decisions relative to	*Union*	*Nonunion*
Faculty welfare:		
Appointments	1.22	1.22
Reappointments or nonrenewal	1.33	.47
Promotions	1.38	.53
Tenure	1.50	.66
Dismissal for cause	1.28	.85
Faculty salary scales	2.00	1.09
Individual faculty salaries	1.89	.92
Average teaching loads	1.78	1.00
Teaching assignments	1.72	1.38
All faculty welfare decisions	1.57	.90
Academic:		
Curriculum	1.56	1.88
Degree requirements	1.56	1.63
Academic performance	2.00	2.00
Types of degree offered	1.33	1.70
New educational programs	1.50	1.78
Admission requirements	.63	1.04
Academic discipline	1.56	1.56
Student extracurricular rules	.81	.94
All academic decisions	1.31	1.50
Administrative:		
Relative staff sizes of disciplines	.33	.81

that faculty participation in the governance of these institutions was significantly advanced and made more important by collective bargaining (Bylsma, 1966; Angell, 1973, pp. 88–89). Another study of faculty collective bargaining in Michigan community colleges reported increased faculty participation on faculty welfare and employment issues but opinion divided on the effect of unionism on faculty involvement in other areas of institutional decision making (Shoup, 1969).

Table 23 gives the extent of faculty participation in institutional decisions at unionized and nonunionized (all California)

TABLE 23
(Continued)

Decisions relative to	Level of faculty participation	
	Union	Nonunion
Administrative: (cont.)		
Programs for buildings	.44	.75
President	.63	1.00
Academic deans	.63	1.01
Department chairmen	1.28	1.44
Short-range budgeting planning (1–3 yr.)	.61	.97
Long-range budgeting planning	.22	.25
Specification of department committees	1.89	1.90
Membership of departmental committees	1.89	1.94
Authority of faculty in governance	1.31	1.56
Specification of senate committees	1.36	1.56
Membership on senate committees	1.75	1.78
Student role in institutional governance	1.06	.84
On all administration decisions	1.02	1.20
Level of participation —all items	1.20	1.25

KEY: *Level of faculty participation*—mean scores of a sample of eight nonunionized (California) community colleges and a sample of nine community colleges with exclusive faculty bargaining agents at the time of the survey. Institutional responses on faculty involvement were weighted as follows: 0 = no faculty involvement; 1 = consultation; and 2 = faculty determination or joint faculty-administration action. Difference in mean scores of union and nonunion samples is significant at the .05 level.

NOTE: The nonunionized community colleges are all in California.

SOURCE: "Report of the Survey Subcommittee of Committee T" (1971, pp. 74–121).

community colleges. Only institutions responding to the survey with a joint faculty-administration response were included. As indicated in the table, the faculty at unionized and nonunionized colleges has a high level of participation in academic matters (sole determination or joint faculty-administration action). Consultation is the extent of both faculties' participation in administrative matters. Decisions on relative staff size of disciplines and building and expansion programs are the only areas in which the nonunionized faculty has a significantly higher level of participation. On faculty welfare matters faculty participation at unionized colleges is significantly higher (joint action). The overall level of faculty participation at the unionized and nonunionized colleges is about the same, but there are some differences in emphasis, although nonunionized faculty involvement in academic and administrative matters is not significantly higher.

The results of these governance comparisons are subject to the usual reservations on measures, sample design, and extraneous factors, but the extent of faculty participation in institutional governance evidently has not been adversely affected by unionism. The impact of unionism on faculty participation in academic and administrative matters awaits more refined analysis.

SOMETHING FOR NOTHING? To date, what is known about community colleges and faculty unionism startles few individuals. Faculty unionism is strongly associated with other public-employee unionism, the emerging community college concept, increased faculty salaries, reduced work load, better benefits, more faculty involvement in governance, more standardized and equitable working conditions, and a more centralized, more rational, and more efficient college management. Faculty unionism is probably not related to the quality of instruction or the conditions of community college students.

What is not known is whether faculty unionism is something for nothing. Unionized community college faculty have clearly obtained better working conditions than K–12 public school teachers and have nearly equaled the best conditions of nonunionized community college faculty. Not known is whether the gains of faculty unionism will be offset by increased management aggressiveness at the bargaining table or have already been offset by increased faculty accountability and less security. Again, it should be emphasized that the gains of faculty unionism in community colleges occurred under extremely favorable financial and political conditions. Under some circumstances faculty unionism may lead to a loss of community support.

The final issue of faculty unionism in community colleges is parity between public two-year and four-year faculty. Parity in base salary with four-year faculty of the same rank was achieved in the CUNY system, but outside of New York State the relationship between four-year and two-year faculty working conditions is not one of parity. However, the bargaining power of community college faculty unions has been considerably enhanced by the new vocationalism, the rapid rise of four-year college tuition and costs, and the demand for teaching-intensive services. The exercise of this power in some states may find district boards and state legislatures coerced into salary and work load parity for public two-year and four-year faculty members.

The establishment of parity in some form will demonstrate to the four-year faculty that faculty unions have produced positive gains for their community college brethren.

7. Academic Unionism in Great Britain

The growth of collective bargaining in the United States has created interest in how similar relationships are working out in the university systems of other countries. In particular, the arrangements in Great Britain have been cited frequently as a possible model for American universities. The British system is regarded as an appropriate model especially by those persons who are concerned about the possible dire consequences of extending the adversary bargaining model to the whole range of academic policy questions that arise in higher education.[1] Underlying this view is the belief that the British approach maintains an apparently successful separation of economic and academic issues. Economic issues are thought to be settled in the main by negotiations at the national level between the Association of University Teachers (AUT) on the one hand and the Committee of Vice Chancellors and Principals and the Department of Education and Science on the other. Academic issues are seen as matters in the province of the internal governance mechanisms of the individual universities.

THE STRUCTURE OF THE SYSTEM Depending on the mechanics of classification, there are 45 universities in Great Britain. In 1972 they enrolled about 235,-000 full-time students and employed some 33,000 academic staff. Between 5,000 and 6,000 of these were librarians, research staff, academic administrators, and other nonteaching profes-

---

[1]The British arrangements were studied during the spring of 1973. Among many others, special appreciation for assistance is expressed to Adrienne Aziz, Assistant General Secretary of the AUT, Derek Ware of the Universities Authorities Panel of the Committee of Vice Chancellors and Principals, and Gareth Williams, Associate Director of the Higher Education Research Unit at the London School of Economics and Political Science. Support for travel was provided by the Institute of International Studies of the University of California, Berkeley.

sionals, leaving 27,000 to 28,000 who were members of teaching staffs.

It has been suggested with varying degrees of seriousness that the system is coming to resemble, however faintly, something like a "University of Great Britain." If the universities are viewed in this way, collectively they would be similar in some quantitative respects to major American systems such as the state and city universities of New York or the California state university and college system. They would have roughly the same total number of students, about twice as many individual geographical locations, and about twice as many academic staff members. As these figures indicate, the separate institutions in Britain are typically considerably smaller in terms of student enrollment than the majority of American universities of similar status. Only the University of London (which is really a federation of more than 30 independent units) has a total student body of more than 30,000 students, putting it in the general size class of, say, the three dozen largest American universities, such as the University of Minnesota or Michigan State University.

Although their enrollment is substantially smaller, Oxford, Cambridge, Glasgow, Edinburgh, and several of the major red brick universities represent concentrations of academic staff approximately equivalent in size to those of larger public universities in the United States. This results from the fact that British universities have only about half the number of students per faculty member as the typical American university.

In fact, of course, there is no University of Great Britain, and British universities are autonomous and independent not only of each other but also of direct control by any other level of government. They are, however, subject to a considerable and increasing coordination and relatively subtle direction by central authority through the agency of the University Grants Committee (UGC).[2] The source of the pressure for increased

---

[2]One observer concluded that British universities are more autonomous than American universities even though "the government now sets faculty salary scales, and imposes a maximum percentage quota for the upper academic ranks, influences by state scholarships the flow of students, affects by its grants the amount and type of research undertaken, and through its coordinating agency allocates funds to the universities in block form, but only after having examined a detailed breakdown of the budget request and having obtained a moral commitment that government funds will not be used for unapproved new programs" (Berdahl, 1971, p. 254).

coordination and the reason for its effectiveness lie in the fact that more than 80 percent of the funds for the universities comes from the national government. In a world of scarce resources it is inevitable that considerations of social and economic policy would produce efforts to influence some of the educational decisions of the components of the system. In no area of university operations, with the possible exception of building construction, has standardization and centralization been carried as far as in academic staff personnel relations. The UGC is only one of the administrative bodies that seem to be evolving toward a version of "management" for the university system, at least in the area of academic industrial relations. The other two are the Committee of Vice Chancellors and Principals and the University Authorities Panel.[3]

The University Grants Committee (UGC) At the peak of the "management" side of the university sector, the UGC is usually regarded as a typically British solution to the problem of channeling governmental funds to an independent university system. The committee dates from 1919 and has been unusually successful in performing its functions. The best description of the function is that of a "buffer" to protect the universities from external interference in the performance of their academic role. The UGC has members drawn from the civil service and from members of the public, the latter often chosen from the lay members of the governing bodies of the universities themselves. Until 1964 the UGC dealt with the Treasury; in that year it was made advisory to the Department of Education and Science (DES), and the DES was given jurisdiction over all education. This reorientation is regarded as a significant step in a gradual transformation of the role of the UGC. As the higher education sector has become absolutely larger and more expensive and relatively more important as an instrument of political and social policy, it is generally agreed that the UGC has almost inevitably begun to take on some of the characteristics of an agency of the government, and its influence on certain major internal decisions (for example, physical facilities and program emphasis) has grown perceptibly.

[3]Information in these sections comes from personal interviews and from Halsey and Trow (1971), Perkin (1969), Burn et al. (1971, Chap. 4), and Williams, Blackstone, and Metcalf (forthcoming).

The DES works with the UGC and scrupulously refrains from directly dealing with university authorities on academic matters in every area but one. Since 1970 representatives of the department have negotiated directly with university representatives and the Association of University Teachers on staff salaries and employment matters. The department claims to have entered this arena reluctantly and only on the receipt of a written request from the universities that it function in this way.

The UGC operates through the device of a quinquennial block grant to the universities, and the latest grant covers the period beginning in 1972. Annual supplementation of at least some expenditures is necessary during the quinquennial period, particularly in the present inflationary times, and this involves a form of more or less genteel negotiation on most matters and more forthright periodic negotiations on salaries in particular.

In its external relations the UGC is vaguely similar to the constitutionally independent boards of regents or the "super-boards" of some of the major American state university systems. Like them and for similar reasons (though probably to a lesser degree), they are becoming rather less of a buffer against outside pressures and more of a transmission belt for pressures from the provider of funds. The committee, however, has much less influence than the American lay governing boards on the internal affairs of the component institutions. The role of the UGC in salary negotiations is essentially that of a mediator in a process that will be described later in detail.

The Committee of Vice-Chancellors and Principals (CVC) The vice-chancellors and principals are the executive officers of the British universities and colleges, and they have been meeting informally to discuss problems of mutual interest since before World War I. The CVC determines its own membership, with the number of members nearly tripling in the 1960s as the university system expanded rapidly. There are now well over 100 vice-chancellors and principals in the British system.

The CVC provides its own budget through self-assessment from the budgets of the component universities. It has a full-time secretary and a number of subdivisions by subject matter. Although opinions differ as to whether the committee is waxing or waning in importance, the majority view seems to be that it is growing in significance and in the range of its activities, primarily because of the need for some organization to serve as a spokesman for the universities as a group. The individual institutions, however, have jealously guarded their independence and resist accepting policy statements of the CVC as automatically binding on the constituent members. From our point of view, however, it is significant that the universities do accept settlements reached by the University Authorities Panel, the negotiating arm of the universities in staff bargaining, as binding agreements.

The Universities Authorities Panel (UAP) The UAP is "technically separate from though administratively linked to" the CVC. It was created to negotiate with the Association of University Teachers on behalf of the universities on salaries and certain employment conditions and is directly responsible to the universities. The panel is made up of six vice-chancellors, one of whom is named by the CVC to serve as chairman, and five lay members chosen from governing boards. The UAP has recently acquired a full-time executive secretary, a former personnel officer of the Open University. The importance of the negotiating and administrative activity of the panel is attested to by the fact that none of the subdivisions of the CVC itself has a full-time secretary.

The Association of University Teachers (AUT) The AUT is the recognized representative of the academic staff in the university system. The Association was established in 1919, roughly in the same period as the American Association of University Professors (AAUP) in the United States, as the professional association of British university teachers. The AUT had its origins mainly in the problems of the nonprofessorial staff at the older red brick universities. It originally was known as the Association of University Lecturers, but a decision in favor of teacher unity resulted in the broadening of its membership base to include professors and the choice of its present name. In recent years the nonteaching staff has grown absolutely in size and relatively in the Association and there is talk of another possible name change, perhaps to something like the Association of University Senior Staff. (Similar speculation has occurred in the AAUP as the composition of its membership has changed.) Both librarians and administrative staff members are scheduled to hold annual conferences within the framework of the AUT, an indication of the growing importance of their special concerns.

H. J. Perkin, the author of a history of the AUT, divides its evolution into two major periods, one from 1919 to 1939, in which it functioned as an "amateur professional body," and a second, over the period 1939 to 1969, in which it developed into a "professional professional body." The principal index of the change was the development of a full-time secretariat and a more systematic organization of its activity in order to participate more energetically in a wider range of problem areas of the profession. Although Perkin does not refer to it, the final year of his history, 1969, almost certainly is the first year of a significant new phase of the AUT's development. Since that time the organization has increasingly become a union of university teachers, employing a full-time general secretary, expanding its headquarters staff, and engaging in direct and formal negotiations with the national administrative structure of the university system. In this it has gone further, earlier and faster, than has the AAUP in the United States.

Significantly, the AUT went outside of the academic profession to hire its new general secretary, Mr. Laurie Sapper, in 1969.[4] It is generally agreed that Mr. Sapper has brought a high degree of trade union professionalism to the representation of the profession's interests before external groups. Prior to his appointment Mr. Sapper was the assistant general secretary of the union of post office employees. The new era of the AUT has seen a further expansion in the full-time professional staff experienced in union representation, which now includes, in addition to the general secretary, a deputy general secretary (primarily concerned with superannuation issues) and three assistant general secretaries as of mid-1973. Policy making is in the hands of a delegate council chosen from the membership and in a set of standing committees, the most relevant for our purposes being the Salaries and Grading Committee. As would be expected, there is considerable expertise on various topics within the Association's membership and this resource is used to produce a stream of studies and reports.

---

[4]Interestingly enough, the AAUP named a new general secretary in 1974.

The trade union flavor that shows signs of permeating the atmosphere of the national headquarters of the AUT is the result of conscious decisions of the Association. Several types of pressures appear to explain the trend:

1 The association has had to function in the past decade as a representative before governmental bodies such as the National Incomes Commission and the Prices and Incomes Board in the pattern set by trade union and industrial organizations. These latter are aggressive pressure groups operating in an atmosphere of competition for advantage in the implementation of a variety of wages and income policies. In addition, it became clear in the latter half of the 1960s that the legal environment in which unions and employee organizations functioned in Britain was going to become more important and more complex, requiring more continuous and expert activity in a number of ways on the part of staff representatives. The industrial relations ferment culminated in the passage of the highly controversial Industrial Relations Act in 1971, but other laws have also affected the operations of unions. The AUT has registered as a trade union under the Industrial Relations Act to secure the advantages it provides in opening up opportunities to secure formal recognition and such other benefits as grievance procedures and requirements for consultation and the provision of information.

2 Some of the association activists view the AUT as operating in a highly organized environment of employee organizations in which strategic and tactical alliances for political and economic action may be increasingly important, and they see a need for knowledgeable and skillful participation in the internal politics of the labor movement. An issue that illustrates this situation is that of the AUT's relations with the Trades Union Congress (TUC), the British equivalent of the AFL-CIO, and, in particular, their relations with other teachers' unions. A large minority within the AUT supports direct affiliation with the TUC, but the membership voted against affiliation in a referendum in 1971 by more than a 2 to 1 ratio. There is considerable support for more extensive cooperative activity among the several teachers' unions, but only limited collaboration has occurred to date, in part because of the trade union movement's adamant boycott of the Industrial Relations Act and its attitude toward those unions that have registered under the act.

3 Finally, the increasing role of the DES in formulating policy in the higher education sector, the UGC's more interventionist stance, and other developments which might threaten the position of the universities in general and the academic staff in particular—all suggest that forthright pressure tactics more familiar in trade union circles may be

useful, at least as part of a reserve arsenal. The prime examples of policy issues of this type are the introduction of government scrutiny of the UGC and university financial accounts by the office of the Comptroller and Auditor General in 1967[5] and the educational reforms introduced in recent years. The most important of these reforms provide for first-degree work outside the university sector through the Council of National Academic Awards, the promulgation of a "binary" system of higher education, primarily through the development of new institutions (the polytechnics), and schemes to promote new programs leading to a diploma of higher education as a possible alternative to traditional degrees. In addition, criticism of the conditions of employment of faculty has been aimed at the same targets in Britain as in the United States, for example, work load, tenure, productivity, and sometimes the earning of outside income.

Many of these issues could be and sometimes have been handled through the traditional machinery of consultation by part-time professional representatives, but the total impact of the new environment seems to have contributed to the feeling that more sustained effort and a broader range of competence is needed in the AUT executive.

The present membership of the AUT is approximately 23,000 out of an estimated potential of 33,000. (At its peak in 1971 the AAUP had about 90,000 members, but these probably represented less than a third of the persons eligible.)

Members of the AUT are organized into 46 local associations in the various universities and in two research councils. Detailed membership data are not available, but the membership of the association appears to be fairly widely dispersed throughout the various institutions and among the various ranks. Oxford and Cambridge are substantially below the average in the percentage of staff enrolled in their local groups; the Oxford local association, for example, claims about 500 of a potential membership of 2,000. A survey of a sample of British academics conducted in 1969 by the Higher Education Research Unit (HERU)[6] found that membership was lowest at Oxford and Cambridge (34 percent) and highest at the new universities and

---

[5]Burn reports that the fears that the inspection of internal records might "lead to more governmental intervention in university affairs are fading" (1971, p. 65).

[6]The HERU survey data are reported in Williams, Blackstone, and Metcalf (forthcoming Ch. 15). This book will be cited in the text henceforth as the HERU study.

the former colleges of advanced technology (75 percent). As far as rank is concerned, 79 percent of the professors, 81 percent of the senior lecturers and readers, and 59 percent of the lecturers reported themselves as members of the union. The HERU survey and interview evidence both confirm that, although the percentage of union membership is lowest among lecturers, staff in this rank are more likely to be activists in the union than are those in the higher ranks.

The HERU survey reported a considerably lower level of union membership in 1969 among the research staff, but since that time the proportion of this group belonging to the AUT is believed to have risen substantially. As noted earlier, the non-teaching staff's absolute and relative position in the AUT has grown, and they have begun to acquire recognition as groups with separate and common interests in the formulation of AUT policy. The possibility of setting up a separate professional group of administrative staff has also been discussed. (Such an organization, the American Association of University Administrators, has been formed in the United States.)

At the national level the AUT has been recognized for many years as the organization representing the academic staff, with the degree of participation in the process of determining salaries and other matters gradually expanding and becoming more formal. At the moment the AUT is the only formally recognized representative of academic staff at the national level, and although British industrial relations practice accepts multiple representation in principle, there is no prospect of a challenge to the AUT's position. At the local level, all but four of the associations had acquired local recognition from their employing institutions by mid-1973. The four exceptions were Oxford and Cambridge and two of the constituent elements of the University of London.[7]

Formal recognition of the local associations as bargaining representatives at the institutional level is new in most of the

---

[7]It was assumed that the two University of London associations would achieve recognition after further negotiation but that it would be more difficult for the Oxbridge units to achieve formal recognition. This seemed to be a result both of the lower degree of membership and the well-known complexity of the employment relationship in the ancient universities. As a result of the latter virtually all generalizations about employment conditions in British universities have to be qualified as they apply to Oxford and Cambridge.

British universities. It seems to be the result of a more aggressive attitude of the AUT units and of the new climate exemplified by the Industrial Relations Act. Many of the universities actually granted local recognition before the passage of the act in 1971, but the concepts of establishing a right to organize, of encouraging recognition and negotiation, and of establishing dispute procedures were clearly part of a policy consensus for several years prior to that date. Not the least of the motives for expanding recognition to the AUT was to avoid problems that would be created by campaigns for recognition for some of the staff by other unions, particularly the militant Association of Scientific, Technical and Managerial Staff, which has some membership among some of the occupational groups represented by the AUT.

Depending on the definition of bargaining, the AUT can be said to have been bargaining on economic issues at the national level for up to 25 years. Any form of negotiation at the local level has been infrequent, but the extension of formal local recognition and the requirements of the new national industrial relations policy, particularly the requirement for formal dispute (grievance) procedures, have created an entirely new situation. Local bargaining is certain to be more vigorous, more frequent, and broader in scope in many universities than it has been in the past.

DEVELOPING THE MECHANICS OF REPRESENTATION Prior to 1949 the AUT functioned primarily as a professional association concerned with general academic matters and used whatever chance it had to influence salaries and other economic affairs through devices such as the publication of salary surveys and joint conferences with representatives of the universities.[8] A new era began, however, with the adoption of a national salary scale for university teachers in that year. Until 1949 the UGC had confined itself to recommending general increases without standardization. The AUT had pressed for a single scale for years, but the scale's adoption was mainly the result of a desire on the part of the universities and the UGC to avoid interuniversity competition in salaries during a period of university expansion financed largely by governmental funds.

[8]Historical material in this section for the years prior to 1970 is from Perkin (1969) and Halsey and Trow (1971).

Although the adoption of the scale provided a point of focus for discussions at the national level that had been lacking before, AUT participation in salary decisions was still minimal.

The first major change came in 1954, when the AUT and the vice-chancellors were both given the "formal right" to approach the UGC at any time on questions of changes in the salary scale. The Chancellor of the Exchequer promised that the UGC would "give a considered reply" to their representations. The AUT continued to press for a more active role, but the government took the view that the "normal type" of negotiating machinery was inappropriate for relations between the governing bodies and academic staff.

In 1960 a formal procedure for consultation with the AUT was established by the UGC, under which, according to one interviewee, a "stately minuet" was choreographed. The AUT prepared a set of proposals whenever a salary review was initiated. At this time the CVC and the UGC were to enter into consultations as to "general considerations" involved in the salary review. The CVC was also to be "freely available" to the AUT for consultation, the exchange of views, and the transmission of information, as well as providing the AUT with "some indication" of the extent to which they would be able to support their proposals.

After the submission of the AUT's proposals to the UGC, the CVC would be asked by the latter for their "advice." The UGC would then meet with the AUT to discuss major points of difference or difficulty. Whether the source of these difficulties was the UGC or the CVC would not be disclosed. A second round of meetings between the UGC and the CVC and the UGC and the AUT would be arranged if necessary.

The UGC would then submit their advice to the Chancellor of the Exchequer and transmit the Chancellor's "considered reply" (the final decision) to the CVC and the AUT, without, in the process, disclosing the substance of what their own advice had been. This concluded the process.

Whatever the other reasons for developing this elaborate procedure, a major objective of its designers was to shield from view the decision-making process on the employers' side and, in particular, as far as possible, to avoid disclosing the source and the exact nature of the objections to the proposals of the AUT.

Although this was a major step toward the AUT's objective of securing an effective voice in salary decisions, the association was far from satisfied. In American terms the AUT had achieved the equivalent of a "meet and confer" procedure, while their objective was to establish a requirement "to bargain collectively in good faith." Specifically, the AUT wanted to deal directly with the final decision maker, to present their proposals, and to get a considered reply not only in the form of decisions on disputed issues but in the form of a rebuttal to the arguments advanced to support their demands. They wanted an opportunity to counter the rebuttal and even, in extreme cases, to take some action against the implementation of the decisions, or to bring the disputed issues to third-party determination.

During the 1960s, major new developments gave the AUT a start toward realizing its goals. These took the form of formal salary reviews by two national commissions set up to deal with wage and salary questions during periods of economic crisis. As part of a general system of central control of income policies, university salaries were reviewed and reported on by the National Incomes Commission in 1963–64 and the National Board of Prices and Income (PIB) in 1968 and again in 1970.[9] The Robbins Committee, which prepared a landmark report on higher education released in 1963, had previously recommended setting up a separate permanent salary review body to advise the government on university pay, but this proposal was not implemented.

The referrals of the salary questions to the pay commissions gave the AUT an opportunity to present their arguments directly to a body that was responsible for making a public recommendation and which produced a relatively detailed response to their arguments in the same pattern used to handle wage and salary claims from other groups. In this sense it represented a step toward assimilating university salary setting into the system in use in other private and public sectors of the economy.

Perkin (1969) describes the hearings before the National Incomes Commission in 1963 as "the nearest thing to real salary negotiation ever achieved by the A.U.T. For the first time, its

[9]National Board of Prices and Incomes (1968, 1970).

negotiators were able to confront, before an independent tribunal . . . the ultimate controllers of the purse strings, the Treasury officials, who found themselves in the unprecedented situation vis-à-vis the A.U.T. of having to provide specific answers to specific arguments and of having their recommendations rejected" (p. 180). Apart from questions of the review procedure, both the substance of the commission's salary award and the principles proposed for determining salary movements were generally satisfactory to the AUT.

Using these principles, particularly those of "fair comparison" and the concept of a "standard rate of advance," the AUT began preparing a new set of proposals. But the new campaign was overtaken by, first, a pay freeze, and then, the referral of salary questions to a new tribunal, the National Board of Prices and Incomes. The AUT was cheered by the fact that the PIB was given a "standing reference" on the question of university salaries, which meant that they would have a continuing responsibility to consider salary questions. The implication that the PIB would be a "general and permanent review body," of course, turned out to be misleading since the PIB itself did not survive long after the installation of the next Conservative government.

In any event, the universities' pay award of the PIB in 1968 was wholly unsatisfactory to the AUT, and Perkin said it was "greeted with astonishment and derision by most university teachers." An average salary increase of about 5 percent was tapered to provide the lower ranks with greater increases, while professors were limited to an average of 2 percent. Most of the opposition, however, was generated by a number of what were essentially obiter dicta, such as the desirability of placing more emphasis in promotion on teaching at the expense of research, an implication that teaching loads might be increased, and a belief that retention and recruitment of quality staff did not seem to be a problem.

From the point of view of the association, the two most objectionable features of the report of the PIB were the blow dealt to the use of the principle of the standard rate of advance of salaries in general and the introduction of a new concept of discretionary payments or merit awards. As far as university staff were concerned, the claim to an increase related to the standard rate of advance of salaries in general became a casualty of the PIB's belief that "the endless chain of increases" must be broken somewhere. (Perkin objected to this as a decision to attack the chain at its smallest and weakest link, which from the PIB's vantage point would have had a certain appealing logic.)

The introduction of the merit awards was influenced by the heavy emphasis in the formulation of general wages policy on "productivity bargains" which encouraged tying pay increases to major improvements in working arrangements, by a belief that teaching should be encouraged, and by a concern with the virtual automaticity of annual pay increments for staff below the professorial rank. The awards were to come from a supplementary grant of 4 percent of the salary bill to be distributed to individuals on a variety of bases, for the most part for accepting a more "exacting teaching load" or for raising the quality of teaching. One of the report's suggestions, that the quality of teaching might be assessed in part by a "carefully drafted questionnaire to students," was not very well received. The merit awards had not been proposed by any element of the university system and had little or no effective support from the university establishment. The full 4 percent recommended by the PIB was never utilized for this purpose, and by 1971 merit awards had been negotiated out of existence, with the money used to raise pay and to add more incremental steps to the lecturer salary scale. In defending itself against criticism of its opposition to discretionary pay, the AUT pointed out that it had no objection to the recognition of merit by accelerating a faculty member's movement up the incremental pay scale, a practice that had always existed.

Whatever the assessment of the experience with national incomes policy machinery, a new and separate system of negotiation was developed in time to handle the next major salary negotiation in 1970, and this machinery is currently in use. The new negotiating procedure was worked out by the AUT, the CVC, and the UGC and accepted by the government. It consists of a two-stage process consisting of negotiations in the framework of two committees, designated A and B. Committee A includes representatives of the AUT and the Universities Authorities Panel of the CVC described in the previous section. Its chairman is drawn from outside and is named by the UGC. If the parties are able to reach agreement on a proposed pay settlement in Committee A, they take it to Committee B as a joint recommendation. If the parties are unable to agree, the chairman has the responsibility to formulate a proposal, which then becomes the official recommendation of Committee A in the Committee B proceedings.

Committee B consists of representatives of Committee A on the universities side and representatives of the Department of Education and Science on the government side. The chairman of Committee B is appointed by the government. If agreement is reached in Committee B, the question can be regarded as settled. If no agreement is reached, the disputed issues are submitted to outside arbitration.

The UGC takes no direct part in the procedure in either committee, participating in Committee A deliberations as a nonvoting "observer" and acting as adviser to the government side in Committee B. In practice the UGC functions in Committee A largely as a mediator, as Americans use the term. The UGC chairman described the process as "running around with an oil can," while another participant described its role more precisely as "conveying a sense of the possible" to each side. The key contribution of the UGC is, on the one hand, to provide the AUT and UAP with an indication of the framework within which the government currently feels the settlement must fit and, on the other hand, to transmit to the government a feel for the realities of the other parties' positions. The DES, for its part, feels that any salary settlement for academics must be compatible with the salary decisions for civil servants in general and with the government's salary policy for the economy as a whole.

Although potential sources of serious stress are evident, the system seems to have worked fairly well through 1973. Four awards have been made, under each of which the average pay increase has approximated that given the main body of civil servants. The parties have reached agreement in Committee A, and the chairman has not had to produce his own version of a settlement. The AUT has not been satisfied with the way in which Committee B has functioned, feeling that conditions specific to the universities have been given less weight than they think appropriate, while considerations of civil service and of economywide incomes policy have had too much influence. The AUT would like to have a voice in appointing the chairman of the arbitration board and has threatened to force the issues to arbitration, but to date this alternative has not been used.

In summary, using our definitions of faculty bargaining in the United States and allowing for the differences in the industrial relations systems in the two countries, the AUT might be said to have acquired bargaining status as early as 1955. At that time they were recognized as the official representatives of the academic staff, had been awarded the formal right of approach to the CVC and the UGC, and were assured of a "considered reply" to their presentations. They would certainly have been listed as an example of faculty unionism after the adoption of the 1960 procedure. The 1970 negotiating arrangements would be classed as faculty bargaining by the most exacting definition. Thus, in 1974 the AUT might be regarded as having functioned as a bargaining agent for 19 years by the most relaxed criteria, as having been bargaining for 14 years by more demanding requirements, and for 4 years by any standard.

COLLECTIVE BARGAINING IN PRACTICE

It will be useful for comparative purposes to review the scope of bargaining and the experience with bargaining in Britain in the context of the issues on which analysis of American experience has been concentrated. The parallels may not always be exact because of the institutional differences that exist in the national industrial relations systems, but on a number of points the similarities are evident. The topics that appear to be relevant in both countries are (1) the selection of the bargaining representative and the appropriate bargaining unit; (2) salary policy; (3) policies on tenure and promotion; (4) dispute procedures; and (5) the relation between the bargaining and the governance systems.

Representation and Bargaining Unit Questions

The most important fact about the issues of the proper representative organization and of the appropriate bargaining unit in Britain is that they are not problems of any consequence. As noted in other chapters, in the United States the choice of the bargaining agent and the definition of the unit are of major importance because of the vigorous competition for bargaining rights that has existed among several teachers' organizations. The bargaining unit problem is important because of its relation to the governance structure and because of its influence on elections to choose a representative.

In Britain the teachers' organizations have well-established jurisdictions over identifiable sectors of the educational system, and competition between organizations is minimal. With two minor exceptions the AUT does not face any serious challenge to its claim to represent academic staff in the universities. The medical faculty tends to shun membership in the AUT in favor of membership in the British Medical Association (BMA), which functions as a de facto bargaining agent for the medical profession as a whole in dealing with the National Health Service and on behalf of the medical staff in dealing with university authorities. The AUT does represent the nonclinical medical staff. The Association of Scientific, Technical and Managerial Staff (ASTMS), a large, aggressive white-collar union, negotiates with the universities on behalf of large numbers of university employees in various grades that are outside the occupational groups classed as academic. The ASTMS represents employees such as the lower ranks of librarians and administrative grades, and in some cases a potential for conflict arises as promotion ladders may carry some of its members over into AUT territory. As a militant organization well over on the political left, the ASTMS attracts some membership from segments of the faculty as well, and it has, on occasion, tried without success to win recognition from individual universities for some of these groups. British industrial relations practice permits multiple representation among the same occupational group, but only when the organizations involved can claim substantial fractions of the eligible membership. The presence of the ASTMS has undoubtedly stimulated the universities' willingness to extend recognition to the local associations of the AUT and has probably also increased the willingness of both the administrations and the AUT to favor some expansion of the group that is considered academic or "academic-related" staff, and therefore in AUT territory.

In recent years the higher education sector has been expanded not only by a dramatic increase in the number of universities but also by the expansion of degree-level instruction outside the traditional university structure, primarily through the development of some 30 "polytechnics." These may grant degrees under the supervision of the National Council for Academic Awards (NCAA). This is the substance of the "binary" system of higher education, which has been the subject of controversy since its promulgation under the Wilson Labour government in 1965.

The colleges of education are another division of higher education and one whose current position is very cloudy.[10] Both the polytechnics and the colleges of education have their own teachers' organization. The Association of Teachers in Technical Institutions (ATTI) has 9,000 members from the staff of the polytechnics as well as another 39,000 members working in other nondegree postsecondary education (known as "further education" in Britain). The Association of Teachers in Colleges and Departments of Education (ATCDE) enrolls some 7,500 teachers in the 155 colleges of education and in the education departments of 7 of the polytechnics and of 28 of the universities. (The great majority of primary and secondary school teachers are represented separately by the National Union of Teachers.)

The relationships among the AUT, the ATTI, and the ATCDE seem to be generally good on practical matters, although they have had difficulty in formulating common stands on broader issues of higher education policy. The boundary lines of jurisdiction seem to be well respected, and cooperative arrangements have been worked out to handle problems such as the representation of ATCDE members who work in universities where they are officially represented by the AUT. A major potential for conflict existed when the colleges of advanced technology were converted into universities, a move which transferred their staffs from the territory of the ATTI to that of the AUT, but this was settled amicably.[11]

A potential trouble spot has recently developed within the ranks of the ATTI because of unrest among a substantial group of the members in polytechnics. Whereas the colleges of advanced technology were shifted as institutions into the university sector, thereby bringing their staff into the domain of the AUT, the binary system provides for the expansion of degree work in the polytechnics and some other institutions,

---

[10]The previous Conservative government proposed the integration of teacher education into the system of higher education by some combination of closing colleges, converting others to more general institutions, and encouraging the affiliation of others with polytechnics and universities.

[11]The AUT also has agreements on the boundaries of representation with the BMA, the British Dental Association, the British Veterinary Association, and the National Association of Local Government Officers. No agreement has been reached with ASTMS.

while keeping them outside the university system. This creates a potential for conflict between the further education and the higher education segments of the membership of the ATTI as the latter press for salaries and conditions of service more like those of teachers in the universities. Since outside the universities degree and nondegree courses not only are taught in the same institution but sometimes are taught by the same individual, a set of new problems has arisen. In 1973 teachers in the polytechnics split off from the ATTI to form a new union. If the higher education work outside the university sector continues to expand, the hitherto orderly division of function among the unions may break down further, but this is not an immediate prospect.

Not only has there been little organizational rivalry for representation rights in Britain, but, partially as a consequence, there has been no serious bargaining unit problem.

In addition to the teaching faculty, a concept of academic-related staff has evolved over the years. This is a fairly nebulous category, but it seems to be defined in terms of the function performed and the level of pay. As a practical matter probably the most important index of whether or not a position is classed as academic staff is whether it is included in the Federated Superannuation System for Universities, the university retirement system. An employee doing work related to the academic programs and paid a salary equivalent to teaching salaries is "academically related."

Finally, probably because there has been relatively little experience with formal local bargaining and also because of the comparatively simple administrative structure in at least the older British universities, there is no counterpart to the debate over the inclusion of department chairmen in the bargaining unit that has occurred in the United States. There is an internal "professorial" problem, but this matter will be discussed in connection with the interaction of bargaining and governance.

In all, the conclusion that emerges from British experience with regard to this set of issues is that the university bargaining system, like the national industrial relations system generally, is (or, better, has been) based on an informal, unstructured, pragmatic approach that minimizes legalism, and thus this type of problem has been unimportant. Unfortunately there seems to be little chance that the British approach could be transferred to the United States. The American reliance on formal, structured relations has its advantages, but in this area it has its costs as well. The aspect of the British system most likely to be transferred in part to the United States is the reduction of organizational competition. This might occur through union mergers, such as those between the AFT and the NEA, or by a division of territory, such as an AAUP withdrawal from competition in some types of institutions.

Salaries In discussing salary policy it is customary to distinguish between the average level of salaries and the internal salary structure, the latter referring to the relationship between the salaries for the various ranks or grades of academic staff. As would be expected from a union of academic professionals, the AUT has developed sophisticated salary presentations over the years and has enunciated a fairly comprehensive and moderately consistent general policy on salary questions. Like other interest groups the Association has adopted the elementary strategic principle that salary claims should be based on the grounds that are most appropriate (those that best justify the desired increases) at the time of submission. Among the alternative criteria that have been identified as lying to hand are changes in wages generally, changes in retail prices, increased productivity, the need to recruit and retain qualified staff, and the salaries of comparable positions.

In the competition for occupational advantage that occurs in highly organized economies, it is unrealistic and probably unfair to expect that any union should fail to use whatever combination of arguments best meets the circumstances of the moment in advancing their claims. In spite of this, two related themes dominate the AUT's arguments for changes in average salaries: (1) recruitment and retention and (2) "fair comparison." In the British situation these two arguments have not been in conflict because the most persistent application of the fair comparison doctrine has been with reference to the civil service, and teachers have not been able to come close to realizing their target salary even during the 1960s, when the expansion of the university system gave the recruitment argument its greatest force. In the labor market of the foreseeable future, the recruitment argument will be subordinated to the fair comparison claim.

The career structure of British academics is organized into three major ranks or titles: *lecturer, senior lecturer,* and *professor.* (The relatively infrequently used title of *reader* is equivalent to, but somewhat more prestigious than, *senior lecturer.*) The often-cited parallel with the American set of ranks—assistant professor, associate professor, and professor—is accurate only in the superficial sense that the rank ordering is the same; the two career systems operate in very different ways.

The lecturer scale has 17 different salary "points" or grades at present (raised from 15 in 1971), and the entry level is usually one of the bottom grades, with a virtually automatic movement up the scale in the form of annual increments for the great majority of the faculty. Senior lecturers and professors are classed as "senior staff," and the proportion of staff in these ranks is limited by a maximum "senior staff ratio." The ratio has been raised over the years to the present level of 40 percent. The senior lecturer scale has eight steps, again essentially automatic annual increments in pay. The eighth step was added in the 1972 settlement. With minor exceptions, there are no set professorial scales; the system specifies a minimum salary and an average salary for all professors, and within these constraints individual bargaining between the faculty member and his university sets actual salaries. As of 1973 the lecturer scale ran from £1,929 to £4,548 with increments of £165 in most cases; the senior lecturer scale began at £4,368 and went to £5,496 with increments of £159; the professorial minimum was £5,625 and the permissible average was £6,777.[12]

The AUT's interpretation of fair comparison starts with the concept of a common labor pool of university graduates, either with advanced degrees or with "good" undergraduate degrees, from which employers draw recruits, with the two major employers being the universities themselves and the government. The AUT's position is that the two major streams from the talent pool ought to yield essentially similar financial rewards to the participants.

Applying this reasoning, the AUT has concluded that the pay at the top of the lecturers' grade ought to be equal to that of the top of the grade of "principal" in the administrative civil ser-

[12]Prior to the PIB's 1968 report there had been a maximum as well as a minimum for professors' pay.

vice. The average honors graduate recruited into the civil service reaches the maximum of the principal's scale in 13 to 15 years from recruitment, assuming that he takes the full 7 years to traverse the seven steps from the top to the bottom of the principal grade.[13] Other graduates move up the same path at a slower rate. Since it is possible to enter employment in the universities at a step above the bottom lecturer grade and for progress up the scale to be accelerated, the average teacher probably reaches the top of the lecturers' scale in about the same number of years as the civil servant takes to reach the top of the principal grade.

The AUT is unlikely to achieve parity under these terms, particularly since the negotiating machinery now seems more closely linked to the civil service pattern than it had been previously. Since 1970 there have been four settlements, which were roughly similar to the awards for the civil service. A major upward shift of approximately 15 percent would be needed to equate the lecturers' and the principals' maximum, and in practice this would mean a major cost increase in addition to the increases that would be in order on other grounds. More important, it would require accepting a permanent change in long-standing "relativities" between the two occupational groups.

The HERU study provides a comprehensive comparison of the salary profiles of the two careers.[14] Based on 1969–70 data, the HERU found that the civil service administrative staff earned less than the universities' humanity and social science faculties in the 24–28 age bracket, leaped ahead substantially at age 29 and maintained a diminishing lead to the end of one's thirties, even though the faculty closed the gap by earning increasing amounts of outside income. Another spurt around age 42 increased the lead of the average civil servant to 20 percent by age 47, and it remained at that level until retirement. The HERU authors calculated the discounted lifetime earnings for the two careers and confirmed the advantage held by the civil servants. Discounting future earnings at 6 percent showed the civil servants with a 25 percent advantage over the humanities and social science faculty, excluding outside earnings for

[13]Association of University Teachers (1972).
[14]HERU study, Tables 13.A.2 and 13.4.

the latter. With outside earnings for faculty included, the differential shrank to 10 percent.

The consistent response of review bodies to the claims for parity has been that, as the PIB put it in Report 145 (1970), "The rewards of university life are not to be measured solely in terms of salary." In the face of the prospects for a long-term surplus in the academic labor market and the long-standing reluctance to accept the parity argument, the AUT, like the American faculty unions, may be satisfied to interpret fair comparison to mean equal increases in the average salary without closing the present gap.

Turning to questions of salary structure, while the AUT follows the common practice of playing the structure "like an accordion," as one participant put it, there is a reiterated call for reducing differentials. The accordion strategy involves calling for greater-than-average increases for the lower ranks or the elimination of the lowest ranks entirely in the name of equity or recruitment problems, followed subsequently by arguments that the upper ranks need greater increases or more steps added to the scale to provide incentive. The union's executive has responded (AUT, 1972) to the call for reduced differentials between grades by arguing that differentials are smaller than they were and by pointing out that the differentials in the civil service are much wider.

A more specific demand has been for the introduction of formal steps in the professorial scale to replace individual bargaining on salary in part; one suggestion is that steps should be specified from the professorial minimum up to the professorial average.

In the light of the experience in some American faculty unions, an important issue is the stand of the AUT on the question of parity of treatment for teaching and nonteaching posts. The nonteaching academics are recognized as lying within the AUT's area of responsibility, and have been the fastest growing segment of the AUT membership. The union has been giving them greater recognition as separate groups with their own problems within the structure of the organization. The policy both of the AUT and of individual universities generally has been to apply increases in benefits uniformly to all segments of the academic staff. Currently a major push in the bargaining sessions has been to develop a national salary structure for the academic-related grades. This would require a major effort to rationalize the titles and work content of hundreds of different positions in the separate universities. In the process of developing a unified national structure, the parity issue in the form of equal pay for equal work would undoubtedly arise among the academic-related groups and quite possibly between the teaching and the nonteaching staff as well. The British universities might not face this issue in the difficult form it has assumed in some American university systems (for example, the City University of New York), but the potential for major conflict exists.

One interesting aspect of negotiating academic salaries in the British system is that the bargaining takes place outside the framework of the quinquennial grant from the UGC. The money needed to pay the cost of general academic salary increases is automatically provided by the government as a supplementary grant. This approach is used only for academic salaries. The amount of increase in other costs of operation, including the negotiated increases in the nonacademic staff salaries, is measured by a special index, the Tress-Brown index, and an annual supplementary grant is provided to offset these increases. In this case, however, the government has agreed to reimburse the universities for only 50 percent of the increase as a guaranteed minimum with the amount of their contribution to the other 50 percent to be negotiated each year. In addition to the effect of automatic reimbursement on possibly reducing the resistance of the vice-chancellors to an academic salary demand, this system tends to encourage the universities to look with favor on expanding the range of positions classed as academic and thus entitled to full, automatic reimbursement of rising costs.

Tenure in Britain The administration of appointment, tenure, and promotion in the British universities is an interesting combination of what Halsey and Trow (1971, p. 190) call "guild unity" and competition. *Guild unity* refers to the principle that, once admitted to the guild of practitioners of an occupation, all members are assumed to be equal and should be treated similarly in similar circumstances. It is a manifestation of professionalism as described in the first chapter and operates to curb competition among members of an occupational group. Halsey and Trow, for example, use the concept to explain the opposition of the AUT to merit pay as proposed by the PIB in 1968. The emphasis of most unions on seniority as a method of allocating rewards and benefits is perhaps the most familiar example of guild unity in action.

All labor markets operate with different mixtures of competition and noncompetition. Competition at the entry level of the academic labor market in Britain is more formal than in the United States, since the advertising of openings in the public press has been traditional. (The requirements of affirmative action programs are making this practice more common in the United States.) Advertising for job openings above the entry level is much less common in Britain,[15] and, of course, there is no way of assessing the competitiveness of the selection process as it actually operates. There is scope for competition, since the HERU study of the academic market found that, on the average, in 1968–69 the number of applications per opening was 13, ranging from 25 in the humanities to 5 in applied science.

Having secured an initial appointment, the new lecturer serves a probationary period of three years (occasionally longer in some institutions) before being considered for tenure. It was surprising to discover that guild unity apparently operates very effectively at this point, since all the persons interviewed agreed that a very high proportion of all candidates were awarded tenure throughout the system. The standard phrases that turned up in the discussions about the proportions securing tenure were "nearly all" or "probably 90 percent."[16] The HERU researchers estimated that during the rapid expansion of the 1960s "over 4 percent" of younger staff left the profession each year, a figure they regarded as representing "heavy wastage." As an estimate of the number failing to obtain tenure in individual universities, however, this figure has serious drawbacks. It understates the number refused tenure because it

---

[15]The HERU authors estimated that a lecturer vacancy was nearly 4 times as likely to be advertised as a professorial vacancy and nearly 10 times as likely as a senior lecturer vacancy, indicating that the market is more competitive at both ends of the scale than in the middle. Unless otherwise noted, HERU data in this section are from HERU, Chapter 6.

[16]The PIB apparently also concluded that the award of tenure and the passage of the efficiency bar (see below) were both largely automatic. See National Board of Prices and Incomes (1968, p. 15).

refers to those "leaving the profession" and some unsuccessful candidates may move from one institution to another. On the other hand, it overstates the true figure because the survey included all academic staff, and about 15 percent of these are not teachers and are not usually eligible for permanent posts. Another source of upward bias is the assumption that all those who leave the profession do so involuntarily. Many academics, even in recent years, have been recruited with little postgraduate training, so it seems certain that some of the departures are voluntary. Each year some proportion of other young professionals in law or medicine must leave the practice of their profession for other activities voluntarily.

The belief that the percentage of successful candidates for tenure is quite high is supported by the HERU finding that 74 percent of their sample held tenure positions in 1968–69, even though more than 60 percent of them had been hired after 1962 and almost 33 percent since 1966. Once again, since a substantial proportion of the sample are not in teaching positions, the percentage of all teachers with tenure is understated. The true proportion is probably—perhaps substantially—over 80 percent. This compares with the consensus guess of our respondents of "almost 90 percent."[17]

The British approach to tenure seems to be in line with that found in many large American state university and college systems and is considerably less exacting than that found in the top tier of American universities. The latter, on the average, award tenure to a smaller proportion of probationary faculty and use a longer probationary period before awarding tenure. According to the Commission on Academic Tenure, in 1971 about 45 percent of public and 36 percent of private universities responding to its survey reported that they awarded tenure to more than 80 percent of those considered; 16 and 23 percent respectively awarded tenure from 0 to 40 percent of their candidates. The commission also found that the median probationary period for institutions in the United States was six years.

The British system, however, has an interesting provision

---

[17]Interestingly enough, although there has been some public criticism of tenure, "tenuring in" does not seem to be considered a very important problem among either the staff or the administrators interviewed in Britain. Halsey and Trow (1971) include very little discussion of tenure in *The British Academics*.

that is not found in American practice. After receiving tenure, the British faculty member below professorial rank receives virtually automatic annual increments in pay (recently amounting to 5 to 6 percent), but after about eight years of service he comes up against an "efficiency bar." In theory this is the equivalent of a promotion step that implies a favorable performance review. Crossing the bar, however, seems to be largely a formality in most cases, according to the HERU study and all other information. In a few universities the administrations have shown interest recently in treating the bar seriously and holding back some of their faculty, and this may become more common. In another example of the application of guild unity the AUT takes the position that the presumption favors advancement at the efficiency bar and that a formal negative evaluation is necessary to deny an applicant passage. This interpretation seems to be in accord with past practice.

To sum up, the British system is at least more formally competitive at the entry level, and probably also more competitive in practice, than is the American system. After entry a substantially larger proportion of the probationary employees achieve tenure in Britain than in comparable American institutions, and as a result between 80 and 90 percent of the recruits can look forward to annual salary advances through the 17 steps of the lecturer grade. At the end of that process, according to the 1972 scale, salary at the last step would be almost $2\frac{1}{2}$ times the salary at the first step of the progression.

Until recently the system was seldom challenged in those instances in which tenure was denied on academic grounds. This reflects the general lack of formal recognition of the AUT at the local level and the lack of formal grievance procedures in the structure of representation. According to a newspaper interview with the general secretary of the AUT, the union is now "pressing for a proper appeals system." The model for such a system is reported to be a newly established procedure at Bedford College, which calls for a three-man committee representing the senate, the AUT, and the lay members of the college council. The committee takes evidence from colleagues, the probationer, and others involved and holds a full hearing.[18]

---

[18]Michael Binyon (1972). According to this report, of three "recently disputed" cases at Bedford, the AUT won two and lost one.

What proportion of all denials of tenure are being challenged and on what grounds is not known, but it appears that what is known as "instant tenure" in the United States may be emerging as an issue in Great Britain. Unlike some of the American union contract clauses providing for review of probationary cases, this approach is not limited to review of questions of procedure. Since the academic labor market suffers from a surplus of supply, this problem will grow in importance, and the AUT is likely to be as protective of probationers' rights as American faculty unions appear to be.

Promotion Once he is appointed, a faculty member's movement through the 17 grades of the lecturer scale is essentially noncompetitive. Competition is introduced, however, at the end of the lecturer series at the point of promotion to the grades of senior lecturer/reader or professor.

This competition arises not only as a result of an internal policy decision but because of the existence of an administratively imposed limit on the proportion of total faculty permitted in the senior ranks. This senior staff ratio has existed for many years and is the subject of negotiation between the AUT and the authorities, although the DES maintains that it lies outside the UAP's jurisdiction. It has risen over the years and is currently set at 40 percent, having been raised from 35 at the time of (but not officially as part of) the 1971 settlement. The actual figure is now somewhat lower for the system as a whole, although some institutions, such as the University of London, exceed the limit. Within the senior staff group, professors account for about one-third of the total of senior staff. Professors make up a little less than one-eighth of all teaching faculty, and the proportion in the range has been 10 to 12 percent for many years. The relatively low proportion of professors among academics is, of course, in marked contrast with the United States, where the title of professor is the normal expectation of most career university teachers.

In Britain the relative lack of advertising for the senior lecturer positions is consistent with the view that this position is usually filled by internal promotion as a reward for worthy institutional service. The relatively few positions with the title of reader, which the HERU study calls a vestige of an earlier system, are more oriented to research and have somewhat higher prestige. The professorship is by far the most clearly competitive prestige title, and in Britain implies both accomplishment in research and responsibility and power in academic administration.

The AUT has dealt with the apparently worsening prospects for promotion into the senior ranks by negotiating an additional step at the top of the senior lecturer scale as well as increasing the permissible ratio of senior to total staff. The union does not seem to have tried to bargain about the ratio of professors to other senior staff. As noted earlier, the AUT has proposed that a series of annual incremental steps be added in the professorial scale that would take all professors up to the permitted average salary in a regularized fashion. Another major issue concerning the professors is the attempt by the AUT to acquire data on the dispersion of actual professorial salaries. Neither of these proposals has been accepted by the university authorities, and the degree of support for them from the professors themselves is not known.

One hypothesis suggested by an analysis of the operation of the British system is that it combines competitive and noncompetitive aspects of an academic career in the same institution, whereas the American system has entire institutions that are competitive while others are largely noncompetitive. In the two or three dozen American universities in the upper reaches of the prestige hierarchy, advancement seems to be more competitive across all ranks and at every stage of the academic's career than it is in the British universities with the possible exception of Oxford and Cambridge. The typical British university provides a relatively noncompetitive career of substantial scope for the great majority of their teachers up to the top of the lecturer scale and then provides for further promotion into the senior lecturer or the professorial rank on a competitive basis for the major portion of the career academics. Perhaps this helps the British universities maintain a reputation for being teaching-oriented while simultaneously providing a reward system that recognizes unusual research accomplishment by elevation to the professorship.

The AUT has consistently tried to extend the career ladder for the majority in the lecturer grades and to expand the opportunity to achieve senior status. They have uniformly supported the egalitarian application of the principles of guild unity, but there is no evidence that they have tried to change the criteria for promotion to senior ranks—particularly to the professorship. The union's attempt to negotiate automatic increments for the lower-paid professors and to make professorial salaries public may be a prelude to questioning the present system of distributing the funds in the salary pool and possibly attacking the legitimacy of differential awards. With that possible exception the AUT to date has shown little tendency to interfere with that part of the career pattern that has traditionally been based on competition.

Grievance Procedures

Until recently grievance procedures were informal, ad hoc, or nonexistent in most individual institutions. With the extension of formal recognition to local AUT chapters, the formalization of appeals procedures has become one of the first orders of business. In the past most individual disputes seem to have centered on problems of implementing national pay awards for individuals or job titles at the local level. More interest is currently being shown in the procedures for appeals from personnel decisions and in the policies to be followed when reductions in programs have to be made, a process that may lead to what the AUT has called "constructive dismissals." (The last section described the development of a grievance procedure used in tenure cases that has been described as a system appropriate for emulation.)

Although appeals from personnel decisions are likely to increase in frequency, for the short-term future the major problem local grievance procedures may have to cope with will result from attempts to develop a national policy for "conditions of service" and a national salary scale for nonteaching academics. *Conditions of service* in this context means work schedules, holidays, job duties, sick leave, additional allowances for additional duties, and similar items. The university authorities are reported to have no objection in principle to bargaining an agreement on this range of issues and may, in fact, be pressed to do so by the provisions of the Industrial Relations Act. The universities have recently negotiated a national system of pay and job classifications for the nonacademic positions represented by the Association of Scientific, Technical and Managerial Staff.

The implementation of national policies on conditions of service and a national salary scale for nonteaching posts will generate many disputes over the interpretation and the implementation of these at the local level. Scores of different job titles, for example, will have to be analyzed and grouped into a systematic classification system that will then be applied uniformly throughout the system. These subjects are likely to dominate the work of the local AUT chapters for some time and will be built very firmly into the local decision-making process.

The fleshing out of the AUT's staff and organizational structure parallels the similar developments in the American faculty unions, including the AAUP, as they become active in bargaining. It portends a higher level of activity over a broader range of subject matter and, in particular, a new and more active role for the local associations in the affairs of the individual university.

Governance In discussions of governance, it is customary to divide British universities into various categories. The HERU study, for example, uses the divisions of Oxford and Cambridge, the University of London, the old civics, the new civics, former colleges of advanced technology, the Scottish universities, and the University of Wales. As usual, Oxford and Cambridge embody the largest divergence from the general pattern in that their colleges are more "collegial" in their internal governance and they are more financially and organizationally independent of their respective university structures. Both the University of London and the University of Wales are, like Oxbridge, federations of colleges, but their governance systems are more like those of other universities. Although there is a great deal of diversity in the details of the governance systems of the various types, in most of them the basic structural forms fit a general pattern.[19]

There are three basic forms of governing bodies in the universities: one oriented to the outside world, one concerned primarily with internal financial affairs, and a third concerned with academic affairs. Although different names are used in different universities, and, occasionally, the same names are

[19]A more general and very useful brief treatment of governance in the British universities can be found in Halsey and Trow (1971, Chap. 5).

used for different types of boards, the most common practice would seem to be the use of the names *court, council,* and *senate,* respectively. The courts are made up mainly of representatives from outside the university with a minority of academics from the staff. They are often quite large, and although they may have substantial formal authority, in practice they tend to be passive, meeting only infrequently. The councils have the principal responsibility for overall financial affairs and at least formally make policy decisions. They have a majority of laymen in their membership but usually also substantial internal academic and administrator representation. The senates are responsible for academic affairs (including their financing) and, in practice, are the most important organs of university governance. Their membership is drawn from the academic staff in a variety of combinations, and in most cases, there is some representation of the administrators and support staff as well. Under the senates lies a system of faculty boards for large subject areas and the university departments, all concerned primarily with academic matters.

The AUT's principal concern in governance is not with the structure of the system or with the distribution of power and function among its various elements. Its concern is with the pattern of membership in the various bodies and with the way that power is exercised within the units, particularly in the departments.

The representation of the academic staff has historically been dominated by professors, reflecting the fact that as recently as the 1930s professors made up between 30 and 40 percent of the teaching faculty. Since World War II the ratio has ranged from 10 to 14 percent, but the governance system has only slowly adjusted to the changed circumstances. The reader will remember that the AUT was originally established as the Association of University Lecturers as a response to the problems of the nonprofessorial staff at that time. Today the AUT is pressing for the representation of nonprofessorial staff in the organs of government and for the democratization of internal processes. As a corollary to expanding the role of other academics, the AUT in some circumstances has suggested limiting the number of professors in the membership and providing that the other academic staff have a voice in the selection of the professors who might be included. Where the senates are very large, for example, an executive committee of some sort may acquire the real power, and the AUT hopes to assure that its membership will not be exclusively or even predominately professorial.[20]

In addition to supporting a broadening of the base of participation in all levels of governance, the AUT has a special concern with the situation within academic departments. Historically many of the departments in British universities have been single-professor departments with the professor serving as administrative head, sometimes for life. In at least some instances administrative power has been exercised in an autocratic manner, with policy, financial, and personnel decisions in the hands of the department head and with relatively little consultation with other staff members. Striking testimony to the importance of this aspect of the professor's role as late as 1969 is provided by the HERU survey. The respondents were asked to indicate the qualities they felt most important for a professor to possess. The most frequently listed quality was administrative and organizational ability (50 percent); the second most frequently cited was the ability to establish good relationships with staff, to be accessible to them, and to control them and foster their cooperation (43 percent). Only a third of the sample listed a good academic record as important, although this may have been taken for granted (HERU study, Chap. 16). This pattern of choice would be inexplicable in an American context.

In some universities multiprofessor departments are common, and in these the chairmanship is often rotated among professors. The AUT proposes the ending of appointments for life, the rotation of the chairmanship, and, most important, the acceptance of the proposition that nonprofessorial staff be eligible to serve as department chairmen. Whatever the policy as to the selection of chairmen, the AUT wants consultation and participation in departmental decisions to be available to all academic staff.

There is some indication that the role of the union in challenging professorial power, especially in departmental affairs, has led to resentment on the part of some professors. In particular, the activity of the AUT, in representing grievants in depart-

---

[20]A report of a working party of the AUT on the government of the universities can be found in the *AUT Bulletin* (1972).

ments, has often turned out to be directed at professors as decision makers. The adoption of the adversary role by the union has led to some questioning of the relation of the AUT to the professorial staff in some universities, although so far this has not been a major problem.

It would be unfortunate if the union were to lose the support of any substantial segment of the professorial group. At present the majority of the professors are members, and this means that the local associations benefit from having a large proportion of the governing bodies staffed by persons who, while they may not identify strongly with the AUT, are, at the least, not antagonistic.

The fact that developments in the universities have frequently tended to coincide with the goals of the AUT does not mean that the AUT has necessarily been the moving force behind the changes that have occurred. In pursuing the twin goals of a broader representation of the nonprofessorial staff in the various institutions of governance and of democratizing decision making in the system generally and in the departments in particular, the AUT has been in tune with the major forces acting on the university. As in the United States, governance structures have been under pressure from various sources to adapt to external and internal forces. Several studies of the governance systems of individual universities in Britain have been conducted and substantial reforms have been proposed, usually calling for broader, more active representation from groups such as students on the governing bodies. The new universities have developed their governance arrangements in a different climate, and, while they have been mindful of tradition, some variations have been tried. The AUT has been supporting a set of proposals that were in the mainstream of change, but it has also been one of the vehicles which has contributed to bringing about change.

AN EVALUATION It is time to return to the principal question posed at the beginning of this chapter: Does the British system of academic collective bargaining illustrate the feasibility of a long-term separation of financial and academic matters, with bargaining limited to economic issues and academic affairs left to academic bodies?

The most appropriate answer seems to be "yes and no."

"Yes" because such a separation has been characteristic of experience in the past; "no" because there is evidence that the boundaries are beginning to erode, although the process is not far advanced and is proceeding slowly. In other words, the situation in Britain is not static but is evolving at an accelerating rate in response to many of the same forces that are bringing about change in the United States.

As we have noted, the British universities and the AUT have unquestionably been engaged in a version of bargaining since the early 1960s at least. The issues have been relatively few and these have been economic in nature, primarily involving salary levels, pensions, and the structure of salaries and positions.

The major reason that the thrust of union-university negotiations in the past was toward economic matters is the organizational structure of the two parties to the relationship. The AUT has been a national organization with relatively ineffective local associations. It was in a position to function best at the national level on matters that were common to all universities. The universities, on the other hand, were (and still are) independent entities with only a rudimentary set of national institutions exercising a coordinating function through the CVC as a voluntary body. The AUT was equipped to function primarily at the national level, while the universities were organized to deal with only a narrow range of issues, largely salaries, pensions, and rank structure questions, at that level. Attempts by the AUT to negotiate on other issues have been met by assertions that the CVC has no power to speak for their constituency as a body. Currently, the AUT is filling out its structure at the lower levels while the universities system is being strengthened at the national level, so that the two sets of structures are becoming congruent. In theory the AUT could demand that the CVC, or its negotiating arm, the Universities Authorities Panel, assume the role of bargaining agent with power to bind its member universities under threat of direct job action, but there is little likelihood that the brandishing of the strike weapon would be taken seriously.[21]

Like other unions the AUT will almost certainly take the

[21]This may be because past negotiations have been over salary questions in which the adversary was the government in the final analysis. A strike for concessions that could be granted directly by the university administrations might be more effective.

position that the scope of bargaining includes any decision that affects the welfare of their members. Their restraint in the past has been based less on principle than on the realities of bargaining relationships. These relationships are now changing.

On the national level the AUT is expanding the range of its concerns from salaries and superannuation to include conditions of service and a uniform salary scale for academically related positions. The CVC do not object in principle to centralizing and standardizing these matters, and the government's only concern is with the cost of any concessions. These are still economic matters, but this development is a step toward expanding the role of the CVC in making decisions that apply collectively to universities as a group. Once this new role is defined, the scope of questions considered may be widened.

The expansion of the scope of bargaining at the national level is illustrated by the recent formation of a new body, the Joint Consultative Committee (JCC), within the CVC. The JCC is a vehicle for dealing with nonsalary issues that are considered to be outside the jurisdiction of the UAP and are brought to the negotiating table by the AUT. As the name suggests, these issues are to be dealt with in a framework of consultative rather than negotiatory procedures, but the two are notoriously difficult to keep separate. The attempt at separation is necessary because UAP agreements are binding, while all other actions by the CVC are only recommendations to the universities.

Regardless of the fate of the current industrial relations law, some form of protection of the right of representation and an accompanying requirement to bargain collectively will be part of the British industrial relations pattern of the future, and under these circumstances the CVC will almost certainly continue to evolve toward the status of the responsible bargaining agent for the universities as a group over a wider and wider range of subject matter.

The AUT has policies and positions on a wide range of academic matters, such as the levels of student grants, the form of internal governance, and the structure of degree and diploma programs. It is not difficult to see some of these issues brought into the orbit of bargaining at the level of the CVC, the UGC, or the DES.

At the local level nearly all universities have granted formal recognition to the AUT's local associations. Once again, the law will play a role in strengthening the hand of the local groups in university affairs. As in American universities, grievance procedures are the main focus of attention at the local level, along with assuring democratic procedures in departmental government and the participation of the nonprofessorial staff in university affairs. The latter two reforms may well be won in many universities without resort to anything resembling direct bargaining. Grievance procedures are likely to have personnel matters as their principal concern, and, insofar as they involve promotions and tenure decisions, the efficiency bar, and reductions in staff, they will move into areas considered at least as much academic as economic. British law now permits a termination to be appealed to an industrial tribunal, and this will encourage the handling of these cases by an internal dispute procedure.

A final example of the trend toward broadening the AUT's concern with noneconomic matters is the advancement of the claim that the union's local associations ought to be involved in the development of their university's quinquennial grant proposal. This is a matter that could not be handled easily by the association at the national level, since each university formulates its proposals independently. With the new status of the local associations some union participation may be achieved in this area.

Once again, this need not imply a bargaining relationship in the sense that adversary positions exist and formal negotiations occur. As in the United States, in some institutions, and on some issues, the regular institutions of faculty governance will be the vehicle of participation. It is not inconceivable, however, that conflict resulting from a combination of financial stringency and educational policy differences with the government or with the administrations will lead to the inclusion of noneconomic matters in the collective bargaining process.

There is enough diversity among the British universities to allow different systems to develop at the local level at different institutions. The AUT may be content at both the local and the national levels to limit the scope of bargaining to the traditional direct salary issues, but union-university relations have become more fully developed and structured and the environment has changed. The potential for negotiations encompassing a wider range of subject matter exists where it did not previously and, in my opinion, this potential will be exploited to some degree in the future. This is not to say that academic issues will be introduced to any substantial degree into bargaining in Britain in the near future, but then the bargaining on academic matters so far in the United States has not been widespread. The conditions that fostered the separation in Britain, however, no longer dominate the situation.

If this analysis is correct, the British model of union-university relations will increasingly come to resemble the American version, tempered by what seems to be a narrower gap between administrators and faculty resulting from a lower level of managerialism in the British system.

8. A Recapitulation

Perhaps the best way to summarize the material presented in the previous chapters is in the form of answers to a series of questions:

Why Do the Faculty of Colleges and Universities Organize?

On the basis of the evidence produced by surveys of faculty attitudes and by studies of the institutions that have chosen union representation, it appears that faculty members organize for reasons that can be grouped under the headings of *status in institutional governance, job security,* and *salaries and other economic conditions.* The categories of positions that are included as "faculty" in discussions of academic unionism are far from homogeneous, and these various groups support unionism for different reasons.[1] The personal motivations that lead to a vote for union representation differ among nontenured assistant professors, research personnel, librarians, middle-aged senior professors in state colleges, financial aid counselors, part-time lecturers, community college faculty, and senior professors in university centers. When the mixture of support in "an appropriate bargaining unit" produces a majority view that the existing machinery for representing faculty interests is inadequate, the institution in question is ripe for organization.

Whatever the reasons for an individual faculty member's decision to support a faculty union, variations in basic faculty attitudes by institution cannot explain the specific geographical and institutional pattern of academic unionism as it has developed to this time.

[1]For a discussion of the heterogeneity of the academic labor market, see Garbarino (1974*a*).

Given the prevailing general attitudes revealed by opinion surveys over most of the system of higher education, it is the thesis of this book that unionization occurs as a response to changes in the environment of higher education as a whole and in the structure and function of individual institutions and systems of institutions.

The environmental changes that have been most important are the rapid expansion of American higher education in the 1960s, followed by the cessation of growth and relatively hard times since that time. The expansion swelled the ranks of the professoriate; raised their personal aspirations with regard to salaries, status, and their professional role in governance; and heightened their aspirations for their institutions. The collapse of the educational boom threatens to lead to at least partial frustration of all of these expectations.

A different, but very crucial, feature of the environment that explains the pattern of organization is the passage of state laws encouraging public-employee unionism and the rapid growth in unionization that followed. The existence of a strong bargaining law touches off a dynamic of organization that is contagious and that forces defensive organization by faculty to participate in the budgetary infighting that seems to be an inevitable consequence of public-employee unionism.

The combination of rapid expansion and a consequent need for consolidation and reevaluation has produced in many states a restructuring of the system of public higher education to secure more coordination and direction. This threatens the position of the faculty of hitherto privileged institutions. The staff of less privileged institutions that are accustomed to thinking of themselves as "emerging universities" may see the new system of control as a threat to their continued evolution, or, alternatively, they may see it as an opportunity to claim "parity" with their colleagues at well-established sister institutions. In either case, the faculty at these colleges may unionize to increase their ability to influence the outcome of the new arrangements.

Many institutions that have expanded their functions—the most important example being the state teachers colleges converted to general-purpose institutions—have undergone structural changes as well. They may have been included in a segmented system made up of their own type of institution or subsumed in a comprehensive system with research universities or community colleges. There is, however, an additional independent effect of functional changes, as illustrated by the single-campus, emerging institutions whose faculty have unionized. With internal strains resulting from a changing mix of students and faculty by discipline and background and with the hope of matching the salary levels and conditions of employment of their university brethren, academic unions seem to them to be a more aggressive and promising vehicle for making faculty desires felt than the traditional methods of representation.

In short, there are two strongholds of faculty unionism. One is the public, multi-institutional system, which includes a strong representation of emerging institutions and which may or may not include the major established university centers in a state. The other stronghold is among the separate public institutions that are also undergoing major academic transformations or have experienced major administrative abuses in the eyes of their faculty.

The stress on the changes in institutional environment, structure, and function as explanations of the incidence of unionism is consistent with the startling difference between public and private institutions in the propensity to organize. Although the financial environment of private institutions worsened more dramatically than that of public institutions, there is no counterpart in the private sector to the upsurge of public-employee unionism in the past decade. The extension of National Labor Relations Board jurisdiction to private colleges and universities in 1970 took place in a mature and stable private-sector industrial relations system. The private sector of higher education has not undergone the dramatic moves toward systemwide expansion and later centralization that have characterized the system of public higher education in almost all states.

During the heady years of expansion private institutions did introduce some functional changes but not to the degree that characterized the public sector. There were many fewer instances of new graduate programs and professional schools in private institutions.

Further indirect support for the argument that change, experienced and anticipated, is the catalyst for organization is provided by the evidence that the institutions that have been unionized had salary levels and levels of participation in governance at least equal and often superior to those in unorganized institutions. In addition, the most highly organized sector, the public community colleges, has enjoyed robust financial health.

Is Faculty Unionism Inevitable?

As of mid-1974 about one out of every five faculty members is represented by a union. The growth has been steady but unspectacular. Faculty unionism is not inevitable and will never be universal, even in public institutions. Nevertheless, it will continue to grow with the spread of public-employee unionism generally. As more states adopt supportive bargaining laws for public employees, the staff of institutions of higher education will be caught up in the movement. To some extent the vagaries of unit determination will decide how extensive organization will be among the various sectors of higher education in a particular state. In general, the community colleges and the state college/university systems will reach the highest degree of organization. Where the operation of the law permits traditional full-time faculty members of the more prestigious university campuses to make their own choice concerning unionization, they will probably remain unorganized for a considerable period. These faculty are likely to feel that some equalization of differentials between themselves and the rest of the system is inevitable in any event, and in the leading institutions an administration that wants to keep its faculty unorganized need only provide them with a reasonable approximation of what they could expect to achieve if they were organized. Governing boards may not have either the will or the financial ability to do this. Much will depend on the willingness of legislatures to resist the continuing steady pressure for egalitarian pay and work load policies among the segments of higher education.

Whether the failure of unionism to penetrate the more prestigious public university systems continues depends more on the policies of the budget makers than it does on the personal characteristics of the faculty at these institutions. As of mid-

1974 perhaps the strongest reason for expecting relatively few first-rank public institutions to remain unorganized in the long run is the strength of the general inflation in the economy. It may or may not be true that unions produce inflation, but it is almost certainly true that substantial inflation produces unions, and faculty are unlikely to prove to be exceptions to this principle.

Even if faculty unionism falls substantially short of spreading throughout higher education, faculty representation in the areas not penetrated by other types of organizations will be more formal and aggressive than in the past. A union is only one form of representative agency, and bargaining will be more pervasive than unionism.

Is Faculty Unionism Irreversible?

As an organizational form unionism is unlikely to be abandoned once it is established. Where the degree of conflict that led to unionization stabilizes at a moderate level, the union will retain its identity but may in the long run behave much like other types of faculty organizations, such as senates. This is particularly likely to occur in guild unions with their homogeneous membership.

What Are the Principal Effects of Faculty Unionism?

If the premise is accepted that faculty unionism is the strongest variant of possible responses to institutional change, then the implication is that unionism creates few new problems but does affect the form of solutions to existing problems.

We concluded that the policies of the faculty unions reflected concerns in three major areas: governance, tenure or job security, and salaries. A summary of the results of this concern follows:

Governance   In the area of governance, in general, unions have tried to replace procedures for consultation that had previously been informal, tacit, and customary with procedures that are formal, explicit, and contractual. In some institutions with undeveloped systems of faculty participation they have succeeded in increasing the influence of faculty in institutional decision making. They have not expanded the area of decisions in which faculty participate beyond those that have been traditional to the governance systems of major universities, but they have raised more institutions to that level of participation.

In some instances unions have won participation rights for groups other than the traditional faculty. At the same time, they may become a vehicle for limiting the ability of such groups as students to influence decisions that have a direct impact on the employment conditions of faculty. This is a legitimate goal of an organization representing an occupational interest group.

Although, to date, the effect of unions on academic senates does not seem to have been major, in the long run the net effect is likely to be a diminution in the role of the senates as there is a reduction in the range and importance of matters left to senate procedure. The concern for the continued existence of senates is largely a concern for the maintenance of administrative initiative and collegiality as a style of decision making. Administrations must evaluate the strength of their desire to maintain traditional practices and face up to the necessity of retaining those that are important to them through the bargaining process.

The most important change the union has·introduced is the concept of an effective grievance procedure available to all members of the bargaining unit on a wide range of issues, both procedural and substantive. The result is an emphasis on the formalization of policy, an attention to fine procedural detail, and a requirement of consistency of treatment and evaluation quite foreign to the practice of the traditional academic bureaucracy.

It is possible that the introduction of third-party determination of some issues through arbitration will have a major impact on institutional decisions, but it is likely that the important effects of the grievance procedure will be felt on the processes of decision making rather than on the substance of decisions.

The costs of the new system will appear in the form of money costs, in dramatic increases in bureaucratization, and in the need for new managerial styles and perhaps new types of managerial personnel.

However, the adoption of a new, frankly adversarial form of faculty-administration interaction may permit more rapid change to occur than the former consensus systems could have produced. This may result from the effect of formal bargaining in legitimizing aggressive administration demands and in permitting a number of separate issues to be "packaged" in a single settlement that has to win the support of only a majority of those voting in a contract ratification.[2] Governance by consensus implies a veto power by minorities on specific issues.

Tenure and job security   The law may be a better protector of the tenure rights of faculty as a whole than the bargaining power of faculty unions. Up to the present, faculty unions have had their greatest impact on the process by which tenure is awarded in individual cases. In this area, unions have been able to open up the process in a number of ways. They have pushed for the adoption of formalized criteria of evaluation and the adoption of detailed procedures for applying these criteria. They have made the information used in the decision-making process more available to the faculty member under consideration and increased his input into the process. They have often been able to secure a statement of reasons for negative action and have made a start on getting third-party review of negative decisions.

The effect of these changes on the selection process depends on how the system worked prior to unionism. A reduction in the "quality" of faculty might occur if the system prior to unionization had actually resulted in a substantial number of negative decisions and if the selection process was successful in identifying desirable candidates and eliminating those less likely to succeed. There is some question as to whether these conditions were met in the typical institution that has been organized. What the unions undoubtedly have done is to slow down a sharp increase in promotion standards that many unionized institutions would have liked to introduce in the current slack faculty labor market.

The most important effect of faculty unionism on job security so far has been the extension of the near equivalent of tenure to groups of academic employees who had previously not enjoyed security of employment. As a general rule, any group included

[2]To date there have been only two rejections of contracts negotiated by bargaining agents, the first at Central Michigan University and the second at the University of Hawaii. In both cases a union with a membership of less than half of the unit negotiated a contract that had to be submitted to the whole unit for ratification.

in a faculty bargaining unit that had not had tenure protection before unionization has made at least some progress toward gaining it.

Tenure, in its present form, will be under attack for the foreseeable future. It remains to be seen if the first line of defense in the courts holds up. If it does not, then the unions will be faced with the necessity of winning job security at the bargaining table.

Salaries Faculty unions' effect on salaries has in general been inversely proportional to the level of salaries prior to unionization. To that extent faculty unions have had an equalizing effect in speeding up a change that might have occurred in any event. Within a given state, unionization has been able to improve the positions of community colleges and state colleges relative to universities. Within institutions lower-paid faculty, "irregular" faculty, and lower-paid nonteaching professionals have benefited most, although this tendency has not been as pronounced as the reduction in salary differences among types of institutions. In some cases administrators of unionized colleges appear to have been willing participants in the drive to narrow pay differences among types of institutions. Faculty at the upper levels of the pay range in their institutions and institutions in the upper levels of the institutional range in their state have been lucky if they have kept up with the general increases for state employees as a whole. It is not clear whether these trends are entirely the results of unionization or the consequence of a general trend toward equalization that is characteristic of higher education generally and that appears to reflect a desire to emphasize the teaching function.

Whether the effect of unions on tenure and salary administration is inimical to maintaining quality of faculty depends, in part, on how determined administrators, legislators, and governing boards are to maintain differentials in pay and status for professionally creative faculty. The individual British universities combine a system of low selectivity (after the initial appointment) and automatic salary increments over many years, with a highly selective screening process at the level of the professorship. Perhaps an American variant of this system will be developed. There is little evidence that faculty unions in general would find this approach unacceptable as a matter of principle.

A great deal has been said about the difficulties that might result from a transfer of the "industrial model" of unionism to the colleges and universities. Evidence to date suggests that what is really occurring is the encapsulation of the faculty of the state systems of higher education much further in the civil service system. At the same time many of these civil service systems are themselves being transformed into a variant of unionism, with many of the traditional characteristics of industrial unionism. The faculty unions are still closer to the civil service union model, and the experience of this and other countries suggests that governmental unions retain significant differences from their industrial counterparts. Unfortunately, it may be that, if the personnel systems of public colleges and universities come to resemble unionized civil service bureaucracies, the results will be inferior to a well-managed, private, industrial-sector system.

In any event, the institutions in the American system of higher education that represent intellectual leadership in the country and that set performance standards for both public and private sectors are probably in more danger from environmental and institutional changes—to which faculty unions are a response—than from the independent actions of those unions. Faculty unions need not prevent state legislators, administrators, and governing boards from maintaining leading systems of higher education as centers of academic excellence if they are determined to do so. In the absence of such a commitment it may be that the elements of their faculty committed to academic meritocracy may be able to make use of a faculty union to protect standards. In general, however, maintaining intellectual leadership in these institutions will require a cooperative effort by the providers of funds, the responsible academic and administrative officers, and the leaders of whatever variety of faculty organization exists.

References

AAUP Bulletin, vol. 58, no. 1, Spring 1972.

American Association for Higher Education: *Faculty Participation in Academic Governance,* Report of the AAHE-NEA Task Force, Washington, D.C., 1967.

American Association of Junior Colleges: *Junior College Directory,* Washington, D.C., appropriate years.

American Association of University Professors: *Statement of Principles and Interpretative Comments on Academic Freedom and Tenure,* Washington, D.C., 1940.

American Association of University Professors: "1968 Standards for Committee T Investigations in the Area of College and University Government," *Faculty Documents and Reports of the American Association of University Professors,* Washington, D.C., 1969.

American Association of University Professors: *Policy Documents and Reports,* Washington, D.C., 1973.

Angell, George W.: "Two-Year College Experience," in E. D. Duryea, Robert S. Fisk, and Associates, *Faculty Unions and Collective Bargaining,* Jossey-Bass Publishers, San Francisco, 1973.

Association of University Teachers: *Future Salary Strategy,* Executive Statement to the Council, London, December 1972.

Aussieker, William: "Bargaining Without Unions in California," *Industrial Relations,* vol. 13, pp. 40–49, February 1974.

Aussieker, William: "Student Involvement in Collective Bargaining," a paper prepared for the Faculty Unionism Project, University of California, Berkeley, 1974. (Mimeographed.)

Aussieker, William, and J. W. Garbarino: "Measuring Faculty Unionism: Quantity and Quality," *Industrial Relations,* vol. 12, pp. 117–124, May 1973.

AUT Bulletin, no. 47, November 1972.

Bayer, Alan E.: *College and University Faculty: A Statistical Description,* ACE Research Reports, vol. 5, no. 5, Washington, D.C., 1970.

Bayer, Alan E.: *Teaching Faculty in Academe: 1972–73,* ACE Research Reports, vol. 8, no. 2, Washington, D.C., 1973.

Begin, James P. (ed.): *Academics at the Bargaining Table,* Proceedings of a conference held by the Institute of Management and Labor Relations, Rutgers University, October 1972, University Extension Division, Rutgers University, New Brunswick, N.J., 1973.

Begin, James P.: *Faculty Governance and Collective Bargaining: An Early Appraisal,* Institute of Management and Labor Relations, Rutgers University, New Brunswick, N.J., 1974.

Benewitz, Maurice C. (ed.): *Proceedings, First Annual Conference, National Center for the Study of Collective Bargaining in Higher Education,* CUNY, New York, 1973.

Benewitz, Maurice C., and Mannix, T.: "Grievance Procedures in Higher Education Contracts," *Community and Junior College Journal,* vol. 44, no. 4, pp. 22–24, December 1974.

Berdahl, Robert O.: *Statewide Coordination of Higher Education,* American Council on Education, Washington, D.C., 1971.

Bergmann, Alexander: "Codetermination in Germany," 1974. (Mimeographed.)

Binyon, Michael: "'Universities need negotiating procedures,' says Sapper," *The Higher Education Supplement, London Times,* June 16, 1972, p. D-6.

Birnbaum, Robert: "Unionization and Faculty Compensation," *Educational Record,* vol. 55, no. 1, pp. 29–33, Winter 1974.

Blaustein, Edward J.: "Collective Bargaining and University Governance," speech to the American Association of Colleges, San Francisco, Jan. 14, 1973.

Bucklew, Neal S.: "State College: Central Michigan," in E. D. Duryea, Robert S. Fisk, and Associates, *Faculty Unions and Collective Bargaining,* Jossey-Bass Publishers, San Francisco, 1973, pp. 156–174.

Burn, B. B., et al.: *Higher Education in Nine Countries,* McGraw-Hill Book Company, New York, 1971.

Bylsma, Donald, Jr.: "Changes in Locus of Decision-Making and Organizational Structure in Selected Public Community Colleges in Michigan Since 1965," Ph.D. dissertation, University of Michigan, Ann Arbor, 1969.

California Community Colleges System, Office of the Chancellor: "Faculty Salary Schedules, 1971–1972," January 1972.

California State Department of Education, Bureau of Junior College Education: *Salary Schedules for Teaching Personnel in California Public Junior Colleges, 1964–65,* Sacramento, November 1964.

Carnegie Commission on Higher Education: *National Survey of Faculty and Student Opinion,* Berkeley, Calif., 1969.

Carnegie Commission on Higher Education: *The Open-Door Colleges,* McGraw-Hill Book Company, New York, 1970.

Carnegie Commission on Higher Education: *Governance of Higher Education,* McGraw-Hill Book Company, New York 1973*a.*

Carnegie Commission on Higher Education: *Priorities for Action: Final Report of the Carnegie Commission on Higher Education,* McGraw-Hill Book Company, New York, 1973*b.*

Carr, Robert, and Daniel Van Eyck: *Collective Bargaining Comes to the Campus,* American Council on Education, Washington, D.C., 1973.

Cartter, Allan M.: *An Assessment of Quality in Graduate Education,* American Council on Education, Washington, D.C., 1966.

Chronicle of Higher Education, Nov. 26, 1973; Mar. 6, 1974*a,* p. 1; May 6, 1974*b,* p. 6.

The College-Rater, College-Rater, Inc., Allentown, Pa., 1967.

Commission on Academic Tenure in Higher Education: *Faculty Tenure,* Jossey-Bass Publishers, San Francisco, 1973.

De Lucia, Lawrence: "Collegiality and Collective Bargaining, Oil and Water," paper presented at the Second Annual Conference of the National Center for the Study of Collective Bargaining in Higher Education, 1974.

Duryea, E. D., Robert S. Fisk, and Associates: *Faculty Unions and Collective Bargaining,* Jossey-Bass Publishers, San Francisco, 1973.

"Election Analysis," *Action,* United States Federation of College Teachers, vol. 4, no. 6, February 1969.

Fearn, Robert M.: "Comment," *Industrial Relations,* vol. 13, no. 1, pp. 90–93, February 1974.

Fisk, Robert S., and E. D. Duryea: "Epilogue: Analysis and Commentary," in E. D. Duryea, Robert S. Fisk, and Associates, *Faculty Unions and Collective Bargaining,* Jossey-Bass Publishers, San Francisco, 1973.

Fisk, Robert S., and William C. Puffer: "Public University System: State University of New York," in E. D. Duryea, Robert S. Fisk, and Associates, *Faculty Unions and Collective Bargaining,* Jossey-Bass Publishers, San Francisco, 1973.

"Further Progress: The Economic Status of the Profession, 1966–67," *AAUP Bulletin,* vol. 53, pp. 136–212, Summer 1967.

Garbarino, J. W.: "Professional Negotiations in Education," *Industrial Relations,* vol. 7, pp. 93–106, February 1968.

Garbarino, J. W.: "Precarious Professors: New Patterns of Representation," *Industrial Relations,* vol. 10, pp. 1–20, February 1971.

Garbarino, J. W.: "Faculty Unionism: From Theory to Practice," *Industrial Relations,* vol. 11, pp. 1–17, February 1972.

Garbarino, J. W.: "Emergence of Collective Bargaining," in E. D. Duryea, Robert S. Fisk, and Associates, *Faculty Unions and Collective Bargaining,* Jossey-Bass Publishers, San Francisco, 1973*a.*

Garbarino, J. W.: "Emerging Patterns of Faculty Bargaining," in James P. Begin (ed.), *Proceedings of the Rutgers University Conference on Collective Bargaining in Higher Education,* Institute of Management and Labor Relations, Rutgers University, New Brunswick, N.J., 1973*b.*

Garbarino, J. W.: "Creeping Unionism and the Faculty Labor Market," in Margaret S. Gordon (ed.), *Higher Education and the Labor Market,* McGraw-Hill Book Company, New York, 1974*a.*

Garbarino, J. W. (ed.): "Symposium: Faculty Unionism in the West," *Industrial Relations,* vol. 13, no. 1, February 1974*b.*

Garbarino, J. W., and W. M. Aussieker, Jr.: *Creeping Unionism Revisited,* IBER Reprint No. 115, Institute of Business and Economic Research, University of California, Berkeley, 1974.

Gold, Lois: "Measuring Faculty Unionism: Quantity and Quality," *Industrial Relations,* vol. 13, no. 3, pp. 325–331, October 1974.

Goldberg, Joseph: "Public Employee Developments in 1971," *Monthly Labor Review,* pp. 56–66, January 1972.

Gordon, Margaret S. (ed.): *Higher Education and the Labor Market,* McGraw-Hill Book Company, New York, 1974.

Gourman, Jack: *The Gourman Report: Ratings of American Colleges,* The Continuing Education Institute, Phoenix, 1967.

Graham, Harry: "Unionism in Higher Education in Illinois, 1971," *Journal of Collective Negotiations,* vol. 1, no. 3, pp. 241–249, March 1972.

Gram, Christine: "Impact of Collective Bargaining on Faculty Salary Structures in Michigan Community Colleges," Ph.D. dissertation, University of Michigan, Ann Arbor, 1971.

Halsey, A. H., and M. A. Trow: *The British Academics,* Faber & Faber, Ltd., London, 1971.

Hodgkinson, Harold L: *Institutions in Transition,* McGraw-Hill Book Company, New York, 1971.

Hodgkinson, Harold L.: *The Campus Senate, Experiment in Democracy,* Center for Research and Development in Higher Education, University of California, Berkeley, 1973*a*.

Hodgkinson, Harold L.: *Research Reporter,* Center for Research and Development in Higher Education, University of California, Berkeley, 1973*b*.

Hodgkinson, Harold L., and Richard L. Meeth (eds.): *Power and Authority,* Jossey-Bass Publishers, San Francisco, 1971.

Hueppe, Frederick: "Private University: St. John's," in E. D. Duryea, Robert S. Fisk, and Associates, *Faculty Unions and Collective Bargaining,* Jossey-Bass Publishers, San Francisco, 1973.

Jencks, Christopher, and David Riesman: *The Academic Revolution,* Doubleday & Company, Inc., Garden City, N.Y., 1968.

Katz, Ellis: "Faculty Stakes in Collective Bargaining," in Jack H. Schuster (ed.), *Encountering the Unionized University,* Jossey-Bass Publishers, San Francisco, 1973.

Kibbee, Robert J.: "A Chancellor Views Bargaining in Retrospect and Prospect," in Maurice C. Benewitz (ed.), *Proceedings, First Annual Conference, National Center for the Study of Collective Bargaining in Higher Education,* CUNY, New York, 1973.

Ladd, E. C., Jr., and S. M. Lipset: *Professors, Unions, and American Higher Education,* Carnegie Commission on Higher Education, Berkeley, Calif., 1973.

Lee, Eugene C., and Frank M. Bowen: *The Multicampus University,* McGraw-Hill Book Company, New York, 1971.

Lieberman, Myron, and Michael H. Moskow: *Collective Negotiations for Teachers,* Rand McNally & Company, Chicago, 1966.

Martorana, S. V., and E. V. Hollis: *State Boards Responsible for Higher Education,* U.S. Department of Health, Education, and Welfare, Office of Education, 1960.

Mason, Henry L.: "Faculty Unionism and University Governance," in Jack H. Schuster (ed.), *Encountering the Unionized University,* Jossey-Bass Publishers, San Francisco, 1974.

Medsker, Leland: *The Junior College,* McGraw-Hill Book Company, New York, 1960.

Medsker, Leland, and Dale Tillery: *Breaking the Access Barriers,* McGraw-Hill Book Company, New York, 1971.

Metzger, Walter P.: "Academic Tenure in America: A Historical Essay," Commission on Academic Tenure in Higher Education, in *Faculty Tenure,* Jossey-Bass Publishers, San Francisco, 1973.

Michigan Education Association: *Salary Schedules, Fringe Benefits and Selected Contract Provisions: Michigan Community Colleges 1971–72,* East Lansing, Mich., 1972.

Mortimer, Kenneth P.: "Faculty Voting Behavior in Collective Bargaining Elections," Center for the Study of Higher Education, Pennsylvania State University, University Park, 1974. (Mimeographed.)

Mortimer, Kenneth P., and G. G. Lozier: *Collective Bargaining: Implications for Governance,* Center for the Study of Higher Education, Pennsylvania State University, University Park, 1972.

Moskow, Michael, J. Joseph Loewenberg, and Edward Clifford Kuziaro: *Collective Bargaining in Public Employment,* Random House, Inc., New York, 1970.

Naples, Caesar: "Collective Bargaining," in Jack H. Schuster (ed.), *Encountering the Unionized University,* Jossey-Bass Publishers, San Francisco, 1974.

National Board of Prices and Incomes: *Standing Reference on the Pay of University Teachers in Great Britain,* report no. 98, cmnd. 3866, HMSO, London, 1968; and report no. 145, cmnd. 4334, HMSO, London, 1970.

National Center for the Study of Collective Bargaining in Higher Education: *Collective Bargaining in Higher Education,* Bibliography no. 2, 1974*a*.

National Center for the Study of Collective Bargaining in Higher Education: "Contracts and Agents," March 1974*b*. (Mimeographed.)

National Center for the Study of Collective Bargaining in Higher Education: *Newsletter,* appropriate issues.

Newton, David: "Management Structure and the Financing of Bargains in Public Universities," in Maurice C. Benewitz (ed.), *Proceedings, First Annual Conference, National Center for the Study of Collective Bargaining in Higher Education,* CUNY, New York, 1973.

Parker, Garland B.: "College and University Enrollments in America, 1971–72," *School and Society,* pp. 115–123, February 1972.

Perkin, H. J.: *Key Profession,* Kelley, New York, 1969.

Pieper, J. W., Jr.: *Financial Support for Institutional Research, 1969–70,* Association for Institutional Research, St. Louis, Mo., 1971.

Pillotte, Joyce: "Faculty Bargaining and Traditional Governance Processes at Central Michigan University," in James P. Begin (ed.), *Academics at the Bargaining Table,* Institute of Management and Labor Relations, Rutgers University, October 1972, University Extension Division, New Brunswick, N.J., 1973.

"Report of Committee A, 1972–73," *AAUP Bulletin,* vol. 59, pp. 150–161, June 1973.

"Report of the General Secretary," *AAUP Bulletin,* vol. 59, pp. 146–149, June 1973.

"Report of the Survey Subcommittee of Committee T," *AAUP Bulletin,* vol. 57, pp. 68–124, Spring 1971.

Seidman, J., L. Kelley, and A. Edge: "Faculty Bargaining Comes to Hawaii," *Industrial Relations,* vol. 13, no. 1, pp. 5–22, March 1974.

Semas, Philip: "AAUP Intensifies Its Interest in Politics, College Finance," *Chronicle of Higher Education,* May 13, 1974, p. 3.

Seyfarth, Shaw, Fairweather, and Geraldson: *Labor Relations and the Law in West Germany and the United States,* University of Michigan, Ann Arbor, 1969.

Shark, Alan R.: "A Student's Right to Collective Bargaining," *Change,* vol. 5, p. 9ff, April 1973.

Sherman, F. E., and D. Loeffler: "Universities, Unions, and the Rule of Law," *Wisconsin Law Review,* Winter 1971, p. 199.

Shipka, Thomas A.: "Collective Bargaining on the Campus," in Maurice C. Benewitz (ed.), *Proceedings, Second Annual Conference, National Center for the Study of Collective Bargaining in Higher Education,* CUNY, New York, forthcoming.

Shoup, Charles A.: "A Study of Faculty Collective Bargaining in Michigan Community Colleges," Ph.D. dissertation, Michigan State University, East Lansing, 1969.

Stevens, Carl: "The Professors and Collective Action," in *Collective Bargaining and the Classroom,* Reprint No. 7, Industrial Relations Center, University of Hawaii, Honolulu, March 1972.

Strauss, George: "The AAUP as a Professional Occupational Association," *Industrial Relations,* vol. 4, October 1965.

Studohar, Paul D.: "The Emergence of the Hawaii Public Employment Law," *Industrial Relations,* vol. 12, October 1973.

"Surviving the Seventies: The Economic Status of the Profession, 1972–73," *AAUP Bulletin*, vol. 59, pp. 188–258, Summer 1973.

"The Threat of Inflationary Erosion: The Annual Report on the Economic Status of the Profession, 1968–69," *AAUP Bulletin*, vol. 55, pp. 192–253, Summer 1969.

Trow, Martin: "National Survey of Higher Education," Carnegie Commission on Higher Education, Berkeley, Calif., 1972. (Mimeographed.)

"Union of Students at N.J. State College Negotiates Pact with Faculty Local," *Chronicle of Higher Education*, Feb. 25, 1974, p. 3.

U.S. Bureau of Labor Statistics: *Dictionary of American Labor Unions*, p. 72ff., Washington, D.C., 1972.

U.S. Office of Education, National Center for Educational Statistics: *Digest of Educational Statistics*, appropriate years.

U.S. Office of Education, National Center for Educational Statistics: *Education Directory: Higher Education*, appropriate years.

U.S. Office of Education, National Center for Educational Statistics: *Financial Statistics of Higher Education: Current Funds, Revenues, and Expenditures*, appropriate years.

U.S. Office of Education, National Center for Educational Statistics: *Number and Characteristics of Employees in Institutions of Higher Education*, appropriate years.

U.S. Office of Education, National Center for Educational Statistics: *Opening Fall Enrollment in Higher Education*, appropriate years.

Walker, J. Malcolm: "Transition to Bargaining in a Multicampus System," *Industrial Relations*, vol. 13, pp. 23–39, February 1974.

Walters, Donald E.: "Collective Bargaining in Higher Education: Its Impact on Campus Life and Faculty Governance," in James P. Begin (ed.), *Academics at the Bargaining Table*, Institute of Management and Labor Relations, Rutgers University, October 1972, University Extension Division, New Brunswick, N.J., 1973.

Williams, G., T. A. V. Blackstone, and D. Metcalf: *The Academic Labor Market*, Elsevier, Amsterdam, forthcoming (cited as HERU study).

Wollett, Donald H.: "Historical Development of Faculty Collective Bargaining and Current Extent," in Maurice C. Benewitz (ed.), *Proceedings, First Annual Conference, National Center for the Study of Collective Bargaining in Higher Education*, CUNY, New York, 1973.

World Almanac, Newspaper Enterprise Association, Inc., New York, 1971 edition.

Index

Academic discipline, 33, 208
Academic matters, faculty participation in governance of, 33, 35
Academic professionals, 111
Academic Senate, University of California, 111*n*.
Academic Senate of California Community Colleges, 185*n*.
Academic student performance, 33
Accountability complex, university institutional change and, 13–16
Administration:
    faculty participation in governance and, 33–35
    faculty relationship at community colleges with, 182
    growth of community colleges and changes in, 194–200
    salary and, 169–171
    unions and, 151–156
Administrators, selection of, 14
Admission requirements, 33, 208
Advisory councils, 117
Age, faculty growth and, 5
Agency shops, 105–107, 145
American Association for Higher Education (AAHE), 40, 69, 97
American Association of University Administrators, 24
American Association of University Professors (AAUP), 24, 44
    faculty bargaining-rights competition of, 84–92
    faculty governance-participation survey of, 32–34, 69–70

American Association of University Professors (AAUP):
    guild unions and, 137
    investigations of, 85
    membership of, 52
    NEA-AFT coalition with, 100–102
    at Rutgers University, 152
    self-grading salary survey of, 46, 204
    University of Hawaii and, 104–105
American Council on Education, 37–38, 52
American Federation of Labor (AFL), 92, 94
American Federation of Teachers (AFT), 18–19, 30, 43–44
    community-college lobbying and, 198–199
    faculty bargaining-rights competition of, 92–96
    membership of, 52
    national NEA merger prospects of, 100–102
    as a trade union, 47–49
Appointments, 33, 208
    in England, 236–240
Apprenticeship regulations, 45
Arapahoe College (Colorado), 184
Assembly of State and Regional Conferences (AAUP), 90–91
Assistant professor, 171–172
Associate professor, 171–172
Association of American Colleges, 90
Association of California State College Professors (ACSCP), 41
Association of Community College Faculty (New York), 193
Association for Institutional Research, 25

Association of Scientific, Technical and Managerial Staff (England), 222, 229, 242
Association of Teachers in Colleges and Departments of Education (England), 230
Association of Teachers in Technical Institutions (England), 230–232
Association of University Teachers (AUT), 147
Association of University Teachers (England), 213, 217–222, 247–249
    governance and, 243–246
    grievance procedures and, 242–243
    promotions and, 240–242
    as representative of academic staff, 229–230
    salaries presentation of, 232–236
    union representation development of, 222–228
Attendance, increase in university, 1–2, 5–6
Aussieker, Bill, 118, 144

Baltimore Community College, 184
Bargaining unit, 55–56, 108
    British, 228–232
Baruch College (New York), 76
Bayer, Alan E., 78
Belleville Area College (Illinois), 87
Benewitz, Maurice C., 154, 166
Berdahl, Robert O., 8, 11
Bergmann, Alexander, 141
Birnbaum, Robert, 170
Blaustein, Edward J., 151–152
Boards of education, 197
British Medical Association, 229
Brooklyn Polytechnic Institute (New York), 54, 76
Budgetary planning, 33–35, 209
Buffalo, State University of, 75–76
Building facility programs, 33, 209
Bureaucratization, 10–11, 115
    at CUNY, 155
Business, university-trained personnel and, 2

California, faculty unionism in, 64
    community-college organizing and, 184–186
    community-college salary structure and, 206
California Federation of Teachers–Community College Council, 185*n.*
California Higher Education Association, 185*n.*
California Junior College Association, 185*n.*
Cambridge University (England), 214, 220, 243
Campus, 4*n.*
Carnegie Commission on Higher Education, 1, 37–38, 69
    community colleges and, 181
    governance survey of, 139
    National Survey of Faculty and Student Opinion of, 5, 52
Carr, Robert, 38, 39, 108
Censured institutes, 85
Central Michigan University, 52, 77
    bargaining model of, 129–130
    salary at, 171, 172
Centralization of higher educational institutions, 9
Chairmen, department, 33, 109–110, 209
Changes and growth in university institutions, 1–21
    accountability complex and, 13–16
    function and, 11–13
    growth of faculty unions and, 67–73
    new legal environment and, 16–20
    size and, 4–6
    structure and, 6–11
    (*See also* Community colleges)
Chicago City Colleges, 62–63, 122, 194
    salary structure of, 207
    union organization of, 184
Citizen groups, multilateral bargaining and, 115–117
City College of New York, 76
City University of New York (CUNY), 4, 28, 31, 51–52, 61, 65, 75–76
    administration-union relations at, 153–155

City University of New York (CUNY):
  community-college faculty in, 193
  end-run multilateral bargaining at, 118–
    120
  faculty senate–union relations at, 146
  Legislative Conferences at, 41–42
  NEA-AFT at, 93, 98, 101
  salary structure at, 172–174, 206
  tenure at, 160
  union membership at, 106
Civil Service Employees Association, 161
Class interest, unionism and, 53
Closed shop, 105
Coalition of American Public Employees,
  64
Coalition multilateral bargaining, 121–
  122
Code of ethics, 45
  of AAUP, 84–85
Codetermination models, 139–141
Cohen, Nathan, 120, 122
College and University Professional
    Association (CUPA), 104–105
College Rater, The, 74
"Collegiality," 147–149
Commission on Academic Tenure in
    Higher Education, 112, 238
Committee of Vice Chancellors and
    Principals (England), 213, 215–217
  salary review and, 223
Community College of Allegheny
    (Pennsylvania), 194
Community colleges, 179–211
  effects of bargaining laws at, 183–186
  California, 184–186
  financial difficulty and educational
    reform at, 186–189
  Michigan, 187–189
  growth of faculty unionism among, 59–
    60
  institutional similarities between four-
    year schools and, 180–183
  organizational change and rapid growth
    of, 189–210
  administrative, 194–200
  compensation and salaries, 204–208
  disorganization, 202–204

Community colleges:
  organizational change and rapid growth
    of:
    functional, 200–202
    governance, 208–210
    structure, 190–194
  recognized bargaining agents for, 87
  salary levels at, 173–175
Company unions, 138
Compensation at community colleges,
  204–208
Competitive union–senate model, 145–147
Comprehensive multicampus institutions,
  6–7
  community-college structural change
    and, 192
  unionism among, 65–66
Comprehensive public-employee union
    laws, 61–64
Comprehensive unions, 135–137
  faculty senate–union relations and, 144–
    145
Compulsory financial contributions, 27
Compulsory union membership, 105–106,
  145
Conditions of service, 242–243
Constructive dismissals, 242
Consultation, 32, 34
Contracts, 27
Cook County College Teachers Union
    (CCCTU), 120, 122, 184, 199
Cooperative union–senate model, 143–145
Cooptative union–senate model, 147–151
Coordinating multicampus agencies, 8–9
Cost of Living Council, 120
Council, British, 244
Council for Democratic Action (CCCTU),
  199–200
Council of National Academic Awards
    (England), 220
Court, British, 244
"Creeping legalism," 152–153
CUNY (*see* City University of New York)
Curricula design and program, 14–15, 33,
  209
  growth of community colleges and, 200–
    201

Deans, 33, 209
Decision making, 10–11, 25
Degree requirements, 33, 208
Degrees, increase in number of, 3–4
    growth of unionism and, 68
Delgado College (Louisiana), 184
De Lucia, Lawrence, 147–148, 161
Department chairmen, 33, 109–110, 209
Department of Education and Science
    (England), 213, 215, 219
    salary review and, 227
Departmental committees, 33
Disciplinary action, 14, 165–166
Discussion, 32, 34
Dismissal, 33, 208
Disorganization, change in community
    colleges and, 202–204
Due process, 152–153
Dues, compulsory union, 105–107

Eastern Michigan University, 77, 130
Educational programs, new, 33
Elections, 107, 108
"Emerging" universities, 68, 71
"Employee-Management Cooperation in
    Federal Service " (1962), 17
Employee Relation Policy Committee
    (New Jersey), 131
Employer identification, 125–126
Employment security, tenure and, 160–163
End-run multilateral bargaining, 118–121
Enrollment, increase in university, 1–2, 5–
    6
Ethnic studies, 200
Exclusive bargaining rights, 27
Executive Order 10988 (1962), 17
Expansion of community colleges, 190–192
External organization for bargaining, 30
Extracurricular behavior, 34, 208

Faculty, 111
    growth of, 5–6
Faculty association, 40–43
Faculty Association of California
    Community Colleges, 185n.
Faculty determination, 32

Faculty distribution among multicampus
    institutions, 6–8
Faculty representation in governance, 9–
    11, 23–50
    collective bargaining and, 27–29
    governance-bargaining continuum and,
        29–31
    management and, 23–27
    models of, 31–49
        faculty association, 40–43
        faculty senate, 31–40
        professional association, 43–47
        trade union, 47–49
    (*See also* Governance of institutions)
Faculty senate, 12, 31–40
    grievance systems of, 138
    patterns of union relations with, 141–
        151
        competitive, 145–147
        cooperative, 143–145
        cooptative, 147–151
"Fair comparison," 232–233
Ferris State College (Michigan), 77
Financial pressures on universities, 15–16
    in community colleges, 186–189
Fordham University (New York), 55n.
Frederick Community College (Maryland),
    184
Full professor, 171–172
Fulton-Montgomery Community College
    (New York), 185n.
Functional changes, 11–13
    community-college growth and, 200–202
    growth of unionism and, 68

Germany, codetermination model of, 139–
    141
Gold, Lois Swirsky, 76
Governance of institutions:
    centralization and coordination agencies
        of, 9–10
    community college growth and, 208–210
    in England, 243–246
    faculty participation in, 9–11
    faculty-unionism effects on, 255–257
    growth of faculty unionism and, 69–73
    structural changes and, 5–8

Governance of institutions:
  unions and, 137, 139
  codetermination, 139–141
  management, 151–156
  union–senate relations, 141–151
  (*See also* Faculty representation in
    governance)
Government, university-trained personnel
  and, 2
Grading standards, 14–15
Graduate student assistants, 117
Grand Rapids Junior College (Michigan),
  185*n.*
Granger, Robert, 161
Great Britain, academic unionism in, 213–
  250
  collective bargaining in, 228–246
    governance, 243–246
    grievance, 242–243
    promotion, 240–242
    representation, 228–232
    salaries, 232–236
    tenure, 236–240
  development of representation in,
    222–228
  structure of, 213–222
Grievance procedures, 27, 152, 154
  in England, 242–243
  tenure and, 164–166
Growth in university institutions (*see*
  Changes and growth in university
  institutions)
Growth trends of faculty unionism, 56–57
Guild unions, 135–137
  faculty senate–union relations and, 144–
    145
Guild unity, 236

Halsey, A. H., 236, 243*n.*
Hawaii:
  community colleges in, 186*n.*
  managerial bargaining model in, 131–
    133
Hawaii, University of, 65, 96, 101, 104–
  105, 168
  bargaining model of, 131–132
Hawaii Employers Council, 132

Hawaii Federation of College Teachers
  (HFCT), 104–105
Hawaiian Government Employees
  Association (HGEA), 104
Higher Education Research Unit
  (England), 220–221, 234
  governance and, 243–245
  tenure and, 237
Hodgkinson, Harold L., 11–12, 26, 68,
  143–144
Hunter College (New York), 76

Illinois, faculty unionism in, 62–64
Inclusive education public-employees
  union laws, 61–64
Independent internal organization for
  bargaining, 29–30
Individual bargaining, 29
Industrial model of unionism, 107
Industrial Relations Act (England, 1971),
  219, 222
Industrial Union Department (IUD), 95–
  96
Instant tenure, unions and, 163–169
Institutional research, 24–25
Institutional structures (*see* Structure of
  institutions)
Institutional systems, 4*n.*
  unionism and, 65–66
Interorganizational bargaining, 116
Intraorganizational bargaining, 116

Job control, professionalism and, 44–45
Joint action, 32, 35
Joint Consultative Committee (England),
  248
Junior colleges, addition of liberal arts
  programs in, 12
  (*See also* Community colleges)

K-12 public school districts, 194–195, 202
Kadish, Sanford, 84
Kibbee, Robert J., 114*n.*, 155
Kirtland Community College (Michigan),
  185*n.*

Labor boards, 108
Ladd, Everett, 52–54
Lake Michigan College, 120
Law schools, 55*n*., 99–100
Lecturer, salary scale of, in Great Britain, 233
Legal environment:
    patterns of unionization and, 61–64
    university institutional change and, 16–20
Legislative Conference (1930), 41, 98
Liberal arts programs, increase of, 11–12
Lieberman, Myron, 51
Lipset, Seymour, 52–54
Litigation, 163
Lobbying, student, 120–121
London, University of, 214, 221, 243
Los Angeles City Colleges, 207

Macomb County Community College (Michigan), 185*n*., 194
Main-branch multicampus institutions, 6–7
    community college structural changes and, 191–192
    unionism among, 65–66, 68
Maintenance-of-membership clauses, 105–107
Management and governance, 23–27, 115
    unions and, 151–156
Managerial bargaining models, 127–133
    of Hawaii, 131–133
    of Michigan, 128–130
    of New Jersey, 130–131
    of New York, 127–128
Mannix, T., 154, 166
Massachusetts, 77, 149
    tripartite bargaining in, 123
Massachusetts, University of, 77, 101
    rejection of union at, 103
Meany, George, 94
Meet and confer public-employee union laws, 61–64, 144
Membership, union, 105–107
Merit pay, 175–176, 226

Michigan, faculty unionism in, 61
    community college educational reform, financial difficulties and, 187–189
    managerial bargaining model in, 128–130
    multicampus unionized community colleges of, 194
Michigan, University of, 77, 130
Michigan Educational Association (MEA), 187–188
Michigan State University, 77, 130
    rejection of union at, 103
Michigan Technological University, 130
Milwaukee Technical Institute, 51
Minnesota, 77
Minnesota Junior College Faculty Association, 193–194
Minority policies, 26
Multicampus institutions, 4*n*.
    bargaining unit determination and, 108–109
    importance of different types of, 7
    unionism among, 65–67
Multilateral bargaining, 115–117
    students and, 118–125
Multiversity, 26

Naples, Caesar, 142
National Association of Community College Faculty, 97
National Association of Higher Education, 97
National Board of Prices and Income (England), 224–225, 235
National Council for Academic Awards (England), 229
National Educational Association (NEA), 18–20, 43–44
    competition for faculty-bargaining rights of, 96–99
    national AFT merger prospects of, 100–102
    New York AFT merger with, 93
National Faculty Association of Community and Junior Colleges, 198

National Incomes Commission (England), 224
National Labor Relations Act, 105
National Labor Relations Board, 19, 47, 57, 67, 109
National Society of Professors, 97
National Survey of Faculty and Student Opinion (Carnegie Commission), 5, 52
New Jersey, faculty unionism in, 61
   managerial bargaining model of, 130–131
New Jersey State Colleges, 30
New York State:
   collective bargaining in, 60–61
   managerial model of, 127–128
   (*See also* City University of New York; State University of New York)
New York State Teachers Association, 41
Newton, David, 154, 155
"No law" public-employee union laws, 61–64, 194
No participation, 32, 35
Nonrenewal, 33
Nonteaching professionals (NTPs), 111, 160–161
   at community colleges, 201
   comprehensive unions and, 137
Normal schools (*see* Community colleges)
Northern Michigan University, 77, 130
   rejection of union at, 103
"Nota Bene" clause, 166

Oakland community colleges (Michigan), 195
Oakland University (Michigan), 77, 86–87
   bargaining model of, 129–130
   salary at, 171
Occupational composition of unions, 111, 135–137
O'Dowd, Donald, 87
Office of Employee Relations:
   New Jersey, 131
   New York, 127
Open admissions, 26
Open files, 164
Open hearings, 117

Oregon, faculty unionism in, 62
Organic internal organizations for bargaining, 29
Organization patterns for faculty unionism, 51–81
   anatomy of, 57–61
   growth trends and, 56–57
   institutional structure and, 65–66
   legal aspects of, 61–64
   public-private dichotomy and, 67–73
   quality and, 73–78
   support and, 51–56
Organizational change (*see* Community colleges, organizational change and rapid growth of)
Organized labor, AFT and, 95–96
Oxford University (England), 214, 220, 243

Parity, 114
Parties and relationships of collective bargaining, 83–133
   American Association of University Professors, 84–92
   American Federation of Teachers, 92–96
   dues and, 105–107
   elusive employer and, 125–127
   managerial bargaining models and, 127–133
      Hawaii, 131–133
      Michigan, 128–130
      New Jersey, 130–131
      New York, 127–128
   mergers and coalitions of, 100–102
   National Educational Association, 96–99
   structure and, 107–125
      department chairmen, 109–110
      faculty bargaining as multilateral, 115–117
      members as professionals or of a profession, 110–115
      student involvement in, 117–125
   unionism and, 102–105
Pass/fail systems, 15
Peer reviews, 162
Pennsylvania, faculty unionism in, 61, 132
Peralta College (Oakland), 207

Performance evaluation, 161–162
  specification for procedures of, 163–164
Perkin, H. J., 218, 224
Personnel decisions, senate faculty and,
  32–35
Policy-making participation, 14
  (*See also* Faculty representation in
  governance)
Political ideology, unionism and, 53
Prairie State College (Illinois), 199
President, community college, 33, 209
Private institutions, 5
  growth of faculty unionism in, 57–61
  recognized bargaining agents for, 87
Private-public dichotomy, public-
  employee union organization and,
  67–73
Producer groups, multilateral bargaining
  and, 116
Productivity bargains, 226
Professional Association, 43–47
Professional Staff Congress (PSC), 155
Professionals, faculty members as, 110–115
Professor, salary scale of, in Great Britain,
  233
Progressive Caucus (AFT), 199*n*.
Promotions, 33, 208
  in England, 240–242
Public Employee Relations Board (New
  York), 120, 154*n*., 161
Public employees' collective-bargaining
  movement, 17–20
  community colleges and, 183–184
Public institutions, 5
  growth of faculty unionism in, 57–61
  recognized bargaining agents for, 87
Public officials, multilateral bargaining
  and, 115–117
Public-private dichotomy, public-
  employee union organization and,
  67–73

Quality of education, unionism and, 73–78

Reagan, Ronald, 64
Recruitment and retention, 232–233

Reform, community-college education,
  186–189
Representation, British academic
  unionism and development of, 222–
  228
  bargaining unit and, 228–232
Reprisal fears, unionizing and, 73
Retention and recruitment, 232–233
Retrenchment, 175–176
Reuther, Walter, 95–96
Review process, student participation in,
  15
Reviews, peer, 162
Revision of the Board of Trustees' Policies,
  162
Robbins Committee (England, 1963), 224
Rutgers University (New Jersey), 76, 116
  AAUP and, 88, 92, 152
  bargaining model of, 130–131
  guild unions at, 136

Saginaw Valley College (Michigan), 77
St. John's University (New York), 101
  guild union at, 136
  salary at, 171
Salaries, faculty, 16, 32, 33
  AAUP survey of, 46, 85
  British collective-bargaining and,
    232–236
  British review procedures for, 222–228
  discussion and, 34–35
  effects of faculty unionism on, 258–
    259
  levels of unionism and, 72–73
  in New York bargaining model, 127–
    128
  structure and, 171–177
  unions and, 169–171
San Francisco State College, 122
Sapper, Laurie, 218
Schenectady County Community College
  (New York), 185*n*.
Seattle Community College, 194
Security of employment, tenure and, 160–
  163
Segmented multicampus institutions, 6–7
  unionism at, 65–66

Selden, David, 102
Selective education public-employee union laws, 61–64
Senate, British, 244
Senate, faculty (*see* Faculty senate)
Senate Professional Association (SPA), 43, 98, 161
Senior lecturer, salary scale of, in Great Britain, 233
Shanker, Albert, 93, 94, 102
"Shared authority," 139
Shop stewards, 110
Single-campus institutions, 6–7, 180
  community college structural change and, 191–192
  unionism among, 65–66
Size, university institutional change and, 4–6
Slichter, Sumner, 152
Southeastern Massachusetts University, 52, 77
Staff sizes, 33
State control of community colleges, 197–198
State University of New York (SUNY), 43, 61, 65, 75–76
  community colleges of, 193
  NEA-AFT at, 93, 98, 101
  tenure at, 160–162
  union membership at, 106
Statewide community college system, 197
Statement of Principles and Interpretative Comments on Academic Freedom and Tenure (AAUP), 84–85
Status equalization, unions and, 157–177
  salaries and salary administration of, 169–171
  salary structure and, 171–177
  tenure and, 157–169
Stevens, Carl, 89
Stockton State College (New Jersey), 124–125
Stony Brook, State University at (New York), 76
Strikes, 27
  students and, 118
Structure of academic unionism in Great Britain, 213–222

Structure of institutions:
  change and, 6–11
  growth of community colleges and, 190–194
  growth of unionism and, 65–66
Student academic performance, 33
Student evaluation of teaching, 15, 118
Student participation in university governance, 26, 32, 34
  in appointment and promotion committees, 15
  collective bargaining and, 117–125
Student Senate (CUNY), 118–120
Student unrest, 3
  challenge to traditional university governance and, 26–27
SUNY (*see* State University of New York)
Support professionals, 111
Syracuse University, 55*n.*

Task Force on Faculty Representation, 40
Taylor Act (New York, 1967), 60–61
  implementation of, 127
Teachers colleges, 12
  (*See also* Community colleges)
Teaching assistants' unions, 14, 117
Teaching loads, 34, 208
Teaching requirements, 33
Technical institutions (*see* Community colleges)
Temple University (Pennsylvania), 100*n.*, 132
Tenure, 14–15, 33, 84–85
  AAUP and, 47
  awarding of, 112–113
  at community colleges, 208, 257–258
  in England, 236–240
  effects of faculty unionism on, 257–258
  unions and, 157–169
Terminal occupational programs, 180
Termination, 14
Third-party arbitration, 107
Third-party intervention, 27, 116
Trade unions, 47–49
Trades Union Congress (England), 219
Trilateral bargaining, 124
Tripartite multilateral bargaining, 122–125

Trow, Martin, 74, 236, 243*n*.
Tuition, 118
Two-year institutions (*see* Community colleges)

Ulster County Community College (New York), 185*n*.
Union shops, 105–107
Unionization of public employees, 17–20 (*See also* Organization patterns for faculty unionism)
United Action Caucus (AFT), 199*n*.
United Federation of College Teachers, 41–42
United Federation of Teachers (UFT), 93
United Professors of California, 94
United Progress Caucus (CCCTU), 199–200
United States Merchant Marine Academy, 51–52
United University Professions, Inc. (SUNY), 111*n*., 148, 161
University of Hawaii Faculty Association (UHFA), 104–105
University Authorities Panel (England), 215, 217

University Grants Committee (England), 214–216, 219–220
development of union representation and, 222–228
Upward-bound studies, 200

Van Alstyne, William, 89
Van Eyck, Daniel, 38, 69, 108

Wagner Act (1935), 17, 84
Wales, University of, 243
Walters, Donald E., 123
Wartofsky, Mark, 89
Washington (state), 77
Wayne State University (Michigan), 76, 77, 91–92, 130
salary at, 170
Webb, Beatrice, 157
Webb, Sidney, 157
Western Michigan University, 130
Winton Act (California), 184–185
Wisconsin, coalition bargaining in, 121–122
Wisconsin Teaching Assistant's Association, 117
Work councils, 139–140